RELATED TITLES

Grammar Source

Math Source

Writing Source

Test Prep and Admissions

WORD SOURCE

The Smarter Way to Learn Vocabulary Words

by Randy Howe

Simon & Schuster

NEW YORK · LONDON · SYDNEY · TORONTO

Kaplan Publishing
Published by SIMON & SCHUSTER
1230 Avenue of the Americas
New York, NY 10020

Editorial Director: Jennifer Farthing
Project Editors: Sheryl Gordon and Anne Kemper
Production Manager: Michael Shevlin
Interior Page Layout: Jan Gladish
Cover Design: Cheung Tai and Mark Weaver

Manufactured in the United States of America
Published simultaneously in Canada

August 2005
10 9 8 7 6 5 4 3 2

ISBN-13: 978-0-7432-5161-7
ISBN-10:   0-7432-5161-X

Contents

About the Author

Randy Howe teaches in New Haven and lives in Madison, Connecticut with his wife, two children, cat, and dog. He has written ten other books, including *Training Wheels for Teachers: What I Wish I'd Known My First 100 Days on the Job*, also published by Kaplan.

Introduction

Dear Reader,

Do unknown vocabulary words you overhear in a conversation or read in a book (or see on a test!) make your head swim? Do you struggle to get through a reading passage because of just one difficult phrase? Do you keep quiet because you're afraid of misusing certain words? Is it frustrating to know how good your essays, papers, and test scores would be if you only had a larger vocabulary? The answer may very well be yes to all of these. Even if you can only relate to just one, then this book is for you. Just by buying *Word Source*, you're already on the road to a better vocabulary!

After reading *Word Source*, not only will you sound more intelligent when talking with family and friends, and not only will you better understand what you are reading, you will find that word knowledge will enhance your professional life, whether it is as a student or an employee. An extensive vocabulary can help you score better on exams, get promoted, or simply save you time when solving everyday problems.

Improving your vocabulary can seem like a tedious process. But learning about word use and meaning doesn't have to be boring. Allow us to introduce the **Building Block Method**.

This teacher-approved method was devised by the experts at Kaplan to make learning vocabulary as painless as possible. It is actually a proven method in several areas of study, including math, grammar, and writing!

Like any other book, you'll begin with the basics—in this case, word roots—and move on from there. The final chapter is "Fifty-cent Words You Can Actually Use," fifty-cent words being the extravagant terminology often found in crossword puzzles and on GRE exams. Speaking of exams, there are also chapters dedicated to words commonly found on both the GRE and SAT exams. If your goal is scoring higher on a test, this is the book for you. Since *Word Source* contains more than 900 vocabulary words, the test makers will be hard-pressed to ask you about a word not contained within these pages.

Within *Word Source*, vocabulary words are often presented in a context that involves situations you might find in your day-to-day life. Some words come with an explanation pertaining to their origin while others are explained using synonyms (words with the same or similar meaning) and/or antonyms (opposites). Not only will you read about these words using varied examples, you will be tested on them in a variety of methods, which is also a part of the Kaplan approach.

There's no smarter way to learn. So get started—a vastly improved vocabulary is only a few building blocks away!

HOW TO USE THIS BOOK

We recommend reading through cover to cover, but if you only have a few days for practice with this book, there are chapter headings to help you find your desired subjects or targets. Within each chapter, you will find Kaplan's systematic approach for improving your vocabulary. Each chapter has been specifically designed with memorization in mind. Each chapter contains four key components as the means to this end:

1. Building Block Quiz

You'll begin each chapter with a short quiz. The first ten questions are a preview of sorts, testing your knowledge of the material to be covered in that chapter. The last two questions will cover material from earlier lessons, so if you get these questions wrong, it's time to go back and review! Taking this quiz helps reinforce what you've already learned, while targeting the information you need to focus on in each chapter. Plus, you'll get even more review from the answer explanations, which tell you why each answer choice is right or wrong.

2. Detailed Lessons

Each chapter focuses on one specific subject area, which will help in the memorization process. Association is one way we can enhance our ability to absorb information. With detailed explanations of the chapter concepts, a multitude of relevant examples, and a variety of strategies to help you remember what you need to know, you will find your vocabulary growing by the minute! Just to make sure you don't forget anything, we will also help you to review the fundamentals from previous chapters, looking back while moving forward.

3. Plentiful Practice

Repetition is the key to mastery. So be prepared to practice, practice, practice! You'll find everything from simple matching exercises to exercises that ask you to apply the skills you're learning to practical, real-life situations. By "learning from all sides," so to speak, you're much more likely to retain the information. And remember, don't start a new chapter if you haven't mastered the earlier material—you'll be building on a weak foundation.

4. Chapter Tests

At the end of each chapter, you'll find a 30-question Chapter Test to help you practice what you've learned and assess how well you remember the new vocabulary. These tests, broken down into true/false and multiple-choice formats, cover material from the chapter and will help to make sure that you've mastered the words before you move on.

5. Cumulative Test

Finally, the book concludes with a 40-question Word Source Cumulative Test covering words from all of the chapters. It will further reinforce your mastery of new vocabulary words and allow you to see how much you've learned.

With a system as easy as this, a fantastic vocabulary is well within your reach. All you have to do is take the first step. Good luck!

SOURCE SERIES CONTEST

Win Paramount Pictures DVDs!

See the last page for full details!

CHAPTER 1

Word Roots

The keys to unlocking unfamiliar words

This first chapter is special because it not only teaches you the most important word roots out there, but it is also an introduction to many of the new vocab words featured in the following chapters!

BUILDING BLOCK QUIZ

DIRECTIONS: Circle the choice that you think best defines the word root.

1. **ver**, as in verisimilitude: very   false   true
2. **prox**, as in proximity: far   approximately   near
3. **mal**, as in malevolent: good   bad   nice
4. **cap**, as in capitulate: seize   full   capsize
5. **am**, as in amorous: love   hate   hug
6. **belli**, as in belligerent: beautiful   war   peace
7. **dic**, as in contradiction: speak   play   promise
8. **anti**, as in antipathy: for   against   feelings
9. **inter**, as in intermission: between   through   besides
10. **omni**, as in omniscient: all   none   rarely

Answers and Explanations

1. **Ver** means true, and has its origins in the Latin veritas, which means truth. Also, for those of you who speak Spanish, verdad means truth. Verisimilitude means the appearance of being true or real.

2. **Prox** means near. Hence, proximity means to be near something: the right answer, the correct location, or something else. Approximately is a trick answer, as it contains the word root but is not a definition. Far is an antonym.

3. Mal means bad. Since the second part of the word, volent, relates back to a Latin word for will (as in to will or wish bad things upon someone else), **mal**evolent means wicked and spiteful. Good and nice are its antonyms.

4. Cap means seize. If you **cap**itulate, it means you are giving in to whoever is trying to seize you or your possessions.

5. Am means love. To be **am**orous is to feel loving. And although you might want to hug someone you feel amorous towards, hug does not define the root. Hate is an antonym.

6. Belli means war and can be found at the beginning of many hateful and violent words: **belli**cose (warlike) and **belli**gerent (aggressive), for example. Beautiful and peace are contrary to all things **belli**.

7. Dic means speak and contra**dic**tion means to speak against another person or against one's own logic. Play and promise are irrelevant.

8. Anti means opposite or against. When a person displays **anti**pathy, he or she is in opposition to something. Although when you are **anti**-something you have feelings against it, feelings is not a definition. For is an antonym.

9. Inter means between. An **inter**mission, for example, is a break between acts during a play. Often, **inter** is used to indicate something done or communicated between people or groups of people. Be careful not to confuse **inter** with intra, which means within. Through and besides are incorrect definitions.

10. Omni means all. When **omni** is used to indicate all it is in a grand sense; not as in she ate *all* the pizza or he stole *all* the money, but as in **omni**scient, which means *all*-knowing. None and rarely are virtual antonyms.

Now that you've tested your skills, it's time to learn some word roots! When you're reading them over, try to absorb not only the definition for each word root, but also the example words provided. You'll find that, in the least, the words share the meaning that comes from the word root.

PART ONE

a-, an- —not, without
Examples: asymmetrical, anonymity

ac-, acr- —sharp, sour
Examples: acuity, acumen

ali-, altr- —another
Examples: alien, altruism

am-, ami- —love
Examples: amorous, amity

ambi-, amphi- —both
Examples: ambidextrous, amphibian

ante-, ant- —before
Examples: antecedent, antediluvian

anti-, ant- —against, opposite
Examples: antidote, antipathy, antagonist

auto- —self
Examples: autonomous, automobile

belli-, bell- —war
Examples: belligerent, bellicose

bene-, ben- —good
Examples: beneficent, benign

bio- —life
Examples: biology, biodegradable

cap-, capt-, -cept, -cip- —take, seize
Examples: capacious, capitulate, precept

chrom- —color
Examples: chromatic, chromosphere

circum- —around
Examples: circumlocution, circumvent

co- —with, together
Examples: cohesion, collaborator

-gno-, -cogn- —know
Examples: agnostic, ignoble

MEMORY TIP

If you've ever taken a **biology** class, what did you learn about? You learned about *life*, right? **Biology** is the study of *life*, and in many high schools the class is now called *Life* Science.

Practice 1

DIRECTIONS: Match the word root (left column) with its definition (right column).

1. **a**		around
2. **ac**		self
3. **ali**		without
4. **am**		know
5. **ambi**		both
6. **ante**		color
7. **anti**		good
8. **auto**		another
9. **belli**		life
10. **bene**		before
11. **bio**		take
12. **cap**		war
13. **chrom**		opposite
14. **circum**		love
15. **co**		sharp
16. **gno**		together

PART TWO

contra- —against
Examples: contradiction, contrary

cosmo-, -cosm —world
Examples: cosmopolitan, cosmos, microcosm

demo-, dem- —people
Examples: democracy, pandemic

dia- —across
Examples: diameter, mediate

dic-, dict- —speak
Examples: dictate, contradiction

dis-, dif-, di- —apart, away
Examples: disheveled, dissemble, disclosure

ex-, e- —out, out of
Examples: exorbitant, extrude, expropriate

fac-, -fic-, -fect, fy-, fea- —make, do
Examples: facile, prolific

frag-, frac- —break
Examples: fragment, refract

MEMORY TIP

You will note that oftentimes these word roots don't just appear at the beginning of the vocabulary words. The **dic** in **contradiction** comes in the middle, for example. **Dic** has to do with spoken words and **contra** means against. If someone contradicts himself, he has gone against something he said previously.

---

gen- —birth, class, kin
Examples: genealogy, genocide

grad-, -gress —step
Examples: graduation, digress

grat- —pleasing
Examples: ingratiate, gratuity

in-, ig-, il-, im-, ir- —not
Examples: incorrigible, intrepid, inviolable

inter- —between, among
Examples: interlocutor, interlude

intra-, intr- —within
Examples: intrapersonal, intramural

MEMORY TIP

Many math teachers use the example of a pizza to teach fractions. The word root **frac** means to break, which makes sense, as a pizza is broken down into slices and distributed to everybody at the dinner table.

Practice 2

DIRECTIONS: Match the word root (left column) with its definition (right column).

17. **contra**	speak
18. **cosmo**	within
19. **dem**	world
20. **dia**	out
21. **dic**	pleasing
22. **dis**	do
23. **ex**	people
24. **fac**	birth
25. **frac**	against
26. **gen**	apart
27. **grad**	not
28. **grat**	across
29. **in**	between
30. **inter**	break
31. **intra**	step

PART THREE

jour- —day
Examples: journal, sojourn

lec-, -leg-, lex- —read, speak
Examples: lecture, illegible

liter- —letter
Examples: literacy, alliteration

mal- —bad
Examples: malevolent, malfeasance, malediction

MEMORY TIP

"Means Anti-Love." Remember that fun little mnemonic device, and you will remember what **mal** means. Any word with **mal** in it is a negative word.

---

man- —hand
Examples: manhandle, mandate

morph- —shape
Examples: amorphous, anthropomorphic

mut- —change
Examples: mutability, immutable

neg- —not, deny
Examples: abnegate, negligible

nom-, -nym- —name
Examples: autonomous, eponymous

nov- —new
Examples: novice, novel

ob- —against
Examples: obdurate, obfuscate, obstreperous

omni- —all
Examples: omniscient, omnipotent

-path-, pass- —feel, suffer
Examples: apathetic, empathetic

phon- —sound
Examples: telephone, cacophony

plac- —calm, please
Examples: implacable, complacent

MEMORY TIP

Rather than envisioning something, when you see the root **phon** think of the *sound* your cell **phone** makes when it rings. Do you have a favorite song programmed in? Is it something funky or just a plain old ringing telephone? Regardless, thinking of your **phone** ringtone will remind you that **phon** means *sound*.

Practice 3

DIRECTIONS: Match the word root (left column) with its definition (right column).

32. **jour**	all
33. **leg**	against
34. **liter**	shape
35. **mal**	read
36. **man**	letter
37. **morph**	feel
38. **mut**	change
39. **neg**	deny
40. **nom**	name
41. **nov**	calm
42. **ob**	day
43. **omni**	new
44. **path**	sound
45. **phon**	hand
46. **plac**	bad

PART FOUR

pot- —power
Examples: impotent, despotism

-prox-, prop- —near
Examples: approximate, proximity

rid-, ris- —laugh
Examples: ridicule, deride

sacr-, sanct- —holy
Examples: sacred, sanctimonious

scrib-, script-, scriv- —write
Examples: scribble, proscribe

sequ-, secu- —follow
Examples: sequence, non sequitur

syn-, sym- —together
Examples: synergy, synonymous

tim- —fear, frightened
Examples: timid, timorous

urb- —city
Examples: urban, urbane

vac- —empty
Examples: vacate, vacuous

ver- —true
Examples: verisimilitude, veracious, aver

> **MEMORY TIP**
>
> When you first pull the **vac**uum cleaner out of the closet, the bag inside should be empty. And when you're done **vac**uuming, you should throw out that bag and put in a new one. One that is also . . . empty! Think of that empty **vac**uum bag and you will be sure to remember that **vac** means empty.

Practice 4

Match the word root (left column) with its definition (right column).

47. **pot**	holy
48. **prox**	follow
49. **rid**	laugh
50. **sanct**	write
51. **scrib**	together
52. **sequ**	near
53. **syn**	frightened
54. **tim**	true
55. **urb**	empty
56. **vac**	power
57. **ver**	city

PRACTICE ANSWERS AND EXPLANATIONS

Practice 1

1. **A**, as in **a**nonymity, is synonymous with without.

2. **Ac**, as in **ac**uity, is synonymous with sharp.

3. **Ali**, as in **ali**en, is synonymous with another.

4. **Am**, as in **am**orous, is synonymous with love.

5. **Ambi**, as in **ambi**dextrous, is synonymous with both.

6. **Ante**, as in **ante**cedent, is synonymous with before.

7. **Anti**, as in **anti**dote, is synonymous with opposite.

8. **Auto**, as in **auto**nomous, is synonymous with self.

9. **Belli**, as in **belli**gerent, is synonymous with war.

10. **Bene**, as in **bene**ficent, is synonymous with good.

11. **Bio**, as in **bio**degradable, is synonymous with life.

12. **Cap**, as in **cap**itulate, is synonymous with take.

13. **Chrom**, as in **chrom**atic, is synonymous with color.

14. **Circum**, as in **circum**locution, is synonymous with around.

15. **Co**, as in **co**hesion, is synonymous with together.

16. **Gno**, as in a**gno**stic, is synonymous with know.

Practice 2

17. **Contra**, as in **contra**diction, is synonymous with against.

18. **Cosmo**, as in **cosmo**politan, is synonymous with world.

19. **Dem**, as in **dem**agogue, is synonymous with people.

20. **Dia**, as in me**dia**te, is synonymous with across.

21. **Dic**, as in ab**dic**ate, is synonymous with speak.

22. **Dis**, as in **dis**tance, is synonymous with apart. A **dis**heveled appearance is *apart* from the expected appearance.

23. **Ex**, as in **ex**orbitant, is synonymous with out.

24. **Fac**, as in **fac**ile, is synonymous with do.

25. **Frac**, as in re**frac**t, is synonymous with break.

26. **Gen**, as in **gen**ealogy, is synonymous with birth.

27. **Grad**, as in **grad**uation, is synonymous with step.

28. **Grat**, as in in**grat**iate, is synonymous with pleasing.

29. **In**, as in **in**trepid, is synonymous with not.

30. **Inter**, as in **inter**lude, is synonymous with between.

31. **Intra**, as in **intra**personal, is synonymous with within.

Practice 3

32. **Jour**, as in so**jour**n, is synonymous with day.

33. **Leg**, as in il**leg**ible, is synonymous with read.

34. **Liter**, as in al**liter**ation, is synonymous with letter.

35. **Mal**, as in **mal**evolent, is synonymous with bad.

36. **Man**, as in **man**date, is synonymous with hand.

37. **Morph**, as in a**morph**ous, is synonymous with shape.

38. **Mut**, as in **mut**ability, is synonymous with change.

39. **Neg**, as in ab**neg**ate, is synonymous with deny.

40. **Nom**, as in auto**nom**ous, is synonymous with name.

41. **Nov**, as in **nov**el, is synonymous with new.

42. **Ob**, as in **ob**durate, is synonymous with against.

43. **Omni**, as in **omni**scient, is synonymous with all.

44. **Path**, as in em**path**etic, is synonymous with feel.

45. **Phon**, as in caco**phon**y, is synonymous with sound.

46. **Plac**, as in im**plac**able, is synonymous with calm.

Practice 4

47. **Pot**, as in im**pot**ent, is synonymous with power.

48. **Prox**, as in **prox**imity, is synonymous with near.

49. **Rid**, as in de**rid**e, is synonymous with laugh.

50. **Sanct**, as in **sanct**imonious, is synonymous with holy.

51. **Scrib**, as in pro**scrib**e, is synonymous with write.

52. **Sequ**, as in non **sequ**itur, is synonymous with follow.

53. **Syn**, as in **syn**ergy, is synonymous with together.

54. **Tim**, as in **tim**id, is synonymous with frightened.

55. **Urb**, as in **urb**an, is synonymous with city.

56. **Vac**, as in **vac**uous, is synonymous with empty.

57. **Ver**, as in a**ver**, is synonymous with true.

CHAPTER 1 TEST

Okay, it's time to put your memory to the test! Take your time, not only when answering the questions, but also when reading the answer explanations that follow. Set a goal for yourself—80% (24 correct answers) is recommended. If you don't reach that goal, go back and read through the chapter again. Good luck!

DIRECTIONS: For questions 1–15, circle T for True or F for False. For questions 16–30, circle the synonym.

1.	T	F	**phon**—sound
2.	T	F	**inter**—within
3.	T	F	**ob**—for
4.	T	F	**urb**—city
5.	T	F	**vac**—full
6.	T	F	**pot**—power
7.	T	F	**ac**—dull
8.	T	F	**altr**—against
9.	T	F	**ambi**—both
10.	T	F	**auto**—mechanical
11.	T	F	**nym**—without
12.	T	F	**ante**—before
13.	T	F	**fac**—fact
14.	T	F	**grat**—pleasing
15.	T	F	**man**—hand

16. **bene**, as in beneficent:	bad	playing	good
17. **cap**, as in capitulate:	give	take	flee
18. **circum**, as in circumvent:	around	between	throughout
19. **dem**, as in demagogue:	statistic	people	list
20. **mut**, as in mutability:	change	table	quiet
21. **tim**, as in timorous:	pleasure	solitude	fear
22. **frac**, as in refract:	object	break	decide

23. **gen**, as in genealogy: birth   clothing   science

24. **intra,**
    as in intrapersonal: without   between   within

25. **morph,**
    as in anthropomorphic: changing   shape   animalistic

26. **a**, as in asymmetrical: combined   without   congruent

27. **chron,**
    as in chronological: time   uncommon   sensational

28. **cosmo,**
    as in cosmopolitan: round   literature   world

29. **jour**, as in sojourn: day   rush   bother

30. **neg,** as in abnegate: note   deny   deliver

Answers and Explanations

1. True. **Phon** is synonymous with sound. Just think of the sound of your best friend's voice coming through your cell **phon**e.

2. False. **Inter** is synonymous with between and should not be confused with **intra**, which means within. An **inter**view, for example, is a discussion between two people.

3. False. **Ob** is synonymous with against, so for is an antonym. Just think, you wouldn't try to **ob**struct something (keep it from happening) if you weren't against it.

4. True. **Urb** is synonymous with city. Just think of **urb**an (in the city) and sub**urb**an (just outside of the city).

5. False. **Vac** is synonymous with empty, so full is an antonym. One example of the word root in use is **vac**uous, which means empty-headed and unintelligent.

6. True. **Pot** is synonymous with power. To be **pot**ent is to be powerful.

7. False. **Ac** is associated with sharp, as in how something offends the senses. Something **ac**rid has a sharp odor, for example. Dull is an antonym.

8. False. **Altr** is synonymous with another, not with against (that word root would be **anti**). **Altr**uistic is a good example, as it refers to one who does nice things for another person.

9. True. **Ambi** is synonymous with both. A person who is **ambi**dextrous can complete tasks with both hands equally well.

10. False. **Auto** is synonymous with self, not with mechanical. For example. something that is **auto**matic will perform a task by itself.

11. False. **Nym** is synonymous with name. Think of ano**nym**ous, which means without a name. The word root meaning without is **a**.

12. True. **Ante** is synonymous with before. **Ante**diluvian, for example, means prehistoric or before modern times.

13. False. **Fac** is synonymous with make and do, not with fact. For example, something that is **fac**ile is easy to do.

14. True. **Grat** is synonymous with pleasing. For example, in**grat**iate means to please someone, but with a motive or purpose in mind.

15. True. **Man** is a word root for hand, as seen in the words **man**handle (to beat up with the hands) and **man**date, which is usually a document granting permission that has to be signed by hand.

16. Bene is synonymous with good. Bad is an antonym and playing is irrelevant.

17. Cap is synonymous with take. Flee does not fit and give is an exact antonym.

18. Circum is synonymous with around. Between and throughout are tempting, because both also deal with direction, but both are wrong.

19. Dem is synonymous with people. A **dem**agogue is a leader of the people, even if she is not a good leader. List and statistic are irrelevant choices.

20. Mut is synonymous with change. The definition of **mut**ability is variations and changes. Quiet is a trick answer (don't be confused by the word mute), and table is just a distracter: an irrelevant word meant to draw attention from the correct answer.

21. Timorous means nervous and **tim** is defined as fear. Solitude (being alone) and pleasure are unrelated.

22. Frac is synonymous with break. Object (either the thing or the action) and decide are both unrelated.

23. Gen is used to signify kin or birth. Although **gen**etics, which is the study of heredity (the traits acquired at birth), is a science, science is incorrect. Clothing is irrelevant.

24. Intra is synonymous with within, as **intra**personal means within one's mind or self. Without is an antonym and between is related to the word root **inter**.

25. Morph is synonymous with shape. Anthropo**morph**ic refers to human characteristics, like shape, attributed to gods or animals. You might be tempted by changing, because the word **morph** is often used to mean changing—but what it really means is to change shape. Animalistic is a distracter.

26. A is a word root that means without. Combined is not synonymous with **a**, and congruent, which means similar, is an antonym.

27. Chron is synonymous with time, or in order (as in chronological order). Uncommon and sensational are unrelated.

28. Cosmo means world and in the case of **cosmo**politan, worldly or international. The world may be round, but that answer is unrelated. *Cosmopolitan* may be a magazine, but literature is unrelated, too.

29. The word root **jour** means day, so rush and bother are irrelevant answers. A so**jour**n is a temporary stay.

30. Neg is synonymous with not and deny. Ab**neg**ate means to give up your rights. Note and deliver are unrelated.

School Days

The basic vocabulary to get you through social studies, science, and math

BUILDING BLOCK QUIZ

This "building block" quiz tests the information you will learn in this chapter, plus two word roots from the previous chapter. By answering the 12 questions below, you will get a sense of how closely you'll have to study this chapter in order to master the vocabulary you'll need to find your way around the classroom!

DIRECTIONS: Fill in the blanks, using the most appropriate of the four multiple-choice answers. The correct answer will always fit into the sentence grammatically.

1. Matt's math teacher suggested he review all of the _____ before his calculus test.

    (A) algorithms (B) refract

    (C) punctuation marks (D) archipelagos

2. On their cruise last summer, the Smiths took a boat around the _____, visiting more than a dozen islands

    (A) cartographer (B) amorphous

    (C) savannah (D) archipelagos

3. The weatherman ruined the bottoms of his favorite pants as he walked among the water-logged, _____ ruins.

   (A) simian (B) diluvial

   (C) sarcastic (D) potable

4. Jen waited until her father made sure the water was _____ before taking a drink.

   (A) arboreal (B) diluvial

   (C) archipelagos (D) potable

5. The science teacher knew that his students would love the _____ exhibit at the zoo.

   (A) arboreal (B) simian

   (C) stubborn (D) aerate

6. They all agreed that calling a town with a nuclear reactor Wellsville was a real _____!

   (A) turgid (B) stratify

   (C) concave (D) misnomer

7. Although Jerry said the spilled milk looked like a dog, everyone else at the table told him it had a(n) _____ shape.

   (A) potable (B) diluvial

   (C) amorphous (D) misnomer

8. To make sure her product was accurate, Nandi consulted a(n) _____ before opening her mapmaking business.

   (A) cartographer (B) placebo

   (C) adjunct (D) acclivity

9. Even if the pills were a(n) _____ and
   simply made of sugar, Kevin was glad they
   made his mother feel better.
   (A) placebo (B) simian
   (C) acclivity (D) archipelago

10. Because he loved studying plant life, Harvey
    knew he wanted a(n) _____ job at the
    nature preserve.
    (A) calamitous (B) circumnavigate
    (C) asymmetrical (D) arboreal

11. **Contra**, as in **contra**diction, is synonymous
    with _____.
    (A) day (B) against
    (C) letter (D) bad

12. **Leg**, as in il**leg**ible, is synonymous with
    _____.
    (A) read (B) take
    (C) change (D) fear

Answers and Explanations

1. A. Since **algorithms** are key to solving math problems, (A) is the only
possible answer. Punctuation marks and archipelagos have nothing to do
with math, as the former relates to exclamation points and semicolons
while the latter is a set of islands. To refract is to deflect sound or light;
besides, the word doesn't fit grammatically in the sentence.

2. D. **Archipelagos** are large groups of islands, making (D) the correct
answer. The other three answers don't fit into the sentence structure,
and their meanings have nothing to do with islands. Savanna is another
geographical word, but it means treeless plains. Amorphous means
shapeless and a cartographer is a mapmaker.

3. B. Anything that is **diluvial** has to do with a flood. The hint of water-logged ruins makes (B) the perfect choice. You might be tempted to choose potable, but since that has to do with safe drinking water, it really isn't an appropriate choice. Simian has to do with apes, and sarcastic, which means mocking and ironic, is used to describe a person.

4. D. Potable has to do with water that is safe for drinking, making (D) the correct choice. Diluvial also has to do with water, but refers to a flood. Since Jen wasn't interested in drinking a flood, (B) is not correct. Arboreal has to do with trees and archipelagos are groups of islands, so neither word applies.

5. B. There might be an arboreal exhibit (one that features trees) on display somewhere. But at a zoo, you are looking at animals and not plant life. Reading in context, the students are going to love the apes in the **simian** exhibit. To aerate is to ventilate and to be stubborn has nothing to do with zoos or exhibits.

6. D. Wellsville is no name for a town with a nuclear reactor; with one leak that town certainly will not be well! Thus, the name is completely unfitting—it is a **misnomer**. In addition, **misnomer** is the only choice that is a noun, so turgid (an adjective meaning pompous), stratify (a verb meaning to divide), and concave (an adjective meaning curved inward) cannot be correct.

7. C. Although someone might drink spilled milk, **amorphous,** which means without clear shape, is a better answer than potable, which means safe to drink. As everyone else contested Jerry's claim about how the milk looked, the answer is apparent. A carton of milk is not enough to cause a flood, ruling out diluvial, and misnomer is a noun, so it does not apply.

8. A. Cartographers are expert mapmakers, so it makes sense that Nandi would want to consult one. Adjunct is something connected to something else; even though that something can be a person, it is too much of a stretch to be correct. Placebo is also a noun, but it refers to a fake medicine (often administered in research studies). Acclivity describes an upward slope, so it is not a possible choice, either.

9. A. After reading the whole sentence you can establish a contrast. Despite taking a **placebo**, or a false remedy, Kevin's mother felt better and he was glad. She did not take a group of islands (archipelago), nor did she take a simian (ape), or an acclivity (upward slope), although those would be interesting things to take!

10. D. Nobody wants a calamitous (disastrous) job. Asymmetrical is also an adjective, but it means uneven, so it does not fit in the context of the sentence. Circumnavigate doesn't work, either, as it means to go around. The hint is that Harvey wanted a job at a nature preserve. Since trees are a part of nature, **arboreal** is the only correct answer.

11. B. **Contra** means against. Bad is close, but it isn't always wrong or bad to be against something. Day and letter are irrelevant choices. If you chose incorrectly for this question, you might want to go back to chapter 1 for some review on word roots.

12. A. **Leg** is synonymous with read and **illegible** means unreadable. Take, change, and fear are all unrelated. If you chose incorrectly for this question, you might want to go back to chapter 1 for some review on word roots.

PART ONE

acclivity n. (uh KLIHV ih tee)—an incline or upward slope, the ascending side of a hill
Climbing up the *acclivity* of Mt. Sizemore took Gemma and Daniel twice as long as they expected.

aerate v. (AYR ayt)—expose to air
One of Rob's jobs at the golf course was to *aerate* the greens in order to keep them looking healthy.

arable adj. (AHR uh buhl)—suitable for cultivation
The class's community service project was to make the land *arable* for a student garden.

arboreal adj. (ahr BOHR ee uhl)—relating to trees; living in trees
The squirrel is an *arboreal* mammal, spending much of its time running up and down trees.

MEMORY TIP

Although you may not celebrate Arbor Day, a celebration of *trees*, keep in mind that it does appear on calendars. As **arboreal** relates to *trees*, thinking of Arbor Day might just help you to memorize the meaning of this word.

archipelago n. (ahr kuh PEHL uh goh)—a large group of islands
In some of the Swedish *archipelago* villages, boat taxis are the only form of transportation.

ballast n. (BAAL uhst)—a structure that helps to stabilize or steady
Bags of sand are often used as *ballast* in hot air balloons.

calamitous adj. (cuhl EH mi tus)—disastrous, catastrophic
Since the annual parade was so *calamitous* last year, the police are working hard to keep everyone safe this year.

cartographer n. (kar TAH gruh fer)—someone who makes maps
Early *cartographers* often had to remake their maps when explorers returned with more and more information about unknown lands.

circumnavigate v. (sir cuhm NAH vi gayt)—to travel completely around
Bobby dreamed of *circumnavigating* the globe in a hot air balloon.

conflagration n. (kahn fluh GRAY shuhn)—large, destructive fire
After the *conflagration* of the night before, Midtown Mall was nothing but a pile of ashes.

contiguous adj. (kuhn TIHG yoo uhs)—sharing a boundary; neighboring
The two houses had *contiguous* yards, so the families shared the landscaping expenses.

cataclysmic adj. (kaat uh KLIHZ mihk)—severely destructive
The hurricane was *cataclysmic* and resulted in a lot of damage, even though it raged overhead for no more than an hour.

despotism n. (DEH spuh ti zuhm)—dominance of a nation through threat of violence
According to some historians, the *despotism* of Stalin outweighed that of Hitler.

diffuse v. (dih FYOOZ)—to spread out widely, to scatter freely, to disseminate
Although the fan helped to *diffuse* the cigarette smoke in the club, Meghan could still smell it on her clothes when she got home.

diluvial adj. (dih LOO vee uhl)—pertaining to a flood
After the hose on the washing machine broke, Hank's laundry room looked absolutely *diluvial*.

Practice 1

DIRECTIONS: Read the three choices, then circle the one most closely related to the word in bold.

1. **acclivity:**	decline	incline	affection
2. **aerate:**	expose	provide	descend
3. **arable:**	soothing	understandable	cultivatable
4. **arboreal:**	stars	fish	trees
5. **ballast:**	stabilize	explode	effect
6. **cartographer:**	maps	trees	sailor
7. **circumnavigate:**	around	sail	dominant
8. **contiguous:**	perpendicular	neighboring	contagious
9. **despotism:**	threatening	delivery	stabilizing
10. **diffuse:**	to threaten	to spread	to describe
11. **cataclysmic:**	catastrophic	hilarious	obvious

Your Words, Your World

Don't have time to sit around repeating these words to yourself, over and over again, in order to remember them? Well, you don't have to! The following exercise tests your knowledge of the material . . . without requiring that you take a test! So your job now is to really *think* about what you read, and to really think about the questions that follow.

Diluvial—The word **diluvial** relates to *flooding*. Right now, in your mind, imagine the scene on the news: cars washed up on curbs, mailboxes down on their sides, telephone poles in the middle of the road, and a rowboat on a roof. Can you see the muddy fields? Can you see cars floating down the street instead of driving? Think of this scene, and then think of the word **diluvial**.

Calamitous—Unfortunately, there are tons of **calamitous** situations in the world. What's the greatest **calamity** that you can think of? Picture your report card in your hands with an F staring you in the face. How about a huge credit card bill? Maybe it's your puppy running away from home? Think of your own personal idea of **calamity** and bring that to mind every time you hear or see the word **calamitous**.

Conflagration—As unpleasant as it may be, the easiest way to remember this word is by picturing a destructive fire. Can you feel the heat? See the huge flames? Hear the sirens and see firefighters rushing to put it out? Envision this scene when you hear or see the word **conflagration**.

Archipelago—The word **archipelago** is most commonly used for a group of islands. Wouldn't that be a nice place to be right now? White sand, blue water, sailboats on the horizon. . . . Imagine a trail of tiny landmasses on a map and then zoom in until you yourself are on one of those islands.

PART TWO

adjunct adj. (AHD juhnkt)—something added, attached, or joined
An *adjunct* professor only works part of the time, so she is not given the same full-time status as other faculty members.

aggregate n. (AA grih giht)—a collective mass, the sum total
When Gerry finally calculated his debt, it came to an *aggregate* of $3,549.

algorithm n. (AAL guh rith uhm)—an established procedure for solving a problem or equation
The accountant used a series of *algorithms* to determine the appropriate tax bracket for her client.

amorphous adj. (ah MOOR fuhs)—having no definite form
The spilled milk was *amorphous* as it spread across the kitchen floor.

antediluvian adj. (ahn tee dee LOO vee uhn)—prehistoric, ancient beyond measure
The *antediluvian* fossils were carefully displayed at the Peabody Museum.

asymmetrical adj. (ay sim EH tri kuhl)—not corresponding in size, shape, position, etc.
The customer refused to pay when she realized the hairstylist had given her an *asymmetrical* haircut.

dominant adj. (DOM uh nent)—most prominent, exercising the most control
At feeding time, Marley showed himself to be the *dominant* puppy in the litter and got the majority of the food.

encroach v. (en KROHCH)—to impinge, infringe, intrude upon
As the human population expands, we continually *encroach* on natural habitats like the rainforests.

extrude v. (ehk STROOD)—to force out or shape something by pushing it through a small opening
Dr. Langley watched with fascination as the volcano *extruded* rock and molten lava.

> **FLASHBACK**
> You will recall that the word root **ex** means *out* or *out of*. It makes sense then that when something is **extruded** it is *forced out*.

misnomer n. (mihs NOH muhr)—an error in naming a person or place
Greenland is a *misnomer*, since the countryside is mostly icy, not green.

oration n. (ohr AY shun)—lecture, formal speech
As class valedictorian, Paulina delivered an impressive *oration* at graduation.

placebo n. (pluh SEE boh)—a substance with no medical value that is given as medication
Dr. Howell was in charge of seeing whether volunteers who swallowed the sugar pill *placebo* felt better afterward anyway.

potable adj. (POH tuh buhl)—suitable for drinking
Though the water was deemed *potable*, it tasted terrible.

prominence n. (PROH mih nens)—importance, eminence
The Homeland Book Store prided itself on having had several authors of *prominence* give readings over the past year.

trajectory n. (truh JEHK tuh ree)—the path followed by a moving object, whether through space or otherwise; flight
The *trajectory* of Stephen's long home run was nearly interrupted by a pigeon.

Practice 2

DIRECTIONS: Consider the definition and then circle T for True or F for False.

12. **T F** **algorithm**—a procedure for solving an equation
13. **T F** **amorphous**—a form with a distinctive shape
14. **T F** **antediluvian**—any structure to help impede a flood
15. **T F** **encroach**—to infringe upon
16. **T F** **extrude**—to give something form by pushing it out
17. **T F** **misnomer**—a mistake made in naming something
18. **T F** **oration**—ability to fly
19. **T F** **placebo**—a non-medicinal medication
20. **T F** **potable**—unsuitable for drinking
21. **T F** **trajectory**—path followed by a moving object
22. **T F** **dominant**—domineering; authoritarian

Your Words, Your World

Don't have time to sit around repeating these words to yourself, over and over again, in order to remember them? Well, you don't have to! The following exercise tests your knowledge of the material . . . without requiring that you take a test! So your job now is to really *think* about what you read, and to really think about the questions that follow.

Adjunct—You may know someone who is an **adjunct** professor or teacher and is only present part of the time . . . but do you know a lazy person who might qualify as an **adjunct** student? Think of that person when you think of **adjunct**.

Aggregate—What's more fun, totaling up the **aggregate** change in your car, jacket pocket, and that jar on your dresser; or totaling the **aggregate** debt you owe your friends for the movies, dinner, and chipping in for gas?

Prominence—Someday will you rise to **prominence** because of what you learned in school, or will you rise to **prominence** despite what you learned in school? Do you think learning more and more vocabulary words will help you rise to **prominence**? We sure do!

Asymmetrical—Is it worse to wear pants that are **asymmetrical** to your width or a shirt that is **asymmetrical** to your height?

PART THREE

austere adj. (aw STEER)—stern, strict, unadorned
Larry signed up his kids for karate class, hoping the *austere* sport would teach them the discipline they lacked.

axiom n. (AKS ee uhm)—premise, postulate, self-evident truth
Halle lived her life based on the *axioms* her grandmother had passed on to her.

biodegradable adj. (by oh de GRAY duh buhl)—capable of being decomposed by microbial action
In earth science, Geraldine learned that fallen leaves are *biodegradable*.

botanist n. (BAH tuhn ihst)—scientist who studies plants
As a *botanist*, Giselle was able to spend hours studying orchids.

coagulate v. (koh AAG yuh layt)—to clot; to cause to thicken
Hemophiliacs are people who can bleed to death from a minor cut because their blood doesn't *coagulate*.

concave adj. (kahn KAYV)—curving inward
The *concave* shape of the bowl held the spaghetti better than a plate.

delineate v. (de LIN ee ayt)—to explain, depict, describe
Coach Goldberg *delineated* the strategy to his team the day before the championship game.

evanescent adj. (ev ihn ESS ihnt)—momentary, transient, short-lived
George paused for a few seconds to enjoy his busy graduation day, knowing that the feeling of accomplishment would be *evanescent*.

inherent adj. (ihn HEHR ehnt)—involving the essential character of something, built-in, inborn
When Tanisha finally saw the *inherent* benefits of memorizing her vocabulary words, she made them a part of her everyday life and did very well on her tests.

posit v. (PAH ziht)—to assume as real or conceded; propose as an explanation
Ms. Franics told the math students that before proving the math formula, they needed to *posit* that *x* and *y* were whole numbers.

prototype n. (PRO toh typ)—early, typical example
Jim and his team were relieved to have finally completed the science project *prototype* so they could go on to building the real model.

recapitulate v. (ree kuh PIHCH yoo layt)—to review by a brief summary
Before handing out the final exam, Mrs. Thompson *recapitulated* ten of the major moments in the history of the United States.

refract v. (rih FRAAKT)—to deflect sound or light
Angela's crystal necklace *refracted* the rays of sunlight so they formed a beautiful pattern on her wall.

regurgitate v. (ree GURJ uh tayt)—rush or surge back; repeat without digesting
Yolanda's mother tried to convince her that she couldn't just *regurgitate* facts; she needed to understand the material to do well on the test.

remission n. (reh MIH shuhn)—a lessening of intensity or degree
Dr. Logan told Herman the good news that that his cancer had finally gone into *remission*.

secrete v. (suh KREET)—release fluids from body; produce from a source
Mr. Mackling explained to John he should start wearing antiperspirant because his body was beginning to *secrete* sweat.

simian adj. (SIH mee uhn)—apelike; relating to apes
Scientists say that early humans were more *simian* in appearance than modern humans.

soluble adj. (SOL yuh buhl)—capable of being solved or dissolved
Sugar is *soluble* in cold water, but it dissolves more easily in hot water.

stratify v. (STRAA tuh fy)—to arrange or divide into layers
Dr. Schliemann found a graduate assistant who was willing to help her *stratify* the layers of soil around Mt. St. Helens.

turgid adj. (TURH jihd)—pompous; pretentious, dull
Although Mr. Schneider was the smartest teacher on staff, he was also the most *turgid,* making students not want to take his class.

Practice 3

DIRECTIONS: Fill in the blanks, using 15 of the 20 words provided below.

evanescent	concave	simian	stratify	biodegradable
botanist	prototype	remission	austere	coagulate
delineated	soluble	refract	secreted	axiom
regurgitating	posit	recapitulate	turgid	inherent

23. DaJuan had always thought that skunks _____ their odor through their fur.

24. Paul worked for years on the _____ of his garbage-burning engine before he started actually building it.

25. Just one _____ look from his father in response to his crazy suggestion, and JoJo knew the answer was no.

26. Every student's position in the classroom was _____ by a chart in the teacher's binder.

27. The class welcomed a _____ in home-work once the state test was finished.

28. Professor Knight based his theory on the _____ that what goes up, must come down.

29. One effect of cancer is that, depending on the treatment, blood can no longer _____.

30. Although George gave her a(n) _____ glance and quickly looked away, Vickie was sure he was trying to send a message.

31. Nobody ever listened to Amjed's political arguments because he was only _____ what he'd heard on TV.

32. Dave knew that the key to building a sound-proof room was being able to _____ the noise.

33. Kenny's father always said that the reward of learning was _____, but Kenny didn't find school to be rewarding at all.

34. Laura defended her littering by saying that everything she had thrown out the window was _____.

35. Since liquid is _____ in a test tube, Mr. Frome had to show his students how to measure it from the bottom of the curve and not the top.

36. Anna thought taking AP Biology was one of the first steps to becoming a _____.

37. Hank wasn't so sure that the equation was _____—he just couldn't find an answer!

Your Words, Your World

Don't have time to sit around repeating all these words to yourself in order to remember them? Well, you don't have to! The following exercise tests your knowledge of the material . . . without requiring that you take a test! So your job now is to really *think* about what you read, and to really think about the questions that follow.

Posit—I'm willing to **posit** that everybody you know would rather order a couple of pizzas than eat liver and onions. Am I right? What is something that you would **posit** about your best friend without question?

Recapitulate—My friends and I used to spend hours on the phone at night, **recapitulating** what had happened in school that day . . . and I don't mean in class. Sound familiar?

Simian—I think that a lot of these new reality shows make human beings seem really **simian** in the way they're forced to fight over limited resources. Do you agree or do you think these shows are harmless entertainment?

Stratify—When a school is several stories tall, the floors are always **stratified** so that the science labs are at the top. What about at your school? Why do you think that is?

Turgid—Although the movies always make wealthy people seem uptight and **turgid**, I've found that, for the most part, they're just as nice as everybody else. Has this been your experience?

PRACTICE ANSWERS AND EXPLANATIONS

Practice 1

1. **Acclivity** is synonymous with incline. A decline goes downhill, so it is an antonym of **acclivity**, and affection is nice, but it has nothing to do with the slope of an object.

2. By definition **aerate** means to expose, usually to air. Provide is close, but not as appropriate. When something descends it travels downward, which has nothing to do with **aerate**.

3. **Arable** is synonymous with cultivatable, or able to be farmed. Soothing and understandable are also adjectives, but have to do with human relations and not farming or gardening.

4. Something **arboreal** relates to trees. Fish and stars also both occur in nature, but are unrelated.

5. **Ballast** stabilizes. Although something that is used for **ballast** will have an effect on the object being stabilized, this answer is not a synonym. Neither is explode, which really has nothing to do with **ballast**.

6. A **cartographer** makes maps. Although a sailor might also dabble in mapmaking, this choice is too much of a stretch to be considered synonymous. Trees have to do with the vocab word arboreal, but not with **cartographer**.

7. By definition, to **circumnavigate** is to travel around. Sail is tempting, as ships often **circumnavigate** storms and continents and the like. But the root **circum**, meaning around, should lead you to the best answer. Dominant has nothing to do with the definition.

8. Contiguous is synonymous with neighboring. Something perpendicular might be **contiguous**, but specifically, that perpendicular thing is at a right angle to something else. Contagious may sound and look like **contiguous**, but has to do with catching diseases.

9. Despotism is synonymous with threatening. Although a despot may have a stabilizing effect on a country, the word is not a good synonym. Delivery is not associated with **despotism** or threatening.

10. Diffuse is synonymous with to spread. To threaten and to describe are unrelated verbs.

11. Cataclysmic is synonymous with catastrophic, both meaning disastrous, as in a disastrous situation. This means that hilarious is out, obviously. Obvious is wrong as well.

Practice 2

12. True. Algorithms are procedures for solving an equation.

13. False. Amorphous is without shape, so to have a distinctive shape is the opposite.

14. False. Antediluvian is ancient and has nothing to do with floods. Careful—the vocab word diluvial, which is very similar, is the word relating to floods.

15. True. To **encroach** is to infringe upon.

16. True. To **extrude** is to give something form by pushing it out.

17. True. A **misnomer** is a mistake made in naming something.

18. False. An **oration** is a formal speech, not the ability to fly.

19. True. A **placebo** is a non-medicinal medication.

20. False. Something **potable** is suitable for drinking, not unsuitable.

21. True. A **trajectory** is the path followed by a moving object.

22. True. To be **dominant** is to be domineering and authoritarian.

Practice 3

23. If an odor is **secreted**, that means it is emitted or produced from the source.

24. A **prototype** is a model, and before companies will put money into developing a product, they want to see a smaller, cheaper example.

25. **Austere** means strict, so JoJo knew he was out of luck.

26. **Delineating** where each person sits helps explain or define the seating arrangement.

27. Who wouldn't appreciate a **remission** in homework (period without it)?

28. An **axiom** is an old saying, and there's nothing professors like more than old sayings.

29. When blood **coagulates** it clots, which is the body's way of putting a stop to bleeding.

30. **Evanescent** means brief, but as we all know, a look can speak a thousand words. Even a quick glance!

31. **Regurgitating** is repetition without digestion, and often, people just repeat the things they've heard others say to sound smart themselves.

32. If you can **refract**, or deflect, sound so that it doesn't travel beyond the border of windows and walls, then you can soundproof a room.

33. If a reward is **inherent**, it is not material. Kenny apparently lacked the natural instinct—which is what inherent means; built-in or preprogrammed—that would allow him to enjoy the process of learning.

34. Throwing something **biodegradable** (able to be broken down by natural elements) out the window may still be considered littering in some places, so Laura had better be careful.

35. If you've ever seen contact lenses, you know what **concave** is. When measuring amounts of liquid, use the lowest point of the downward curve.

36. A **botanist** studies plants, so Anna should like biology, although dissecting frogs might not be what she bargained for.

37. Soluble means capable of being solved or dissolved. In this case, Hank was stumped and made the all-too-quick assumption that it was the equation's fault and not his!

CHAPTER 2 TEST

Okay, it's time to put your memory to the test! Take your time, not only with the questions, but also when reading the answer explanations that follow. Set a goal for yourself—80% (24 correct answers) is recommended—and if you don't reach that goal, go back and read through the chapter again. Good luck!

DIRECTIONS: For questions 1–15, circle T for True or F for False. For questions 16–30, circle the synonym.

1. T   F   **soluble**—impossible to solve
2. T   F   **stratify**—to divide into layers
3. T   F   **turgid**—pretentious
4. T   F   **prototype**—typing with just two fingers
5. T   F   **recapitulate**—to give in
6. T   F   **evanescent**—short-lived
7. T   F   **inherent**—to be given something
8. T   F   **austere**—stern
9. T   F   **coagulate**—to clot
10. T   F   **simian**—of an earlier era
11. T   F   **contiguous**—next to
12. T   F   **prominence**—unimportant
13. T   F   **calamitous**—peaceful
14. T   F   **botanist**—scientist
15. T   F   **aerate**—expose

16. **to explain:**	delineate	coagulate	recapitulate
17. **to assume as real:**	inherent	posit	encroach
18. **without definite form:**	amorphous	prototype	turgid
19. **added or attached:**	diffuse	adjunct	inherent
20. **to infringe:**	encroach	despotism	austere
21. **sharing a boundary:**	diffuse	coagulate	contiguous
22. **disastrous:**	calamitous	simian	amorphous

23. **having to do with trees:**	adjunct	arboreal	turgid
24. **rule by threat:**	austere	stratify	despotism
25. **to spread widely:**	diffuse	soluble	evanescent
26. **an incline:**	decline	acclivity	delineate
27. **the total:**	aggravate	segregate	aggregate
28. **a naming error:**	misty	misnomer	marginal
29. **a formal speech:**	oration	amorphous	ovation
30. **to deflect:**	retract	refract	detract

Answers and Explanations

1. **False.** **Soluble** is capable of being solved, and the opposite of impossible.

2. **True.** To **stratify** is to arrange or divide into layers.

3. **True.** **Turgid** is pretentious.

4. **False.** **Prototype** is an early or typical example, and has nothing to do with typing.

5. **False.** To **recapitulate** is to review by a brief summary. This is a confusing one, because it contains the word capitulate, which does mean giving in. Just another example of how tricky vocab can be!

6. **True.** **Evanescent** is momentary, transient, short-lived.

7. **False.** **Inherent** is involving the essential character of something, not to be given something. Careful not to confuse **inherent** with an inheritance.

8. **True.** **Austere** is stern.

9. **True.** To **coagulate** is to clot.

10. **False.** **Simian** is apelike, not anything to do with an earlier era.

11. **True.** **Contiguous** is sharing a boundary, or next to.

12. **False.** **Prominence** is important; to say unimportant would be incorrect.

13. **False.** **Calamitous** is disastrous, so peaceful is almost its opposite.

14. **True.** A **botanist** is a scientist who studies plant life.

15. **True.** To **aerate** is to expose to air.

16. To explain is synonymous with **delineate**. Coagulate is to clot, as blood does when forming a scab, and to recapitulate is to review.

17. To assume as real is to **posit**. Inherent means built-in, as in human nature, and encroach means to intrude.

18. **Amorphous** means to be without definite form. Prototypes are models or examples, so they have a definite form. Turgid means pompous.

19. Added and attached are both synonymous with **adjunct**. Diffuse means to spread out and inherent means built-in.

20. To infringe is to **encroach**; despotism (tyranny) is a noun and austere (severe) is an adjective.

21. Contiguous means sharing a boundary. Diffuse means to spread out and coagulate means to clot.

22. Disastrous is synonymous with **calamitous**. Simian is apelike and amorphous is without definite shape.

23. Arboreal means having to do with trees. Adjunct is synonymous with attached and turgid is synonymous with pretentious, neither of which makes mention of trees or nature.

24. Despotism is rule by threat. Although austere, which means severe, is in the same neighborhood, it is not synonymous. Stratify is a verb meaning to break down into different levels.

25. To **diffuse** is to spread widely, which might be confused with soluble (to dissolve or solve), but the two definitions are not synonyms; also, diffuse is a verb and soluble is an adjective. Evanescent is also an adjective, and means brief or passing.

26. An **acclivity** is an incline. Decline is the obvious opposite, while delineate (define) does not fit.

27. An **aggregate** is the sum total, whereas aggravate (upset) and segregate (separate) simply rhyme. Don't fall for the rhyme!

28. Misty is a weather condition and marginal means unimportant. A **misnomer** is an error in naming something.

29. An **oration** is a formal speech and not an ovation, which is a round of applause. Amorphous, or without definite shape, is also incorrect.

30. To retract is to take back and to detract is to take away from. Both sound close but are not synonyms. To **refract** is to deflect, especially light or sound.

CHAPTER 3

The Job Market

Words to know for your résumé, interviews, and thank-you letters

BUILDING BLOCK QUIZ

This "building block" quiz tests the information that you will learn in this chapter, plus two words from the previous chapter. By answering the 12 questions below, you will get a sense of how closely you'll have to study this chapter in order to master the vocabulary of the job market. If you choose incorrect answers for the final two questions, you'll want to go back to chapter 2 for some review.

DIRECTIONS: Fill in the blanks, using the most appropriate of the four multiple-choice answers. The correct answer will always fit into the sentence grammatically.

1. Dean Higgins was pleased when Myles chose to
   _____ to his request and describe the
   details of the fight.
   (A) ascent (B) assent
   (C) rudeness (D) disagree

2. Frances was _____ with her hands, so it
   only made sense that she was a fantastic typist.
   (A) abrupt (B) disagree
   (C) adept (D) polite

3. In his senior year, Chris stopped being so
_____ and started answering questions
in class and going to parties.
(A) agree (B) different
(C) diffident (D) callous

4. Tanner came from a(n) _____ family
and could afford the best, but chose to drive an
old, beat-up pickup truck.
(A) affluent (B) impoverished
(C) allergic (D) flattering

5. With three younger siblings, Jake often felt that
the _____ of cooking and cleaning was
unfairly placed upon him.
(A) only (B) onus
(C) apelike (D) first and foremost

6. The announcement that the music store would
be closing in five minutes was _____ and
so Helen decided to take her business else-
where.
(A) dimpled (B) unskilled
(C) shy (D) brusque

7. Del couldn't believe that his _____
gambling debt was over $500.
(A) importunate (B) aggravate
(C) responsible (D) finances

8. When he started making fun of several students, the class advisor's graduation speech
became quite _____ and very few people
applauded when he was done.

   (A) stylish (B) indecorous
   (C) flood-ridden (D) aristocratic

9. Paul's _____ at the dinner table embarrassed Vicky in front of her friends and she was
sure to let him know afterward.

   (A) repay (B) kindness
   (C) intrapersonal (D) insolence

10. Although Mrs. Lovell's background was very
_____, she actually understood the lives
of her poor students well enough to be a
school favorite.

   (A) burden (B) diluvial
   (C) patrician (D) happenstance

11. Mr. Perkins was disliked as he was a(n)
_____ disciplinarian.

   (A) rich (B) austere
   (C) despite (D) unreturned

12. As a child Hillary had loved dinosaurs, so it
only made sense that she was interested in
_____ studies.

   (A) pester (B) antediluvian
   (C) double (D) despotism

Answers and Explanations

1. B. To **assent** is to agree and Myles, much to Dean Higgins's relief, agreed to share the information. Ascent means climb, and is a trick answer. Rudeness and disagree wouldn't make sense in the context of the sentence, as they are negative words and a positive word is required.

2. C. Frances was skilled, or **adept**, with her hands, so typing came easily to her. Abrupt sounds similar to **adept**, but since it means sudden, it does not fit. Disagree and polite don't sound right, nor do they fit grammatically.

3. C. Be careful—different may sound like **diffident**, but since it doesn't mean shy, it doesn't fit. Chris became more outgoing, so he was no longer **diffident**. He was not callous (insensitive) and agree does not work in the context of this sentence.

4. A. The word but establishes contrast. The best example of contrast is an **affluent** (wealthy) guy driving an old pickup truck. This automatically rules out impoverished as an answer. Allergic and flattering are adjectives, but they don't make sense here.

5. B. Jake had his own life to live but was helping out his family by bearing the responsibility, or **onus**, of so many chores. The other words and phrases—only, apelike, and first and foremost—are off base.

6. D. An announcement may be described as shy and unskilled, but those adjectives would apply more to the announcer than to what the announcer says. Helen, feeling either rushed or offended by this **brusque**, or abrupt, announcement, decided not to make a purchase. The fourth choice, dimpled, is an adjective that does not make sense in the context of the sentence.

7. A. Although it might aggravate Del to have gambled and lost, the blank needs to be filled with **importunate**, which means urgent. Debt like this certainly isn't responsible and although the subject of this sentence is finances, the word is a noun and doesn't fit.

8. B. To be **indecorous** is to be improper—the only way to describe the advisor's comments. They weren't stylish, even though he was probably trying to be cool, and they weren't aristocratic because wealth had nothing to do with his jokes. Flood-ridden isn't relevant to this dud of a speech.

9. D. Vicky wasn't angry about kindness, and both repay and intrapersonal just don't make sense at that point in the sentence. Reading in context, only **insolence** (rudeness or disrespect) works. Paul needs to work on his manners!

10. C. A background can be **patrician** if it is snobby and upper class. Once again, contrast hints at the answer as Mrs. Lovell's poor students liked her despite her aristocratic roots. Burden is a noun that cannot be used to describe an upbringing. Diluvial relates to a flood and happenstance is something that happens by accident.

11. B. Mr. Perkins was an **austere**, or stern, disciplinarian, so nobody liked him. It doesn't matter whether he was rich and neither despite (careful not to confuse this with despot!) nor unreturned fits into the sentence. If you chose incorrectly for this question, you might want to go back to chapter 2 for some review.

12. B. Antediluvian makes the most sense as it is synonymous with prehistoric. To pester is to bother, double is two or twice, and despotism is tyranny—none of those work in the context of the sentence. If you chose incorrectly for this question, you might want to go back to chapter 2 for some review.

PART ONE

adept adj. (ah DEPT)—very skilled
Lisa was so *adept* at computer programming that three different companies offered her a job.

abeyance n. (ah BAY ens)—temporary suppression or suspension
Michelle's evening routine was in a state of *abeyance* as she put everything on hold to wait for the phone call from the college recruiter.

assent v. (ah SENT)—to express agreement
Many recent college grads *assent* to low pay and benefits just to land their first job.

auspicious v. (aw SPISH iss)—having favorable prospects, promising
Tamika thought that the boss inviting her out to lunch was an *auspicious* start to her new job.

bombastic adj. (bohm BAA stihk)—ostentatious and lofty in style, but ultimately meaningless
The CEO's speeches were *bombastic* and all of Linda's coworkers told her not to take them too seriously.

circumvent v. (suhr kuhm VEHNT)—to go around; avoid
Laura was able to *circumvent* the hospital's rules, slipping in to see her mother after visiting hours had ended.

commensurate adj. (cah MEN suhr eht)—proportional
Steve was given a salary *commensurate* to his knowledge and experience.

concord n. (KOHN koord)—agreement
The board of directors was in *concord* that Stanley was the man to hire for the job.

conventional adj. (kuhn VEN shun uhl)—typical, customary, commonplace
Conventional wisdom says that a getting good job today requires having a college education.

diffident adj. (DIF ih dint)—shy, lacking confidence
Even though he was the funniest of all his coworkers, for some reason Stan was always *diffident* around girls at work.

digress v. (diy GREHS)—to turn aside, especially from the main point; to stray from the subject
The company CEO tended to *digress* when trying to make a point to the employees.

flippant adj. (FLIH puhnt)—marked by disrespectful lightheartedness
Haley's *flippant* explanation for the mistake angered her supervisor, and she was immediately put on probation.

genealogy n. (jee nee AHL oh gee)—a recorded history of a person's ancestors
For the independent project, Max traced his *genealogy* all the way back to the *Mayflower*.

importunate adj. (ihm pohr CHUH niht)—troublesomely urgent; extremely persistent in request or demand
Tanya's *importunate* need for money compelled her to ask her family for help.

incisive adj. (in SY sihv)—perceptive, penetrating
Dr. Rhode's *incisive* analysis of the patient's chart helped him to better understand the situation.

Practice 1

DIRECTIONS: After reading the three choices, circle the one that you think is the *antonym* of the word in bold.

1. **adept:**   skilled   not proficient   pleased
2. **abeyance:**   proceed   wait   anticipate
3. **auspicious:** promising   pessimistic   fortunate
4. **bombastic:** modest   pretentious   ignitable
5. **circumvent:** go around   undeviating   nonconfrontational
6. **commensurate:**
                          proportional   disproportional to compensate
7. **concord:**   disagreement   peace   harmony
8. **conventional:**
                          conformist   atypical   archetypal
9. **digress:**   straightforward deviate   wonder
10. **importunate:**
                          demanding   kind   persistent

Your Words, Your World

Don't have time to sit around repeating these words to yourself, over and over again, in order to remember them? Well, you don't have to! The following exercise tests your knowledge of the material . . . without requiring that you take a test! So your job now is to really *think* about what you read, and to really think about the questions that follow.

Genealogy—Have you ever asked your grandparents what your Mom and Dad were like as kids? Have you ever asked them about the generation that immigrated to the United States? At the next family dinner, look into that **genealogy** of yours.

Incisive—If someone is **incisive** that's a good thing. It's a combination of being *smart* and *observant*, kind of like a spy! Who is the most **incisive** person you know? This is the guy or girl who always has *insight* into why someone is in a bad mood or a good mood. Are you incisive?

Assent—To **assent** is to *concur* or to *consent*. While you're being so incisive, decide whether or not you are an *agreeable* person. You might even want to ask a close friend or family member. In using the word, you will grow more comfortable with it, increasing your ability to remember it. Better yet, you'll learn a little something about yourself.

Diffident—The world is full of *shy* people and all too often these **diffident** folks aren't asked for their opinion. You must know at least one *introvert*, right? One *quiet*, hang-out-in the corner, keeps-to-himself kind of person? At school, at home, in the office, out at a party, try and engage someone who usually doesn't say much. What does he think of a current event? What is his opinion? **Diffident** people usually enjoy talking, just so long as it's a one-on-one situation and not in a group. If you yourself are **diffident**, this exercise is twice as challenging. Good luck!

Flippant—We all appreciate being around funny people. Saying someone is funny can mean many things, though. There are those who like to laugh along with others and then there are those who use humor in a less constructive way. If someone is *sarcastic*, *mocking*, or *superficial*, is she trying to make others feel better or worse? Being funny is fun for all, but being **flippant** . . . not necessarily so.

PART TWO

affectation n. (ah feck TAY shun)—pretension; false display
When Robert came home with a southern drawl after one month of working in Atlanta, everyone knew it was an *affectation*.

affluent adj. (ah FLOO int)—rich, abundant
As an *affluent* woman, Enid was able to give large sums of money to charity.

amity n. (aah muh TEE)—friendship
Correspondence over the years contributed to a lasting *amity* between the colleagues.

assimilation v. (ah sim ih LAY shun)—act of blending in, becoming similar
Language classes were offered to help new immigrants with their *assimilation* into the American culture.

brusque adj. (bruhsk)—rough and abrupt in manner
Vivian's *brusque* treatment of the bank customers quickly cost her the position of teller.

callous adj. (CAHL us)—thick-skinned, insensitive
Bud's *callous* personality allowed him to not only survive, but to thrive, in the high-pressure office.

chagrin n. (shuh GRIN)—shame, embarrassment, humiliation
With much *chagrin*, Lenny told his parents that he hadn't been hired for the job.

civility n. (sih VILL ih tee)—courtesy, politeness
The new train conductor treated the commuters with such *civility* that he quickly became their favorite.

ingratiate v. (ihn GRAY shee ayt)—to gain favor with another by deliberate effort, to seek to please somebody so as to gain an advantage
Helen *ingratiated* herself with her fellow interns by volunteering for some of the less-desirable tasks.

levity n. (LEH vih tee)—an inappropriate lack of seriousness, overly casual
Trey's joke added needed *levity* to the otherwise serious meeting.

objective adj. (ob JEHK tihv)—impartial, uninfluenced by emotion
Hector knew he had to try and be *objective* when his daughter asked whether or not she should go away to college.

onus n. (OH nuhs)—a burden, an obligation
Antonia was beginning to hate the *onus* of having to answer the phone for her boss at work.

MEMORY TIP

When you and your family, or group of friends, is dealing with a problem, just think: "The **onus** is *on us*." An **onus** is a *burden* and burdens should be shared.

---

panegyric n. (paan uh JEER ihk)—elaborate praise; formal hymn of praise
The director's *panegyric* letter to the donor kept the charitable donations coming.

persistence n. (puhr SIS tuns)—the act, state, or quality of not giving up
Jamie's *persistence* at getting the petition signed impressed everyone
on the team.

pertinent adj. (PUHR tih nent)—applicable, appropriate
Greg felt his complaints were *pertinent* and did not hesitate to mention
them at his first staff meeting.

Practice 2

DIRECTIONS: Consider the two word choices in the parentheses and
circle the one that best fits in the context of the sentence.

11. As soon as Tisha won the lottery, she began to
    hang out with a more (affluent OR panegyric)
    crowd.

12. Mike had no idea how to help his son find
    (amorphous OR amity) in his new school.

13. When the two elementary schools joined as
    one, the process of (assimilation OR
    persistence) included a Saturday barbecue for
    all of the families.

14. A parent phoned the school to complain that
    Mr. Kroenig was too (callous OR prominent)
    in his written feedback on student essays.

15. With the hopes of creating an atmosphere of
    politeness, Mrs. Young's students voted to
    make (concave OR civility) the class theme
    for the year.

16. Jonah liked to (ingratiate OR chagrin)
    himself with teachers by staying after school
    and offering to help clean, make copies, and
    get coffee.

17. When the seniors started a Peer Court system,
    they unanimously elected Sascha as school
    judge because he was the most (callous OR
    objective) person in the class.

18. Nobody took Frankie's music reviews seriously because she always wrote (panegyric OR affluent) articles that never contained a harsh word.

19. Marny won the Coach's Award because of her (persistence OR amity) in recovering from knee surgery and returning to the basketball court.

20. Greg tended to be too wordy and Miss Dickens reminded him to just include the (pertinent OR onus) information in his research paper.

Your Words, Your World

Don't have time to sit around repeating these words to yourself, over and over again, in order to remember them? Well, you don't have to! The following exercise tests your knowledge of the material . . . without requiring that you take a test! So your job now is to really *think* about what you read, and to really cement an image in your mind. You never know when you'll need that image to pop up again.

Affectation—To have an **affectation** is to have a *quirk* or *mannerism*. Picture a soap opera actress who uses her hands dramatically when she speaks. This is an **affectation**. Although **affectation** is a noun, it is synonymous with *posing* (and is usually used in a critical manner). Posing in a pretentious way is not a new thing. The word **affectation** has its roots in the Latin *affectatio*.

Brusque—Derived from the British *broosk* and the Italian *brusco*, **brusque** is to be *rude*; to be *curt* or *short* with someone. Have you ever been handled *briskly* by someone? You wanted a job and the manager pushed you out of the door after a 30-second interview? If you can remember a time when someone was abrupt and brushed you off, then you know what it means to be **brusque**.

Chagrin—Do your cheeks turn red when you feel embarrassed? Do you drop your gaze to the floor? Shuffle your feet? Dig your hands down deep into your pockets? Picture just one off these things and you will remember what it means to feel the *mortification* that is **chagrin**.

Levity—The Latin *levitas* means light, a physical state used today to describe the way some people can keep a situation from becoming too serious. As a matter of fact, to *levitate* is to raise something up. By bringing **levity** to a situation, you are raising it from something plain, or worse—uncomfortable or confrontational—to something *enjoyable*.

Onus—In a way, **onus** is the opposite of levity. An **onus** is a *burden* that someone must bear. It is a *weight* on the shoulders, like the weight of the world. Speaking of which, have you seen the image of Atlas with the world on his shoulders? If not, find it. This is a surefire way to remember what **onus** means. Atlas was accountable for the world's safekeeping. He was responsible. The **onus** was on him.

PART THREE

conformity n. (kon FORM ih tee)—similarity in form or character
Bruce made it his business to act in *conformity* with the rules and traditions of the law firm.

disheveled adj. (di SHEHV uld)—marked by disorder, untidy
The employment counselor suggested Bruce do something about his *disheveled* appearance before the interview.

emulate v. (EHM yoo layt)—to strive to equal or excel, to imitate
For better and for worse, eager employees often *emulate* their superiors.

feign v. (fayn)—to pretend, to give a false appearance of
James *feigned* enjoyment during the golf outing, to give his boss a good impression.

gauche adj. (gohsh)—lacking social refinement
When Eddie snapped his fingers for the waiter, Mr. Swanson quickly told him to stop acting so *gauche*.

indecorous adj. (in DEHK uh rus)—improper, lacking good taste
Gloria was shocked at the *indecorous* behavior at the company holiday party.

indiscretion n. (in dis KRESH un)—lack of prudence, mistake
Jerry's *indiscretion* at the convention cost his company the new account.

insolence n. (IN su lehns)—rudeness, impertinence
Mark's boss refused to promote him because his *insolence* was so insulting.

opportune adj. (ah puhr TOON)—appropriate, fitting
Her investment in microchips, just before the technological revolution of the 1990s, was *opportune*.

patrician adj. (puh TRIH shuhn)—aristocratic
Though she really couldn't afford an expensive lifestyle, Cleo had *patrician* tastes.

plebian adj. (plee BEE uhn)—crude or coarse; characteristic of commoners
Although Anders & Co was a top-notch accounting firm, its office parties were often *plebeian* to the point that security had to be called.

prepossessing adj. (pree puh ZEH sing)—attractive, engaging
Terry's *prepossessing* appearance made him the most eligible bachelor in the office.

propriety n. (pro PRIY ih tee)—correct behavior; appropriateness
At the company lunch, *propriety* demanded that the employees all wait for the CEO to taste his soup first.

provincial adj. (pruh VIHN shuhl)—limited in outlook, narrow, unsophisticated
Having grown up in the city, Anita had to adjust to the *provincial* attitudes of her country cousins.

requite v. (rih KWIYT)—to return or repay
Ben knew that Melinda had forwarded the e-mail with his inappropriate joke to personnel and planned to *requite* her backstabbing ways.

sybarite n. (SIH buh riyt)—a person devoted to pleasure and luxury
A confirmed *sybarite*, Judge Noonan only held court two days a week; the other days he played golf or went sailing.

versatile adj. (vuhr suh TIYL)—adaptable, all-purpose
By being *versatile* around the office, Lila hoped never to lose her job.

Practice 3

DIRECTIONS: Fill in the blanks, using 12 of the 15 words provided below.

propriety	conformity	feign	sybarite	prepossessing
gauche	requite	indiscretion	patrician	opportune
versatility	provincial	emulate	plebian	disheveled

21. Despite his uncle's generous job offer, Vincent just couldn't _____ interest in a mortuary career.

22. Mandy's _____ ideas forced the advertising firm to hire someone more worldly and creative.

23. Everybody in the office was very suspicious when the boss hired the _____ young woman as his new secretary.

24. When Francine's parents saw her, they knew that her _____ appearance would prevent her from getting the job.

25. Ray vowed to _____ the coworker who had told the boss about his long lunch.

26. Dave was lacking in experience, but his _____ during the job interview let the firm know he could handle himself when talking to important clients.

27. The director decided not to hire Lucy as she was known as a _____ who often skipped rehearsals for manicures and deep-tissue massages.

28. Since Wednesday was payday, it seemed an _____ time for George to buy a new suit.

29. The private school demanded _____ in its teachers, so Wally decided to accept the job teaching in the city where he had more freedom to be original.

30. Grace proved her _____ by making well-received changes to the newsletter's layout, writing, and photography.

31. Carla would have gone to the party with Bo, but his suggestion of renting a horse-drawn carriage to get there was way too _____ for her.

32. No one in Larry's family minded when he decided to _____ Bill Gates's love of computer programming.

Your Words, Your World

Don't have time to sit around repeating these words to yourself, over and over again, in order to remember them? Well, you don't have to! The following exercise tests your knowledge of the material . . . without requiring that you take a test! So your job now is to really *think* about what you read, and to really think about the questions that follow.

Gauche—Nobody wants to eat with a **gauche** dinner guest. Would you invite somebody **gauche** out to dinner, or to your house for dinner? What would you do if you were on a blind date and your date turned out to be *vulgar* and *rude*? To further cement this image in your mind, think of the most **gauche** person you know. And the next time you see this *tasteless person*, remember to thank him or her for helping you remember a word.

Plebian—Bourgeoisie is to proletariat as patrician is to **plebian**. The bourgeoisie and the patricians are upper class; from money; well-off. The proletariat and the **plebians** are of the lower classes. It seems mean, but when using the word as an adjective, **plebian** is synonymous with *vulgar*, *coarse*, and *common*.

Indiscretion—Okay, honesty time. Have you ever been the gauche one, the person who, in a fit of plebian **indiscretion**, told somebody's secret? Maybe you got careless and shared a joke that probably shouldn't have been shared? Discretion means good judgment and who doesn't want to show good judgment?

Insolence—To be **insolent** is to be *rude* and unfortunately, the world is full of **insolent** people. How do you react when faced with a *disrespectful* person? Situations like these are difficult enough to manage, but especially so when you are an employee and the **insolence** is being displayed by a customer. If you've been in this situation, did you handle it professionally or end up losing your job? Who knows why people allow themselves to be *audacious* and *impudent*?

Indecorous—*Impolite*? *Rude*? *Inappropriate*? Nobody likes these characteristics in a date or customer, but oftentimes, these traits make for the most memorable characters. Who is your favorite *rude* dude? How about an *impolite* woman? Think about books you've read and some of the movies and TV shows you've watched.

PRACTICE ANSWERS AND EXPLANATIONS

Practice 1

1. **Adept** means skilled or proficient, which is the opposite of not proficient. One who is adept might be pleased, but even so, this choice is irrelevant.

2. **Abeyance** means suspension or postponement, both opposites of proceed. Wait and anticipate are virtually synonymous with one another, as well as with **abeyance**.

3. **Auspicious** means promising or having favorable prospects. Therefore, its opposite is pessimistic, which means having a negative outlook. Fortunate is another positive word that is similar to **auspicious**.

4. **Bombastic** means pretentious, which is the opposite of modest, which means shy or diffident. If something is ignitable it is flammable, which is unrelated to **bombastic**.

5. To **circumvent** is to go around, which is the opposite of being undeviating (not departing from one's course). If someone is nonconfrontational, he or she also might **circumvent** a situation to get out of it.

6. Commensurate means proportional, which, as you can tell by the word root dis, is the opposite of disproportional. Compensate has a similar sound but means to make a payment.

7. If two things are in **concord**, they are in harmony, which is also similar to peace. The opposite of peace and harmony is disagreement.

8. Someone **conventional** is a conformist, which is the opposite of atypical. Notice the word root a, meaning not. Archetypal may sound the same as atypical, but means that something is a classic example, or a prototype.

9. To **digress** is to deviate, which is the opposite of being straightforward. Wonder sounds like wander and wander is a distant cousin of **digress**, but hopefully you were not fooled.

10. To be **importunate** is to be demanding and persistent. Kind is the antonym.

Practice 2

11. Affluent is correct, as panegyric means elaborate praise. After winning the lottery, Tisha started to hang out with other wealthy, or affluent, friends.

12. Amity is defined as peace and friendship. Amorphous means a shapeless blob, and does not make sense here.

13. Assimilation can lead to amity and in the case of these two elementary schools, a barbecue was used as a way of building friendships. Persistence means to keep trying, so it does not work here.

14. Nobody wants to be criticized, and if a teacher is **callous** (heartless and abrupt), the student will not feel very good about his or her work, let alone that teacher. Prominent means famous and does not apply to Mr. Kroenig's feedback.

15. Concave is curved inward while **civility** is a form of being polite and fair. So **civility** it is for Mrs. Young's class!

16. To **ingratiate** yourself to someone else is to gain favor through deliberate, contrived effort (such as offering to get coffee!). Chagrin is a state of embarrassment and it seems that Jonah isn't ashamed of his behavior.

17. To be **objective** is to be impartial and unbiased; this quality is critical when legal matters are considered. If he's an **objective** person, chances are Sascha will not be callous as a Peer Court judge.

18. Apparently, Frankie was a fan of music, but not of being objective. Her **panegyric**, or elaborate praise, did little to inform her readers, thus she was losing those readers.

19. Marny didn't get herself back on the basketball court through friendship and peace—amity just doesn't fit. No, it was through hard work, through sweat and tears, through **persistence**, that she was able to recover from knee surgery and win the Coach's Award.

20. Greg needed to know what was important and relevant to the topic of his paper. He needed to just write about the **pertinent** information. This may have been his burden, or his onus, as he sat down to write, but the answer is clearly **pertinent**.

Practice 3

21. To **feign** is to pretend and Vincent just couldn't put on a show for his uncle.

22. **Provincial** is an adjective that describes a lack of worldliness. It also means a lack of sophistication. The advertising agency obviously is looking for someone who has grand ideas that will have a nationwide, if not worldwide, appeal. Unfortunately for Mandy, she isn't that person.

23. The boss hired an attractive, **prepossessing** secretary and right away, everybody started gossiping about it.

24. Francine looked **disheveled**, or messy, so she probably won't get the job. Even if she gets rejected for another reason, showing up for an interview looking sloppy is never a good idea.

25. Ray was looking for revenge and when someone avenges a wrong done to him, he **requites**.

26. Decorum and manners will get you far, and in this case, Dave's **propriety** got him the job.

27. Lucy was a slave to her expensive tastes and this makes her a **sybarite**. That's fine as long as she could pay for that manicure, not to mention the fees at the spa.

28. Opportune means appropriate or fitting and payday is a fitting day to go and get fitted for a suit. Speaking of suits, suitable is also synonymous with **opportune**.

29. Conformity means to follow a preestablished pattern; to stick to the norm. If Wally saw teaching as an art, he probably wanted to make sure he could use his own style and not have to follow some sort of code of **conformity**.

30. Way to go, Grace! Being able to edit writing, layout, and photography: now that's **versatility**!

31. If Bo was hoping to impress Carla with his money, he failed. To be **patrician** is to be aristocratic and it sounds like Carla just wasn't into that.

32. To **emulate** is to imitate and Larry's family must have hoped that he would emulate Bill Gates's earnings, as well.

CHAPTER 3 TEST

Okay, it's time to put your memory to the test! Take your time not only with the questions but when reading the answer explanations that follow. Set a goal for yourself—80% (24 correct answers) is recommended—and if you don't reach that goal, go back and read through the chapter again. Good luck!

DIRECTIONS: For questions 1–15, circle T for True or F for False. For questions 16–30, circle the synonym.

1. T F **affluent**—extremely poor
2. T F **concord**—in a state of disagreement
3. T F **adept**—unskilled
4. T F **digress**—to deviate from the point
5. T F **incisive**—perceptive
6. T F **callous**—thick-skinned
7. T F **assent**—to express displeasure or disagreement
8. T F **ingratiate**—to offend on purpose
9. T F **persistence**—refusing to give up
10. T F **provincial**—limited in outlook; unsophisticated
11. T F **affectation**—a pretentious habit
12. T F **conventional**—atypical
13. T F **brusque**—abrupt
14. T F **levity**—a lack of seriousness
15. T F **diffident**—outgoing and friendly

16. **pertinent:**	relevant	irrelevant	trustworthy
17. **conformity:**	dissimilar	similar	conceded
18. **indiscretion:**	careless	discrete	introverted
19. **opportune:**	inappropriate	insignificant	appropriate
20. **onus:**	burden	desirable	undesirable
21. **versatile:**	unchanged	adaptable	high-quality
22. **objective:**	solid	partial	impartial

23. **prepossessing:**

	unattractive	ownership	attractive

24. **feign:** pretend   state   decide

25. **commensurate:**

	commiserate	proportional	promise

26. **flippant:** respectful   acrobatic   lighthearted

27. **amity:** friendship   conformity   bombastic

28. **emulate:** criticize   divert   imitate

29. **propriety:** polite behavior   impolite behavior   real estate

30. **panegyric:** criticism   high praise   epidemic

Answers and Explanations

1. **False.** **Affluent** is not being extremely poor; it is possessing wealth.

2. **False.** **Concord** is peaceful agreement, not disagreement.

3. **False.** **Adept** means skilled, not unskilled.

4. **True.** To **digress** is to deviate from the point.

5. **True.** To be **incisive** is to be perceptive.

6. **True.** **Callous** is thick-skinned.

7. **False.** **Assent** is agreement, not displeasure or disagreement.

8. **False.** To **ingratiate** is to please so it is not to offend, and certainly not to offend on purpose.

9. **True.** When someone has **persistence**, he or she refuses to give up.

10. **True.** **Provincial** is unsophisticated and limited in outlook and perspective.

11. **True.** An **affectation** is a pretentious habit.

12. **False.** **Conventional** is the opposite of atypical, as it means usual and predictable.

13. **True.** To be **brusque** is to be abrupt in mannerisms.

14. **True.** **Levity** is a lack of seriousness.

15. **False.** **Diffident** is shy, so an antonym of outgoing and friendly.

16. **Pertinent** is relevant, not irrelevant. Trustworthy is unrelated.

17. **Conformity** is traditional and similar, so not dissimilar or conceded.

18. **Indiscretion** is careless, and the opposite of discrete. Introverts are rarely indiscrete.

19. **Opportune** is appropriate and not insignificant (unimportant) or inappropriate.

20. An **onus** is a burden or responsibility and neither desirable nor undesirable.

21. Versatile is adaptable and has nothing to do with high-quality. Unchanged is an antonym.

22. Objective is impartial and not partial. The final choice, solid, is irrelevant.

23. Prepossessing is attractive. Ownership of something may be attractive, but it isn't an acceptable definition, nor is unattractive.

24. To **feign** is to pretend; not decide or state, although one might **feign** approval by stating approval.

25. Commensurate is proportional and although promise sounds similar to proportional and commiserate (to express pity for) sounds similar to **commensurate**, neither choice is correct.

26. To be **flippant** is to be disrespectfully lighthearted, so respectful is an antonym. And don't be fooled by the choice of acrobatic (flexible), as it is a distracter based on the flip in **flippant**.

27. Amity is a positive word meaning friendship. Bombastic (pompous) is a negative word and conformity (sticking to the norm) is irrelevant.

28. Emulate is the highest form of flattery, as it is to imitate. To criticize is the opposite and to divert is to redirect, which is unrelated.

29. Propriety means decorum, or polite behavior. Impropriety is impolite behavior, so it qualifies as an antonym, while real estate is a distracter based on the word property.

30. Panegyric is the opposite of criticism. It is actually high or elaborate praise. Epidemic is irrelevant as it means plague.

CHAPTER 4

Business Headlines

Words for your banker, broker, and even the bully who wants your lunch money

BUILDING BLOCK QUIZ

This "building block" quiz samples the information that you will learn in this chapter, plus two words from the previous chapter. By answering the 12 questions below, you will get a sense of how closely you'll have to study this chapter in order to master the vocabulary you'll find in the professional world, in business classes, and when reading the financial pages. If you choose incorrect answers for the final two questions, you'll want to go back to chapter 3 for some review.

DIRECTIONS: After reading the four choices, circle the one that you think most accurately defines the word.

1. Quentin tended to _____ when he told stories, but no one minded the exaggeration as his wild tales were so funny.
   (A) antagonize (B) denigrate
   (C) aggrandize (D) aggravate

2. When Sal _____ the book club funds to pay for the homecoming dance band, the librarian was not happy.
   (A) appropriated (B) described
   (C) defended (D) improper

3. By not telling anyone about the kids breaking into the vending machine, Jackson was also _____ of the crime.

(A) concave (B) culpable

(C) interested (D) innocent

4. Reading Theresa's report card, Mr. and Mrs. Hammill were pleased to see several references to how _____ their daughter was.

(A) retired (B) indolent

(C) industrious (D) conflagration

5. During the holidays, the Future Business Leaders of America club collected canned goods for the _____.

(A) penurious (B) legible

(C) controlled (D) prosperous

6. The CEO of a local bank came to speak to the class, but everyone quickly lost interest in what the _____ man had to say.

(A) turgid (B) diluvial

(C) aggrandize (D) algorithms

7. In receiving over $30,000 in scholarship money, Talia finally _____ the rewards of all her hard work.

(A) dispersed (B) reaped

(C) contested (D) bereaved

8. Working summers at the bank, Leroy used to
_____ every little detail, hoping to one
day open a bank of his own.

(A) cleanse (B) produce

(C) potable (D) scrutinize

9. Although Paulo was voted Most _____
in the high school yearbook, he went on to be
an honest insurance salesman and chairman of
the city's Ethics in Business Committee.

(A) Fast (B) Slow

(C) Wily (D) Banal

10. Although Jennell could not _____ her
sister's athletic successes, she excelled in the
classroom and received an academic scholarship.

(A) replicate (B) create

(C) renegotiate (D) adjudicate

11. To impress women, Tomas often _____
having thousands of shares of Google stock.

(A) fixed (B) feigned

(C) permanent (D) fainted

12. Since childhood, Gretchen had wanted to live
in a(n) _____ neighborhood with huge
lawns and swimming pools.

(A) forgetful (B) reverence

(C) remembrance (D) affluent

Answers and Explanations

1. C. To **aggrandize** is to exaggerate and although one may **aggrandize** while antagonizing (provoking) or denigrating (belittling) another person, those answers are not synonymous. Aggravate means to bother. It sounds like **aggrandize** and rhymes with exaggerate, but has nothing to do with the answer (even if those who exaggerate do aggravate you!).

2. A. Appropriated is to have allocated or distributed. Sal took every last penny from the book club and spent it on the homecoming dance band. He did not describe anything and he did not defend anything. And although his actions were improper in the eyes of the librarian, this adjective does not work here, where a verb is needed.

3. B. Culpable is guilty, so innocent is an antonym and interested is an unrelated word. Concave means curved inward, so it has nothing to do with being guilty (or with stealing snacks!).

4. C. Industrious is productive and hardworking, and although retired people can certainly be **industrious**, productive is the best choice for what Theresa's parents would read on her report card. To be indolent is to be lazy, thus an antonym of **industrious**. A conflagration is a destructive fire and completely unrelated.

5. A. Penurious means poor. Legible and controlled are irrelevant. Prosperous may sound a little like **penurious**, but it actually means the opposite: well-off.

6. A. Turgid is synonymous with pretentious, pompous, and affected. Diluvial has to do with flood debris, and to aggrandize is to exaggerate (which may or may not be a trait of the **turgid**, but is a verb, so does not fit as a possible answer). Algorithms have to do with math and the word does not fit in with the rest of the sentence. (If you got this one wrong, you might want to return to chapter 2 for some review.)

7. B. To **reap** is to collect. Contested means competed and dispersed means distributed, so both are unrelated. The bereaved are in mourning, which has nothing to do with reap . . . unless you want to stretch and make a connection to the Grim Reaper.

8. D. To **scrutinize** is to examine very closely, so Leroy carefully studied every detail that summer so as to learn how banking works. He may have even cleansed the bank in hopes of getting ahead, but the definition just doesn't fit here. The same can be said of produce as he certainly didn't produce every detail of the bank. Potable is out of the question as it is an adjective that describes drinkable water.

9. C. **Wily** is cunning and neither fast, slow, nor banal (commonplace) work in the context of the sentence, especially given the contrast of Paulo's subsequent accomplishments.

10. A. To **replicate** is to duplicate. Adjudicate (to settle a dispute) and renegotiate (to revise) are verbs that might sound like possibilities, but their definitions rule them out. Create means to make something original, and is almost an antonym of **replicate**, so it does not work, either.

11. B. **Feigned** means lied or pretended. Fixed would mean he had repaired, and fainted would mean he had passed out, so both of those are incorrect. Permanent is an adjective that does not fit in the context of the sentence, either. If you answered this question incorrectly, you might want to go back to chapter 3 for some review.

12. D. To be **affluent** is to be wealthy, and can describe people and places. None of the other answers, from forgetful (absentminded) to reverence (respect and admiration) to remembrance (commemoration), describes a neighborhood someone would want to live in. If you answered this question incorrectly, you might want to go back to chapter 3 for some review.

PART ONE

accrue v. (ah CROO)—to accumulate, grow by addition
Timmy's aunt gave him a savings bond that would *accrue* in a bank account over the years to help pay for college.

aggrandize v. (ah gran DIYZ)—to make larger than what really is; to exaggerate
The parents were extremely upset to learn that the principal had *aggrandized* the test scores to make the school look good.

> **MEMORY TIP**
>
> You will find the word *grand* right smack in the middle of **aggrandize**. And to **aggrandize** is to *exaggerate* or make seem bigger and better than is really the case. When trying to remember what **aggrandize** means, look to the word in the middle.

ancillary adj. (ayn sil AHR ee)—accessory; subordinate; helping
Absorbing the bottling business as an *ancillary* was part of a larger plan for the young cola company.

appropriate v. (uh PROH pree ayt)—to assign to a particular purpose, allocate
As class treasurer, Clark suggested they *appropriate* $2,000 for the school's library and spend less on the trip.

arrears n. (uh REERZ)—unpaid, overdue debts or bills; neglected obligations
After the expensive lawsuit, Dominic's accounts were in *arrears*.

beget v. (bee GEHT)—to produce, especially as an effect or outgrowth; to bring about
Principal Browning was sure that his charitable acts would *beget* charitable acts by the students.

bilk v. (bihlk)—to cheat, defraud
Though the lawyer seemed honest, Enrique feared he would try to *bilk* him out of all his money.

cache n. (kaash)—a hiding place; stockpile
Everyone believed that the assistant principal had a *cache* of leftover class funds hidden in a Swiss bank account.

clientele n. (kly ehn TEL)—body of customers or patrons
The Chili Dog was proud to count the high school students among its *clientele*.

cohesion n. (ko HEE zhun)—act or state of sticking together; close union
Charlie felt a sense of of *cohesion* as he and his sister begged for a family vacation to Disney World.

collaborator n. (koh lahb ehr AY tohr)—someone who helps on a task
Lucy had no qualms about working with a *collaborator*, just so long as the project was finished on time.

compensate v. (kohm pehn SAYT)—to repay or reimburse
The moving company *compensated* Tom for the furniture it had broken.

cull v. (kuhl)—to select, weed out
As the Future Business Leaders considered student proposals, they used errors in spelling and grammar to *cull* the pile of paperwork to a more manageable size.

culpable adj. (KUHL puh bull)—guilty, responsible for wrong
The class treasurer was found *culpable* in the scheme to steal from the prom funds.

deficit n. (DEH fih sit)—shortfall, debit, disadvantage
With the nation nursing a staggering *deficit*, the Philanthropy Club had a hard time choosing a charity to support.

Practice 1

DIRECTIONS: Consider the definition and then circle T for True or F for False.

1.	T	F	**ancillary**—an accessory
2.	T	F	**arrears**—unpaid debts
3.	T	F	**bilk**—to cheat
4.	T	F	**cache**—a collection of goods that is valueless
5.	T	F	**clientele**—telephone operators
6.	T	F	**cohesion**—team unity
7.	T	F	**collaborator**—a partner
8.	T	F	**cull**—to distribute
9.	T	F	**culpable**—to be upset
10.	T	F	**deficit**—a shortage

Your Words, Your World

Don't have time to sit around repeating these words to yourself, over and over again, in order to remember them? Well, you don't have to! The following exercise tests your knowledge of the material . . . without requiring that you take a test! So your job now is to really *think* about what you read, and to really think about the questions that follow.

Accrue—What's more fun, **accruing** money from each paycheck so you can get that car you want, or taking on a second job to pay off credit card debt? To **accrue** is to *amass*, *increase*, *accumulate*, and *grow*.

Aggrandize—Do you have a friend who tends to **aggrandize** with great *exaggerated* details when she tells a story? By the same token, do you get tired of acquaintances who **aggrandize** every time they open their mouths? You know they're *exaggerating* and *lying* and not to be believed. To **aggrandize** can be positive: think of the friend who tells those entertaining stories. But, it can also be negative: think of the person who *overdoes* it and cannot be trusted.

Appropriate—*Budgeting* is a skill beyond compare. To be able to *allocate* money in the right way is one of life's challenges. When you get your hands on some money, do you spend it right away or do you **appropriate** it for bills or for big purchases somewhere down the road?

Beget—Will you **beget** positive changes in your life or negative changes? Breaking bad habits is one of the hardest things to do, but the second you start, you will *produce*, *cause*, and *bring about* positive results. Just to become aware of your spending habits is a step in the effort to **beget** financial stability.

Compensate—Just as you are **compensated** for whatever work you do, all of the folks you do business with expect to be *paid* for their goods and services. Have you appropriated enough money to *cover* your expenses? Have you accrued enough cash for both bills and fun? When answering these questions for yourself, don't aggrandize!

PART TWO

disclose v. (dihs CLOHZ)—to make known, expose to view
The journalist was kept in jail for four hours because she would not *disclose* the source of her article.

discourse n. (DIHS kohrs)—verbal exchange, conversation
Mr. Hemmings knew that he might convince Colby to apply to college if they engaged in a calm *discourse*, one-on-one.

discretion n. (dihs KREH shin)—ability to judge on one's own
Sales at Starburst coffeehouses quickly grew, aided in part by the fact that store managers could choose the day's special at their own *discretion*.

divulge v. (diy VULJ)—to make known
Pat was fired for *divulging* the company's secrets to its competitor.

inauspicious adj. (ihn aw SPIHSH ihs)—unfavorable
Telemarketers always seem to call at the most *inauspicious* times.

industrious adj. (ihn DUHS tree uhs)—hardworking, diligent
Growing up with an *industrious* father, Ron couldn't help but have a good work ethic.

liability n. (liy uh BIHL uh tee)—handicap, something holding one back
When Team Blue complained that Darren was a *liability*, Mrs. Sweetney subtracted a point, reminding them that good teammates are never critical of one another.

patronize v. (PAY truh niyz)—to adopt an air of condescension toward, to buy from.
Mrs. Berger *patronized* the honors students with smiley-face stickers and pats on the head.

peculate v. (PEHK yoo layt)—to embezzle
No one in the front office could believe it when the superintendent was accused of *peculating* transportation funds so that he could pad his retirement fund.

pecuniary adj. (pih KYOO nee ehr ee)—relating to money
As an economics teacher, Ms. Jackson hoped her students would make wise *pecuniary* decisions for the rest of their lives.

penurious adj. (puh NOOR ee us)—poverty-stricken; destitute
The *penurious* people in Scrooge's neighborhood could not believe his Christmas spirit.

pragmatic adj. (prag MAH tihk)—practical; moved by facts rather than abstract ideals
Because he prided himself on his *pragmatic* ways of thinking, Paul chose not to take the philosophy class with his friends.

prohibitive adj. (proh HIHB ih tiv)—excessive; too expensive
Gutierrez fought for lower prices on produce nationwide, saying that the cost was *prohibitive* to the impoverished and a contributor to their poor health.

propel v. (proh PEHL)—to cause to move forward
Mr. Sanders promised the board that the research and development would *propel* the company into the next century.

prophetic adj. (proh FEH tik)—foretelling events by divine means
The secretary's early warnings proved *prophetic*, as the security guard was fired for using school computers to shop online.

Practice 2

DIRECTIONS: Read the three choices and then circle the *antonym*.

11. **disclose:**	conceal	reveal	announce
12. **discourse:**	discussion	study	uncommunicative
13. **discretion:**	recklessness	care	secret
14. **inauspicious:**	poor	favorable	infamous
15. **industrious:**	business	creative	lazy
16. **patronize:**	salutary	respect	crass
17. **pecuniary:**	barter	financial	stingy
18. **penurious:**	wealthy	poor	middle class
19. **prohibitive:**	disallowed	affordable	restricting
20. **prophetic:**	hindsight	foresight	nearsighted

Your Words, Your World

Don't have time to sit around repeating these words to yourself, over and over again, in order to remember them? Well, you don't have to! The following exercise tests your knowledge of the material . . . without requiring that you take a test! So your job now is to really *think* about what you read, and to really cement an image in your mind. You never know when you'll need that image to pop up again.

Divulge—In **divulge** we find the Latin *divulgare*, *di* meaning "apart" and *vulgare* meaning "to make public." Imagine, if you will, a large crowd of people standing before a stage with a podium. And guess who is standing behind the podium? That's right: you. And you're about to **divulge** something very important. Something very secretive. Your hand reaches for the microphone and . . . what do you say?

Liability—The French *lier* means "to bind." Oftentimes, people feel a huge *responsibility* as a noose around the neck or handcuffs binding their hands. Having a **liability** can be pretty stressful, so these images aren't exaggerated. When you imagine this word, synonymous with *obligation*, imagine that you are bound by ethical laws to take care of this **liability**. (Otherwise, you're **liable** to get yourself into some serious trouble!)

Peculate—Remember those handcuffs? Well, you can picture them once more, but this time they don't represent a responsibility. You really have been arrested. Everybody told you not to embezzle that money. But you did. You **peculated** other people's life savings and so now you must pay; pay back the money and pay your debt to society.

Pragmatic—Picture, if you will, a robot that takes out the trash, washes the dishes, vacuums, does laundry, balances the checkbook, answers cold callers with a definitive no, and sends all junk email to the spam police. Borrowing from the Greek, this robot will be called *Pragmatikos*, which has to do with taking care of business—with being *sensible* and *down-to-earth*—and is the origin of **pragmatic**.

Propel—*Propellere* is the Latin root of **propel**, *pro* meaning "forward" and *pellere* meaning "to drive." Can you see a **propeller** starting up in anticipation of *driving* this plane forward? See the blades spin faster and faster as you get more and more excited for your week in some exotic location. It was the new, high-paying job that helped **propel** you on this luxurious vacation. It was your idea to interview for a new job, so you have **propelled** yourself physically (on the plane) as well as figuratively (thinking to change jobs).

PART THREE

proximity n. (prok SIM ih tee)—nearness
Shovanda worked in close *proximity* to her crush, Dan, at her after-school job at Pizza World.

proxy n. (PRAHK see)—a person authorized to act for someone else
Janet acted as *proxy* for Diana at the debate when Diana lost her voice.

quid pro quo n. (kwid proh KWOH)—something done or given in return for another thing.
After working four Saturdays in a row, Kyle reminded Bob of their *quid pro quo* agreement and moved into the corner office.

reap v. (reep)—to obtain a return, often a harvest
While the grasshopper starved in the winter, the ant *reaped* the benefits of his hard labor.

remiss adj. (ree MIS)—negligent or careless about a job
After reviewing the class checkbook, Mrs. Edgars informed Jon that he had been *remiss* as class treasurer and should resign.

remuneration n. (rih MYOO nuh ray shuhn)—payment for goods or services or to recompense for losses
Oliver expected *remuneration* for his business travel expenses and was surprised when his boss returned his receipts and said no.

replicate v. (REP lih kayt)—to duplicate, repeat
Wendy knew that, in order to *replicate* the grades she earned in the second quarter, she'd have to get at least a 90 percent on the test.

requisition v. (re kwi ZIH shun)—to demand the use of
Monty *requisitioned* access to the executive bathroom and was pleased when the boss personally handed him a key.

retroactive adj. (reh troh AHK tiv)—applying to an earlier time
Mrs. Linden announced that all of the high school kids who stayed on at the restaurant would receive raises *retroactive* to their date of hiring.

scapegoat n. (SKAYP goht)—someone blamed for every problem
Devon always told his mother that he was the teacher's *scapegoat*, but she knew better.

scrutinize v. (SKROOH tihn iyz)—to observe carefully
Outside consultants were hired to *scrutinize* the company's finances, but doubled the company's debt with their expensive billing.

status quo n. (stah tus KWOH)—the state of affairs at a particular, usually current, time.
The *status quo* was good enough for Nancy, so she never pushed for a raise—and, outside of cost-of-living increases, never got one.

> **MEMORY TIP**
>
> **Status quo** is a Latin phrase that is used in the business world, but also as a common phrase. It means "state in which" or, more specifically, *the state of affairs at the current time.*

subterfuge n. (SUB ter fyooj)—deceptive strategy
Everyone knew that Zana had climbed the company ladder by use of *subterfuge*, but nobody was ever able to prove it.

toady n. (TOH dee)—one who flatters in the hope of gaining favors
Whenever Ray was being a *toady* with Ms. Hollingsworth, somebody in class would say, "Ribbit! Ribbit!"

usury n. (YOO zuh ree)—the practice of lending money at exorbitant rates
Wesley was accused of *usury* when the customer discovered that he was charging 40 percent interest to cash a check.

wily adj. (WIY lee)—clever; deceptive
Susan was *wily*, but couldn't get out of doing her day of community service, a requirement of every student in Mr. Mayall's class.

Practice 3

DIRECTIONS: Consider the two word choices in the parentheses and circle the one that best fits in the context of the sentence.

21. Max wouldn't take cash from his neighbor; instead he preferred a barter system that was (quid pro quo OR status quo).

22. When Miss Fiona asked Chico for an update on his project, he told her that everything was as she would expect—all was (quid pro quo OR status quo).

23. After Coach Cranston called Jonesy out for being such a kiss-up, everyone on the team knew that he was indeed (a toady OR wily).

24. The first thing Bernice learned in her ethics class at business school was that corporate (subterfuge OR proximity) is unacceptable.

25. Larry refused to be a (scapegoat OR toady) for the bullies in the bathroom and went straight to the assistant principal.

26. The English professor reminded her students to (subterfuge OR scrutinize) their bibliographies so as to ensure that all sources were cited.

27. Teddy knew to keep his friends near, but his enemies in even closer (proxy OR proximity).

28. Will had learned from experience that sports-betting bookies practiced (usury OR wily).

29. On his deathbed, Randall changed his mind and named his first wife the (scapegoat OR proxy) for his estate.

30. It was no surprise to learn that Ernie was a (wily OR scapegoat) businessman, as he had always made money selling baseball cards and Blow-Pops on the playground when no teachers were looking.

Your Words, Your World

Don't have time to sit around repeating these words to yourself, over and over again, in order to remember them? Well, you don't have to! The following exercise tests your knowledge of the material . . . without requiring that you take a test! So your job now is to really *think* about what you read, and to really think about the questions that follow.

Reap—Have you **reaped** what you've sown? Every day, you make certain efforts. Are you being *rewarded* for your efforts? If your earnings or grades don't measure up to the efforts you're making, what can you do about it? When you use this book, the more work you put into the reading and the activities, the more you'll learn. You will **reap** the rewards of your hard work in the form of a vastly improved vocabulary.

Remiss—How long until the SAT or GRE? Not long, huh? Well, if you've been working hard, there should be no problem, right? However, if you are being **remiss** in your work, then you are right to be worried. To be **remiss** is to be *irresponsible*. It is to be *negligent*. You haven't been *neglectful* of this book and its activities, have you? Well, good. No need to worry then!

Remuneration—Is there a light at the end of the tunnel for you, hard-working student? Is there some sort of **renumeration** for this improved vocabulary? Of course there is! In the long term, this *reward* may very well be financial. If you only hope to be wiser with your words, well then that's a **remuneration** of a different sort: a compensation in brainpower and skills, as well as the self-satisfaction of knowing that you have improved yourself.

Replicate—Although it may seem that there is no need to *duplicate* the word "duplicate," there is another word for it—**replicate**. When you get dressed every day, do you **replicate** someone? And if not, whose wardrobe would you **replicate** if you had the money? Have you ever **replicated** somebody's test answers? *Copied* someone's written work by cutting and pasting an online essay? That was a dishonest move, but at least it will help you remember what **replicate** means!

Requisition—How did you come to own this book? Was it a gift? Or did you **requisition** it, demanding that a parent, aunt, uncle, or grandparent purchase it for you? Did you use a guilt trip to get this book? What form of **requisition** do you use most often?

Retroactive—Have you ever received **retroactive** remuneration for a job done in the past? Have you ever requisitioned funds, **retroactive** to a previous time? *Retro* means *prior to* or back in the *past* while *active* actually means *applied to*. Think of something you did a few weeks ago. If it was around the house, you might want to bring this back up again when you want something (like the car for the night). If you did this chore or favor for a friend or coworker, you might want to remind him or her before asking a favor of your own.

PRACTICE ANSWERS AND EXPLANATIONS

Practice 1

1. **True.** Something **ancillary** is an accessory.

2. **True.** **Arrears** are unpaid debts.

3. **True.** To **bilk** is to cheat.

4. **False.** A **cache** is a stockpile, usually of something valuable.

5. **False.** **Clientele** refers to a business's customers and not telephone operators.

6. **True.** **Cohesion** is unity in a team or group.

7. **True.** A **collaborator** is a partner.

8. **False.** To **cull** is to select, a near-antonym of distribute.

9. **False.** To be **culpable** is to be guilty.

10. **True.** A **deficit** is a shortage.

Practice 2

11. To **disclose** is to reveal or announce something. Conceal means to hide, and so it is the antonym.

12. **Discourse** is a form of communication, so uncommunicative is a perfect antonym. Discussion is a synonym and study is unrelated.

13. **Discretion** is a means of being careful, so recklessness is the antonym.

14. Inauspicious indicates unfavorable or poor conditions, so favorable is the antonym. Infamous contains the same root, but means having a bad reputation.

15. Industrious is productive and conscientious, so lazy is the antonym. Business is a noun and someone industrious could be considered creative.

16. Patronize is to condescend to someone—sometimes in a crass manner, sometimes not—so respect is the antonym. Salutary is a positive word meaning good for your health.

17. Anything **pecuniary** relates to money, while to barter is to trade goods, making it the antonym. Financial also relates to money, and stingy is synonymous with cheap.

18. Penurious is to be poor, so wealthy is the best antonym. Middle class is very different from poor, but wealthy is at the exact opposite end of the spectrum.

19. Prohibitive is to be too expensive, so affordable is the antonym. Restricting and disallowed are both negative words similar to prohibitive.

20. Prophetic is to be able to see the future—to have foresight—so hindsight is the antonym. Nearsighted people simply need glasses.

Practice 3

21. Quid pro quo is the best choice, as it means "something for something." Status quo indicates the state of current affairs, so doesn't fit.

22. Status quo works best in this sentence, as it indicates the state of current affairs (even if Chico might have been lying). Quid pro quo means something done in return for something else.

23. To be wily is to be cunning. In this case, Jonesy was not cunning, he was a **toady**. When someone is a **toady**, he isn't that smart. His efforts to ingratiate himself are clear to all involved.

24. Deceptive ploys fall into the **subterfuge** category, and the students were being warned about the negatives of being deceptive. No need to teach about proximity, or closeness.

25. In this choice of animalistic terms, toady may sound right, but the answer is **scapegoat**. Larry was refusing to let himself be blamed for somebody else's wrongdoings in the bathroom.

26. Subterfuge just doesn't fit in the context of this sentence. The professor is giving a warning about plagiarism and wants to make sure that every detail is **scrutinized**—examined and reexamined—in particular, the list of the books, articles, and websites that the students used in putting together their papers.

27. Proximity is synonymous with nearness and closeness, so works best in Teddy's case. A proxy is a substitute, so the word doesn't work here.

28. Usury is a situation in which those in debt find themselves paying an extremely high interest rate. Although someone who practices usury might be cunning, wily is an adjective that does not work in the context of the sentence.

29. A **proxy** is a substitute, and although Randall might have wanted to blame his first wife for everything and anything before passing away, the scapegoat option just doesn't make as much sense. In legal terms, Randall was trusting his first wife to handle his estate.

30. Ernie was **wily**—he was so cunning that he always got away with business practices that border on the illegal. There is no scapegoat, or someone being falsely blamed, here.

CHAPTER 4 TEST

Okay, it's time to put your memory to the test! Take your time not only with the questions but in reading the answer explanations that follow. Set a goal for yourself—80% (24 correct answers) is recommended— and if you don't reach that goal, go back and read through the chapter again. Good luck!

DIRECTIONS: For questions 1–15, circle T for True or F for False. For questions 16–30, circle the synonym.

1.	T F	**retroactive**—back to an earlier time	
2.	T F	**usury**—using someone as a consultant	
3.	T F	**subterfuge**—under the surface	
4.	T F	**quid pro quo**—the state of affairs at a certain time	
5.	T F	**remiss**—doing a job carelessly	
6.	T F	**prophetic**—psychic and visionary	
7.	T F	**pragmatic**—practical	
8.	T F	**peculate**—to speculate	
9.	T F	**inauspicious**—unfavorable	
10.	T F	**discourse**—verbal exchange	
11.	T F	**status quo**—the usual	
12.	T F	**appropriate**—to allocate	
13.	T F	**propel**—to slow down	
14.	T F	**industrious**—easygoing	
15.	T F	**proxy**—an authorized representative	

16. **guilty:**	culpable	inculpable	liability
17. **to select:**	bilk	cull	aggrandize
18. **a helper:**	clientele	collaborator	culpable
19. **a hiding place:**	cache	cull	status quo
20. **to cheat:**	accrue	bilk	aggrandize
21. **overdue debts:**	arrears	accrue	bilk

22. **to accumulate:**	cull	usury	accrue
23. **to exaggerate:**	cache	culpable	aggrandize
24. **patrons:**	collaborators	liabilities	clientele
25. **a responsibility:**	accrue	usury	liability
26. **additional:**	ancillary	inaccessible	summary
27. **reveal:**	conceal	divulge	unknown
28. **obtain:**	reap	replicate	proximity
29. **flatterer:**	critic	froggy	toady
30. **deceptive:**	prophetic	candid	wily

Answers and Explanations

1. True. **Retroactive** refers back to an earlier time.

2. False. **Usury** is actually lending money at an extremely high rate, not the hiring of a consultant.

3. False. **Subterfuge** can be thought of as a deception that is "under the surface," but that definition is not close enough for the answer to be true. **Subterfuge** is a noun.

4. False. **Quid pro quo** is Latin for "something for something." The definition given is actually for status quo, not **quid pro quo.**

5. True. **Remiss** is, indeed, doing a job carelessly. Do not be **remiss** in your vocabulary work!

6. True. To be **prophetic** is to anticipate the future; it is to be visionary and psychic.

7. True. To be **pragmatic** is to be practical.

8. False. To **peculate** is not to speculate, even if it does rhyme. To peculate is to embezzle.

9. True. Something **inauspicious** is unfavorable.

10. True. **Discourse** is discussion, dialogue, verbal exchange—all of the above.

11. True. The **status quo** is the state in which things usually are. It is normal.

12. True. To **appropriate** is to allocate or assign.

13. False. To **propel** is not to slow down. It is to drive or push forward.

14. False. To be **industrious** is to be very productive, not to be easy-going.

15. True. A **proxy** is an authorized representative, often named in legal or medical situations.

16. Guilty is **culpable.** Inculpable is innocent and a liability is a legal responsibility.

17. To select is to **cull.** The other two choices are also verbs, but not synonymous with selecting. To aggrandize is to exaggerate while to bilk is to deceive.

18. A helper is a **collaborator**. Clientele receive the help, and culpable means guilty.

19. A hiding place is a **cache**. Status quo is the current state of affairs while to cull is to select, so neither fits.

20. To cheat is to **bilk**. To accrue is to gather while to aggrandize is to exaggerate.

21. Overdue debts are **arrears**. To bilk is to cheat and to accrue is to gather.

22. To accumulate is to **accrue**. Usury is the practice of loaning money at an extremely high rate of interest. To cull means to select.

23. To exaggerate is to **aggrandize**. To be culpable is to be guilty, while a cache is a hiding place of sorts. Neither fits the definition.

24. Patrons are a business's **clientele**. They can be liabilities and they may even be collaborators, but to be a patron is to be among the **clientele**.

25. A responsibility is a **liability**. Usury and accrue do not fit, grammatically or in terms of meaning.

26. An **ancillary** is a supplementary (additional) thing, most often an added-on document. Inaccessible (unable to get through) and summary (a review) are unrelated.

27. To **divulge** is to reveal. Conceal (hide) and unknown are virtual antonyms.

28. To **reap** is to obtain or acquire. To replicate is to duplicate, and proximity occurs when one thing is near another, so both are incorrect.

29. A **toady** is a flatterer. A critic is the opposite while froggy is a silly answer.

30. To be **wily** is to be deceptive. To be candid is to be honest, which is almost an antonym. To be prophetic is to be a visionary.

CHAPTER 5

Political Headlines

Words most likely heard on the news regarding politics and world events

BUILDING BLOCK QUIZ

This "building block" quiz tests the information that you will learn in this chapter, plus two words from the previous chapter. By answering the 12 questions below, you will get a sense of how closely you'll have to study this chapter in order to master the vocabulary of politics.

DIRECTIONS: Fill in the blanks, using the most appropriate of the four multiple-choice answers. The correct answer will always fit into the sentence grammatically.

1. When Billy tried to _____ the remote control, his sister reminded him that she'd let him watch football the day before.

   (A) arrogate (B) accede
   (C) autonomous (D) vacillate

2. The senator was the perfect choice to delay the passing of the tax bill since his _____ usually lasted for hours on end.

   (A) abdicates (B) arrogates
   (C) filibusters (D) harangues

3. Margaret's favorite part of social studies was learning about the U.S. Constitution and her _____ rights.

(A) inviolable (B) discord

(C) intransigent (D) oligarchy

4. What Troy hated most about being student body president was feeling compelled to _____ between concentrating on student concerns and the concerns of the principal.

(A) arrogate (B) accede

(C) abeyance (D) vacillate

5. The press conference was a total _____: the air conditioning blew warm air, the lights flickered off twice, and the microphones did not work.

(A) pandemic (B) dogmatic

(C) debacle (D) austere

6. As a freshman, Joan had been such a(n) _____ class president, refusing to change her stance on many issues, that the staff was shocked to learn she'd been reelected.

(A) oligarchy (B) inviolable

(C) stratify (D) intransigent

7. No one thought that a(n) _____ could rule the Middle Eastern country for much longer.

(A) inviolable (B) oligarchy

(C) filibuster (D) harangue

8. From coast to coast, the lack of flu shots was a concern of _____ proportions.
   (A) pandemic (B) turgid
   (C) paean (D) propel

9. History teaches that dictators tend to be _____ and cruel to their people.
   (A) cartographer (B) misnomer
   (C) aerate (D) dogmatic

10. The letter informed Hillary that because of five unpaid tickets, her license was in a state of _____ until further notice.
    (A) abeyance (B) potable
    (C) accede (D) diluvial

11. The teenagers felt frustrated and _____ when the town adopted a 9 P.M. curfew for everyone age 18 and younger.
    (A) prominenced (B) propelled
    (C) patronized (D) debacled

12. Ms. Jenkins liked to _____ her students' research papers to make sure they hadn't been plagiarized from the Internet.
    (A) pandemic (B) vacillate
    (C) feign (D) scrutinize

Answers and Explanations

1. A. To **arrogate** is to claim as your own without right; one example is claiming the remote control when you already had a turn. To accede is to agree, autonomous is independent, and to vacillate is to waver back and forth.

2. C. The senator was known for his **filibusters**, or prolonged speeches, which are often used in politics as delay tactics. Abdicates (renounces) and arrogates (to claim without right) are verbs. Harangues are angry lectures or speeches. While this is a potential choice, **filibusters** makes more sense in the context of delaying a bill.

3. A. **Inviolable** rights are sacred rights and Margaret likes to know that she has such unbreakable rights. Discord, which is disagreement, and oligarchy, which is rule by a group, are nouns that do not fit within the context of the sentence. Intransigent is an adjective synonymous with stubborn, which cannot be used to describe rights.

4. D. Troy was trying to make everyone happy, thus the feeling of wavering (or **vacillating**) back and forth between staff and students. To arrogate is to claim without right and to accede is to agree, both of which do not work in the context of the sentence. Abeyance is the temporary suppression of something, but that answer must be suppressed in this case because it is incorrect. **Vacillate** perfectly describes Troy's situation.

5. C. A **debacle** is a total mess or disaster, as this press conference was. Since the conference took place in one room, it couldn't possibly be pandemic (over a widespread area). The situation also can't be considered austere (strict or severe), even though it sounds like it was less than pleasant. Dogmatic is synonymous with austere, so it is ruled out as well.

6. D. To be **intransigent** is to be stubborn, so the fact that such an inflexible person could get reelected was surprising. An oligarchy is rule by a group, so does not apply to Joan's situation or style. Inviolable is unbreakable and sacred, so it is an inappropriate choice. To stratify is to break into layers for further study, so it is also irrelevant.

7. B. An **oligarchy** is a group that rules. A filibuster does not work as it is a long speech. To harangue is to lecture and inviolable is unbreakable.

8. A. Pandemic is over a widespread area, as in an epidemic: in this case, the flu. The other three choices are unrelated: turgid (pompous), paean (an artistic tribute), and propel (to drive forward).

9. D. By nature, a leader who takes control—usually through military power—is **dogmatic**, meaning inflexible and strict. These leaders are not cruel mapmakers (cartographer), they are not cruelly misnamed (misnomer), and they do not have anything to do with cruel ventilation (aerate).

10. A. Abeyance is a noun meaning a state of temporary suspension. Diluvial and potable relate to water and are irrelevant. To accede is to agree and for Hillary, there was nothing agreeable about this situation!

11. C. When a group feels **patronized**, it feels it has been talked down to and treated unfairly. Propelled is in the right neighborhood, as the teens may be pushed into action, but that's just too much of a stretch to be correct. In turn, prominenced and debacled aren't real words. If you answered this question incorrectly, you might want to go back to chapter 4 for some review.

12. D. Ms. Jenkins **scrutinized** those research papers, meaning she searched them carefully for language and style that didn't seem like it would come from one of her students. Pandemic (something occurring over a widespread area) does not apply or fit, grammatically, and to vacillate is to waver. To feign is to fake, which is relevant but incorrect—Ms. Jenkins did not fake her students' research papers. If you answered this question incorrectly, you might want to go back to chapter 4 for some review.

PART ONE

abdicate v. (aab dih KAYT)—to give up a position, right, or power
Facing impeachment, Nixon decided to **abdicate** the presidency and resigned.

abrogate v. (AAB ruh gayt)—to annul; to abolish by authoritative action
Students, staff, and parents were all upset when Principal Redford decided to **abrogate** the student council's controversial decision.

accede v. (aak SEED)—to express approval, to agree to
Harry hinted to the political party that he would **accede** if asked to run for mayor.

accentuate v. (aak SEN choo ayt)—to stress or emphasize; intensify
It's natural for a politician to **accentuate** positive aspects of a situation in a campaign speech, while speaking little about the negative.

actuate v. (AAK choo ayt) to put into motion, to activate; to motivate or influence to activity
Mara's speech **actuated** the crowd of usually apathetic students and they marched towards the governor's mansion.

ameliorate v. (ah MEEL yor ayt)—to make better, improve
Crime statistics in the city were **ameliorated** under the last mayor.

arrogate v. (AA ruh gayt)—to claim without justification; to claim for oneself without right
With Soviet support, Castro **arrogated** the personal property of the wealthy and turned Cuba into a communist country.

autonomous adj. (aw TOHN uh muss)—separate, independent
The history teacher told the class that the goal of America's founding fathers was to make the colonies *autonomous* from England.

FLASHBACK

In the first chapter, you learned that the word root **auto** means *self*. As long as you can remember this, you will remember that to be **autonomous** is to be *independent*. It is to be able to rely on your*self*, to answer only to your*self*, and to be responsible for your*self*.

---

belligerent adj. (buh LIJ ehr ent)—hostile, tending to fight. Latin for "to wage war."
When the class clown became *belligerent*, Mrs. Ivans finally decided it was time for a parent-teacher conference.

beneficent adj. (buh NEHF ih sihnt)—pertaining to an act of kindness
Anonymously, somebody made a *beneficent* donation of $50,000 to the Boy Scouts.

caucus n. (KAW kuhs)—smaller group within an organization; a meeting of such a group
Gus was proud to be a part of the student *caucus* asked to help the police combat teen drinking and driving.

collusion n. (kuh LOO zhen)—collaboration, complicity, conspiracy
When they learned that Coach Woodson was in *collusion* with the opposing coach to get his quarterback the county record, the Booster Club refused to hold a banquet for him.

conciliatory adj. (kuhn sil ee uh TOR ee)—overcoming distrust or hostility
Fred made the *conciliatory* gesture of buying Abby flowers after she'd defeated him in the race for student body president.

concordant adj. (kon KOR dint)—harmonious, agreeing
Bruce told his mother how her advice had helped him and the *concordant* words brought a smile to her lips.

convoluted adj. (KON vuh loo tid)—twisted, complicated, involved
Joel lost the election because his speech was too *convoluted* for anyone to understand.

Practice 1

DIRECTIONS: Consider the two word choices in the parentheses and circle the one that best fits in the context of the sentence.

1. Expecting to see only A's and B's on their son's report card, Mack's parents were shocked at the chemistry teacher's (belligerent OR toady) criticisms of him.

2. The mayor and superintendent were in (a caucus OR collusion) to lie about their citywide test scores just to keep real-estate values high.

3. Although Craig had his books inside already, Troy (arrogated OR abrogated) the locker as his own, even putting a lock on it with a secret combination.

4. Dean Harris had a hard time following Christy's (abdicated OR convoluted) story about why she was late, and simply gave her a detention.

5. After four years of (beneficent OR belligerent) leadership, Principal Adams was honored when the seniors asked her to deliver the speech at their graduation.

6. Darryl's heartfelt letter led Mr. Pike to (abrogate OR arrogate) his decision to bar Darryl from running for student body president.

7. In their graduation card, Jack's parents described watching him with pride as he became so much more (convoluted OR autonomous) between his freshman and senior years.

8. The (concordant OR caucus) of concerned parents convinced the school to cancel the prom, much to the disappointment of everyone at school.

9. When the head of security (abdicated OR arrogated) his cushy position, everyone wondered if it was to avoid a scandal.

10. Miss Inkster dimmed the lights and played (belligerent OR concordant) music from South America before the final exam, hoping to calm the anxious students.

Your Words, Your World

Don't have time to sit around repeating these words to yourself, over and over again, in order to remember them? Well, you don't have to! The following exercise tests your knowledge of the material . . . without requiring that you take a test! So your job now is to really *think* about what you read, and to really think about the questions that follow.

Conciliatory—Have you ever been caught in the middle of an argument between two friends or family members? Of course you tried to patch things up, and when you did so, you were acting in a **conciliatory** manner. In trying to *pacify* both people, in trying to get them to start communicating with one another again, you were *defusing conflict*.

Actuate—When was the last time you **actuated**, or *instigated*, a plan of action? And how did you do it? How did you *motivate* everyone to follow suit? Did you convince one other person first? If you can't recall a time you played *leader*, how about second-in-command?

Accede—And when a good idea comes along, an idea so good that everyone is in *agreement*, why not celebrate it? To **accede** is to *agree* and once in a while there is a plan that nobody can find fault with: a great movie, a great restaurant, a theme for a party or dance, or a road trip. Then it's time to **accede**! When was the last time you **acceded**, or *agreed*, with a good plan? What did you and your friends do? Remember this and you will remember what **accede** means: to *agree*!

Ameliorate—To **ameliorate** is to *upgrade*. When you've got a little extra cash in your pocket, how do you *upgrade*? At the diner, do you get a milkshake instead of a soda and ask for melted cheese and gravy on your fries? When shopping, do you splurge a little? Have you ever flown first class on an airplane? This is yet another form of *upgrading*.

Accentuate—Have you ever heard the phrase "Accentuate the positive"? When you **accentuate**, you *highlight*; you *emphasize*. For example, do you always look at life as if your glass were half full or as if it were half empty? If you see your glass as half full, then you are **accentuating** the positive.

PART TWO

demagogue n. (DEH muh gahg)—a leader, rabble-rouser, usually appealing to emotion or prejudice
Taking on the role of *demagogue*, Will almost won the election for student council president as a write-in candidate.

disavow v. (dis uh VOW)—to refuse to acknowledge
When his son announced he'd be running against him as a Democrat, Senator Dowd *disavowed* him, refusing to even shake his hand.

discord n. (DIS kord)—lack of agreement; inharmonious combination
The *discord* at the environmental summit was quickly reported to the press.

FLASHBACK

In the examples **disavow** and **discord**, it is clear that the word root **dis** means *apart* or *away* from. **Disavow** is often used to describe someone who is physically or politically moving *away* from someone else, and **discord** is a description of two people or parties that are *apart*.

---

dogmatic adj. (dawg MAA tik)—rigidly fixed in opinion, opinionated
The students thought Principal White was unfairly *dogmatic*, but the parents loved her.

equitable adj. (eh KWI tuh buhl)—fair; just and impartial
Everyone appreciated that Governor Brown had at least tried to find an *equitable* solution to the problem.

filibuster n. (FIL ih buh stuhr)—the use of obstructionist tactics, especially prolonged speechmaking, in order to delay something
Terry's *filibuster* included everything from intimidating security guards to protesting unfair policies, but the assistant principal couldn't be distracted from handing down the suspension.

galvanize v. (GAAL vuh niyz)—to shock; to arouse awareness
The shutting down of a third homeless shelter *galvanized* the activist group into action.

harangue v. (huh RAANG)—to give a long speech
Maria and her friends *harangued* the school board to the point that it finally agreed to allow seniors to drive to school.

imperious adj. (ihm PEER ee uhs)—commanding, domineering; urgent
Though King Edgar had been a kind leader, his daughter was *imperious* and demanding during her rule.

intransigent adj. (ihn TRAANZ uh jihnt)—uncompromising, refusing to abandon an extreme position
Superintendent Townsend's *intransigent* stance on Saturday detentions actually led to a decrease in behavior problems at the high school.

malfeasance n. (maal FEE zuhns)—wrongdoing or misconduct, especially by a public official
The president's *malfeasance* made it difficult for teachers to decide what was appropriate during discussions of current events.

mandate n. (MAN dayt)—a command or instruction. Latin for "to put into one's hand."
The *mandate* of the new SAT exam left teachers and students scrambling to prepare for a test none of them had ever seen before.

maxim n. (MAK suhm)—fundamental principle
The students were taught the *maxim*, "Do unto others as you would have them do unto you."

mediate v. (MEE dee yayt)—to resolve a dispute between two other parties
The training of students to *mediate* disagreements between other students became popular during the 1990s.

megalomania n. (mehg uh loh MAY nee uh)—obsession with great or grandiose performance
The student council jokingly accused its advisor of *megalomania* when she suggested a "royal wedding" theme for the prom.

Practice 2

DIRECTIONS: Read the four choices and circle the word that does not fit with the other three (which are synonymous with the vocabulary word in bold).

11. **disavow:**
    renounce   deny   reject   pledge

12. **discord:**
    conflict   dispute   agreement   dissension

13. **dogmatic:**
    accommodating assertive   rigid   inflexible

14. **filibuster:**
    obstruct   hinder   impede   brief

15. **galvanize:**
    shock   restrain   stimulate   rouse

16. **harangue:**
    scold   praise   lecture   criticize

17. **imperious:**
    arrogant   subservient   commanding   authoritarian

18. **intransigent:**
    inflexible   uncompromising obliging   stubborn

19. **mandate:**
    permission   consent   refusal   authorization

20. **megalomania:**
    humility   delusional   exaggerative   grandiose

Your Words, Your World

Don't have time to sit around repeating these words to yourself, over and over again, in order to remember them? Well, you don't have to! The following exercise tests your knowledge of the material . . . without requiring that you take a test! So your job now is to really *think* about what you read, and to really cement an image in your mind. You never know when you'll need that image to pop up again.

Demagogue—*Dem* is Greek for "the people" and *agagos* means a leader. A **demagogue** is a *leader* who uses the people as a tool for personal gain. Imagine one of the troublemakers you know standing before a large crowd. What is she thinking about? Is she thinking about what's good for all of those people? Or is she thinking about what's good for her? That's a **demagogue**.

Equitable—Think of the most *reasonable, fair, objective* person you know; someone with an *unbiased, impartial* outlook on the world. Has this person ever acted greedily (like a demagogue)? Has he ever pretended to care about others while really only looking out for his own interests? If you consider him to be **equitable**, then chances are, he hasn't. To remember this word, you can think of this person.

Malfeasance—*Mal* is a word root that means *bad* or *wrong*, while the Latin *facere* means "to do." **Malfeasance** translates to *misconduct*, but is most often applied to *wrongdoing* by public officials. In recent weeks, chances are some politician was in the news for doing something wrong. Think of this person's face on your television set or on the front page of the newspaper.

Mediate—The Latin *mediatus* describes the act of *resolving* a problem between two people. This is also the definition for **mediation**. To **mediate** is to *intervene* in a positive manner. *Mediare*, also Latin, means "to divide in the middle." So, to remember the definition of **mediate**, picture a babysitter placing a line of tape right down the middle of a bedroom. On one side is one brother and on the other side, the other brother. They've been fighting and in the effort to **mediate** a peaceable solution, this babysitter is getting them separated.

PART THREE

paradigm n. (PAAR uh diym)—an outstandingly clear or typical example
Mr. Bloomfield used the great difference in payrolls of professional
baseball teams as a *paradigm* of the capitalist system.

paramount adj. (PAAR uh mownt)—supreme, dominant, primary
Since many voters still didn't know who he was, Harrison knew it was of
paramount importance to get face time on the news before election day.

parity n. (PAAR ih tee)—equality
In discussing feminism, Mrs. Lutskaya agreed that life had improved for
women, but pointed out that there were still many *parity* issues to be
dealt with.

polarize v. (POH luhr iyz)—to tend toward opposite extremes
Gay marriage *polarized* many voters in the 2004 election.

polyglot n. (PAH lee gloht)—a speaker of many languages
Ling's extensive travels have helped her to become a true *polyglot*.

precept n. (PREE sept)—principle; law
The justices of the Supreme Court do their best to abide by the
precepts of the United States Constitution.

prudent adj. (PROO dihnt)—careful, cautious
Considering how close the election was, the mayor was *prudent* about
not making too many changes right away.

puissant adj. (PYOO sihnt)—powerful
Pat Johnson was a *puissant* student leader, not because of her good
grades but because of her athletic ability and achievement.

reconciliation n. (reh con sil ee AY shun)—the act of agreement after a
quarrel, the resolution of a dispute
The juniors attempted *reconciliation* with the seniors by returning their
homecoming float and personally delivering to them 10 large pizzas.

succumb v. (suh KUHM)—to give in to stronger power; yield
The principal decided to *succumb* to the students' request as a means
of rewarding their activism.

vacillate v. (vah sil AYT)—to waver, show indecision
Governor Wiggins cost himself countless votes when he *vacillated* on
the health care question during the debate.

vacuous adj. (vah kyoo UHS)—empty, void; lacking intelligence, purposeless

The congresswoman's *vacuous* speech angered the voters, who were tired of hearing her empty promises.

Practice 3

DIRECTIONS: Consider the definition and then circle T for True or F for False.

21.	T	F	**paradigm**—a poorly explained example
22.	T	F	**paramount**—supreme
23.	T	F	**parity**—equality
24.	T	F	**polarize**—to motivate
25.	T	F	**polyglot**—someone who can speak several languages
26.	T	F	**precept**—a preconceived notion
27.	T	F	**prudent**—to be careful
28.	T	F	**puissant**—a French militiaman
29.	T	F	**succumb**—to stand your ground
30.	T	F	**vacillate**—to waver
31.	T	F	**vacuous**—lacking intelligence

Your Words, Your World

Don't have time to sit around repeating these words to yourself, over and over again, in order to remember them? Well, you don't have to! The following exercise tests your knowledge of the material . . . without requiring that you take a test! You will find that each of these words can be used in both political and nonpolitical conversations.

vacillate—Getting annoyed with a friend who can't make up his or her mind? Tell that friend to stop **vacillating**. Are you going with us to the movies or aren't you? By the same token, nobody likes politicians who *waver* back and forth, especially on an important issue.

succumb—Whereas having a friend who will **succumb** to your requests is a good thing, if a politician **succumbs** too easily to pressure, that can't be good—not for her career and certainly not for the people who voted her into office. If your friend is tired or has to study or has another excuse, you know you can usually convince him to go out because he always **succumbs**. Deep inside, he wants to be talked into having fun. But what lies in the heart of the politician who **succumbs** to other leaders, no matter what her voters want?

reconciliation—Whereas the tendency to succumb is sometimes good and sometimes bad, any kind of **reconciliation** is good. Whether between friends or politicians, the ability to *mend* relationships and return to happier times is always a positive. When friends argue, they must be able to come to a *resolution*. The same thing can be said of politicians. If anything is to be accomplished, first there must be a cease-fire and then there must be *compromise*.

PART FOUR

cede v. (seed)—to surrender possession of something
Argentina *ceded* the Falkland Islands to Britain after a brief war.

compatriot n. (KOHM pay tree oht)—fellow countryman
Halfway across the world, Jeff felt most comfortable in the company of his *compatriots*.

debacle n. (dah BAAH kuhl)—disastrous collapse, total failure
The Inauguration picnic turned into a *debacle* soon after the rain started.

emissary n. (EHM ih ser ee)—an agent sent as a representative
After cutting class, Paul sent Heather as his *emissary*, armed with a note of apology.

hegemony n. (heh jeh MOH nee)—the domination of one state or group over its allies
In the traditional flag football game, the senior girls claimed *hegemony* over the junior girls.

impotent adj. (IMP uh tent)—powerless, ineffective, lacking strength
Senator Cliff was *impotent* to prevent the media from learning of his daughter's arrest.

indomitable adj. (in DOM ih tu buhl)—fearless, unconquerable
Sam was the most *indomitable* goalkeeper in the county, until the underdogs from Jefferson High scored three goals off of her.

inviolable adj. (in VY uh lu buhl)—safe from violation or assault
The relieved refugees felt *inviolable* as UN troops stood guard over the camp.

oligarchy n. (ah lih GAAR kee)—a government in which a small group exercises supreme control
During the class president's extended absence, the treasurer, secretary, and vice president would share all duties as an *oligarchy*.

pandemic adj. (pahn DEH mikh)—occurring over a wide geographic area and affecting a large portion of the population; often said of a plague or disease
Pandemic alarm spread throughout the area after the devastating earthquake.

unanimity n. (YOO nahn ih mih tee)—state of total agreement or unity
The *unanimity* of the council members on this issue was surprising—they rarely agreed on anything.

Practice 4

DIRECTIONS: In completing the sentences, use 8 of the 10 words below. Use each of the words just once.

debacle   oligarchy   indomitable   cede   impotent

hegemony   emissary   pandemic   inviolable   precept

32. A small group that is in control of a government is a(n) _____.

33. A _____ can be a disastrous collapse, or a fun way to refer to a harmless-but-chaotic situation.

34. Benjamin Franklin spent many years living and working in Paris, as a(n) _____ of the United States government.

35. The United Nations usually gets involved when one country tries to exercise _____ over another.

36. A "lame duck" president who doesn't have to face another election is often _____ to pass legislation.

37. When a military man is voted president, it is usually because the American people want a(n) _____ leader.

38. Every politician knows that the people have certain rights and laws that they consider _____, and therefore can never be altered.

39. A national election is _____ in importance and participation.

Your Words, Your World

Don't have time to sit around repeating these words to yourself, over and over again, in order to remember them? Well, you don't have to! The following exercise tests your knowledge of the material . . . without requiring that you take a test! So your job now is to really *think* about what you read, and to really think about the questions that follow.

cede—In recent weeks, have you had the confidence to *yield*, to *surrender*, to **cede**? Well, good for you. Do you think that most politicians are willing to admit defeat, back off on an issue, or let an argument go? That seems doubtful. It's as if the word **cede** weren't in their vocabulary.

compatriot—What do you have in common with your **compatriots**? As Americans, what are the traits that we all share? Think about your **compatriots**: those who live in your neighborhood and those who live a thousand miles away. In what ways are they like you?

unanimity—Who in your family do you share absolute **unanimity** with? Who is the one person you *agree* with most often? Maybe within political parties there can be *harmony*, *union*, and *unity*. However, these qualities are rare in politics in general.

PRACTICE ANSWERS AND EXPLANATIONS

Practice 1

1. To be **belligerent** is to be hostile. A toady is a flatterer, something Mack's teacher definitely was not.

2. To be in **collusion** is to be in a state of collaboration, which perfectly describes the mayor and superintendent. A caucus is a small group within a group, so it is not relevant to the topic.

3. To **arrogate** is to claim without justification, as Troy did with the locker. To abrogate is to cancel, which does not fit in context.

4. If something **is convoluted**, it is twisted and complicated. To abdicate is to give up power, which does not describe a story.

5. **Beneficent** is a word to describe an act, or acts, of kindness. Someone belligerent is argumentative or prone to fighting.

6. To **abrogate** is to annul or terminate, and is the best choice to describe Mr. Pike's decision. Arrogate may rhyme with **abrogate**, but its meaning, to claim without justification, is far different.

7. To be **autonomous** is to be independent. To be convoluted is to be twisted, as in distorting the truth, which does not work in the context of the sentence.

8. To be concordant is to be harmonious and although those parents were in agreement, concordant is not the best word to describe them. A **caucus** is a group or committee and the goal of this group had been to cancel the prom, a mission they accomplished.

9. When something is **abdicated** it is relinquished (as in resigning a position like head of security). If something is arrogated it is claimed without right.

10. **Concordant** is harmonious, as in pleasant-sounding music. Miss Inkster would not play belligerent, or angry, music if she wanted to calm the class.

Practice 2

11. To **disavow** is not to pledge, but rather to renounce, deny, and reject.

12. **Discord** is not agreement, but rather conflict, dispute, and dissension.

13. **Dogmatic** is not accommodating, but rather assertive, rigid, and inflexible.

14. To **filibuster** is not to be brief, but rather to obstruct, hinder, and impede in a long-winded manner.

15. To **galvanize** is not to restrain, but rather to shock, stimulate, and rouse.

16. To **harangue** is not to praise, but to scold, lecture, and criticize.

17. To be **imperious** is not to be subservient, but rather arrogant, commanding, and authoritarian.

18. To be **intransigent** is not to be obliging, but rather inflexible, uncompromising, and stubborn.

19. A **mandate** is not a refusal, but rather permission, consent, and authorization.

20. **Megalomania** is not humility, but rather to be delusional, exaggerative, and grandiose.

Practice 3

21. False. A **paradigm** is not a poorly explained example, but a model that is held up as an example.

22. True. To be **paramount** is to be supreme.

23. True. **Parity** is equality.

24. False. To **polarize** is not to motivate, although a polarizing issue might motivate a person to act. To **polarize** is to push people to opposite extremes, usually based around a divisive issue.

25. True. A **polyglot** is someone who can speak several languages.

26. False. A **precept** is not a preconceived notion, but a principle or a law.

27. True. To be **prudent** is to be careful.

28. False. **Puissant** is not a French militiaman, but an adjective meaning powerful.

29. False. To **succumb** is to give in, the opposite of standing your ground.

30. True. To **vacillate** is to waver.

31. True. To be **vacuous** is to lack intelligence or to share empty sentiment.

Practice 4

32. An **oligarchy** is a small group in charge of a government.

33. A **debacle** is an absolute mess. At its best, **debacle** is sometimes used to describe a humorous situation.

34. An **emissary** is like an ambassador; it is somebody who lives in another country in order to represent his or her homeland.

35. Hegemony is when one country tries to dominate another country. Most often, this attempt at supremacy comes through the use of force.

36. If a president is powerless to pass legislation, then he or she is **impotent.**

37. An antonym to impotent is **indomitable.** This means strong and unconquerable, but it can also be used to mean stubborn.

38. Inviolable laws and rights are unbreakable and virtually sacred. The Bill of Rights is a set of **inviolable** rules established to protect individual rights.

39. Pandemic is most often used in a negative sense, especially to describe disease. But in this case, **pandemic** is simply used to describe an event of interest to people all across the country.

CHAPTER 5 TEST

Okay, it's time to put your memory to the test! Take your time not only with the questions but in reading the answer explanations that follow. Set a goal for yourself—80% (24 correct answers) is recommended—and if you don't reach that goal, go back and read through the chapter again. Good luck!

DIRECTIONS: For questions 1–15, circle T for True or F for False. For questions 16–30, circle the synonym.

1.	T	F	**impotent**—to be powerless
2.	T	F	**debacle**—a disastrous mess
3.	T	F	**succumb**—to overcome
4.	T	F	**prudent**—lacking care
5.	T	F	**precept**—a principle or law
6.	T	F	**polarize**—opposite extremes
7.	T	F	**capitulate**—to overcome
8.	T	F	**mediate**—to leave a dispute unresolved
9.	T	F	**mandate**—authorization
10.	T	F	**imperious**—submissive
11.	T	F	**unanimity**—disagreement
12.	T	F	**accede**—approval
13.	T	F	**collusion**—adversarial
14.	T	F	**puissant**—powerful
15.	T	F	**indomitable**—afraid

16. **discord:**	harmony	disagreement	accord
17. **disavow:**	deny	acknowledge	accept
18. **concordant:**	grumpy	agreeable	argumentative
19. **convoluted:**	elaborate	concerned	disastrous
20. **beneficent:**	malice	compassionately	indifference
21. **belligerent:**	intoxicated	hostile	cheerful
22. **ameliorate:**	improve	devolve	amenable

23. **abrogate:**   delegate   cancel   succumb

24. **paradigm:**   example   migration   bureaucracy

25. **paramount:**   trivial   mountainous   supreme

26. **accentuate:**   gloss over   emphasize   arrogate

27. **galvanize:**   shock   placate   appease

28. **autonomous:**   dependent   equitable   independent

29. **emissary:**   enemy   demagogue   delegate

30. **malfeasance:**   wrongdoing   parity   compatriot

Answers and Explanations

1. True. To be **impotent** is to be powerless.

2. True. A **debacle** is a big mess.

3. False. To **succumb** is to give in, not to overcome.

4. False. **Prudent** is not lacking care, it is to proceed with care.

5. True. A **precept** is a law or principle.

6. True. **Polarize** has do with positions—usually political opinions—that are at opposite extremes.

7. False. To **capitulate** is to surrender, not to overcome.

8. False. To **mediate** is to resolve an issue and not to leave it unresolved.

9. True. A **mandate** is an authorization.

10. False. To be **imperious** is to be domineering, not to be submissive.

11. False. **Unanimity** is a state of agreement, so disagreement is an antonym.

12. True. To **accede** is to give approval.

13. False. **Collusion** is to be in a state of collaboration, so to be adversarial is the exact opposite.

14. True. To be **puissant** is to be powerful.

15. False. To be **indomitable** is to be fearless and unconquerable, so afraid is an antonym.

16. Discord is to be in disagreement, not to be in harmony or in accord.

17. To **disavow** is to deny and not to acknowledge or accept.

18. Concordant is to be neither grumpy nor argumentative; it is to be agreeable.

19. Convoluted is elaborate, but not concerned or disastrous.

20. Beneficent is to do something compassionately and not with malice or indifference.

21. Belligerent is hostile and not cheerful, nor intoxicated.

22. **Ameliorate** is to improve and not to be amenable; devolve means to pass on by succession or to degenerate and is not synonymous with **ameliorate**.

23. **Abrogate** is to cancel and not to succumb or delegate.

24. A **paradigm** is an example and has nothing to do with migration or the slow and unreliable systems (often governmental) associated with bureaucracy.

25. **Paramount** is not synonymous with trivial (unimportant) or mountainous. The closest definition is supreme.

26. To **accentuate** is not to gloss over (ignore); nor is it to arrogate (claim without justification), although both are verbs. To emphasize is actually to accentuate.

27. To **galvanize** is to shock into action. While placate and appease are synonymous with one another, they are antonyms of **galvanize**. They involve calming people down and making them happy and comfortable.

28. To be **autonomous** is to be independent. To be dependant is to rely on others and to be equitable is to be reasonable and fair; not necessarily a way **autonomous** people, especially leaders, have to act.

29. An **emissary** is a delegate or representative. Enemy is nearly an antonym while demagogues (troublemaking popular leaders) are rarely representative of anybody or anything other than themselves.

30. **Malfeasance** is wrongdoing, usually by a politician. A compatriot is a fellow countryman, and parity is equality, both of which do not fit.

CHAPTER 6

Arts and Leisure

Using these words is an art form unto itself

BUILDING BLOCK QUIZ

This "building block" quiz samples the information that you will learn in this chapter, plus two words from the previous chapter. By answering the 12 questions below, you will get a sense of how closely you'll have to study this chapter in order to master the vocabulary of the world of arts and leisure.

DIRECTIONS: Fill in the blanks, using the most appropriate of the four multiple-choice answers. The correct answer will always fit into the sentence grammatically.

1. Harvey's wearing Dartmouth football shorts _____ the fact that he never went to Dartmouth, let alone played football there.

   (A) versatile (B) vilified
   (C) belied (D) elaborated

2. The _____ film festival cost the student council over $3,000 and hardly seemed worth the expensive decorations and refreshments.

   (A) licentious (B) vernacular
   (C) paean (D) lavish

3. Vargas was not the first to go into politics after a successful career as a(n) _____, in this case as a published author.

   (A) artisan (B) ornate

   (C) paean (D) interlude

4. Melody, who'd always had an eye for fine detail, quickly became famous for her _____ stained glass.

   (A) versatile (B) proxy

   (C) allusive (D) ornate

5. Upon moving out to Brooklyn, Gabe made sure to engage everyone he met in conversation, so as to learn the local _____.

   (A) vernacular (B) lavish

   (C) censure (D) hackneyed

6. Surprisingly, when the film was _____ by the president, donations poured in to the director and he was able to distribute the film nationally.

   (A) belied (B) censured

   (C) ancillary (D) proxied

7. The loft was perfect in that it was _____ enough to host everything from painting lessons to dancing lessons to yoga!

   (A) vilify (B) ornate

   (C) versatile (D) lavish

8. Giovanni welcomed the brief _____ during his book tour, allowing him to catch up on e-mails and work on his new novel.

   (A) constant (B) proxy

   (C) licentious (D) interlude

9. Some saw Annette's paintings as beautiful portrayals of the human body, while others called them _____.

   (A) interlude (B) vernacular

   (C) licentious (D) nonchalant

10. The _____ was intended to be a tribute to Robert Frost, but ended up celebrating some other poets who were fantastic in their own right.

    (A) paean (B) ornate

    (C) artisan (D) gourmand

11. Mr. Marcus couldn't understand why the superintendent would _____ on approving the skate park proposal, as there was a funding source and a petition signed by over 100 interested students.

    (A) vacillate (B) allusive

    (C) belligerent (D) proxy

12. The students voted for a(n) _____ of the vice president, secretary, and treasurer after the student council president was expelled.

    (A) versatile (B) oligarchy

    (C) megalomania (D) lavish

Answers and Explanations

1. C. To **belie** is to misrepresent. Vilified (spoke badly about) and elaborated (explained) are grammatically correct, but do not make sense. Versatile means multitalented and does not make sense in context.

2. D. **Lavish** means extravagant, as indicated by the $3,000. A paean is an artistic tribute. Licentious (immoral) is an adjective, but does not work as well as **lavish**. Vernacular means common language and doesn't make sense.

3. A. An **artisan** is an expert in the creative arts, including everything from tile work to writing. Ornate (intricate) and paean (an artistic tribute) are both related to the arts, but they don't fit in the blank. Interlude is irrelevant, as it means a break or brief interval.

4. D. **Ornate** means elaborate. Allusive (always making indirect references), versatile (capable of doing many things), and proxy (substitute) do not make sense in context.

5. A. **Vernacular** is a common dialect; in this case, the way people in Brooklyn speak. Lavish is extravagant, so that answer can be ruled out. Censure is finding fault and this is not what Gabe was doing. Finally, hackneyed is clichéd, and although some may call any accent or **vernacular** clichéd, the word is an adjective and does not work in context.

6. B. Proxy and ancillary both indicate substitutions, so they are irrelevant. To **censure** is to criticize and this is what the president did. To belie is to disprove or contradict, which is close, but not as acceptable as **censure**.

7. C. Ornate and lavish are synonymous (detailed and extravagant), so they rule each other out. To vilify is to belittle, and the blank must be filled with a positive word like **versatile**, which means adaptable.

8. D. An **interlude** is an interval, and is the best choice. Constant is an antonym, proxy is a substitute, and licentious is immoral, so none of these works in context.

9. C. Licentious is immoral and fits in with the contrast of the sentence. Vernacular (current language) and nonchalant (casual) may seem to be decent choices, but they fall short of the criticism of **licentious**. Interlude (interval) does not make sense in context.

10. A. A **paean** is a tribute and in this case, a tribute to Robert Frost. Ornate (intricate) and artisan (a creative person) are topical but don't fit. Gourmand is a glutton or gourmet, and has nothing to do with poetry.

11. A. To **vacillate** is to waver, so it's no wonder Mr. Marcus was confused. The superintendent's delayed response may have been a belligerent move to delay approval, but that adjective is not the correct choice. Proxy (substitute) and allusive (indirect references) are also wrong. If you answered this question incorrectly, you might want to go back to chapter 5 for some review.

12. B. An **oligarchy** is government-by-group—in this case, the other student council officers. To be versatile is to be adaptable and although those three students may be adaptable. . . . Megalomania (a misconception of power) may explain why the president was expelled, but it's still an incorrect choice. Lavish (abundant) just doesn't fit. If you answered this question incorrectly, you might want to go back to chapter 5 for some review.

PART ONE

abnegate v. (ahb nuh GAYT)—to deny; renounce
Citing artistic freedom, Arnold decide to *abnegate* the honors project and submit his poem rather than the required research paper.

allusive adj. (ah LOO siv)—making many indirect references
Although Gabrielle's presentation dealt with the 2000 election, it was more *allusive* than factual and she received a C—.

apotheosis n. (ah poh thee OH sis)—glorification; glorified ideal
As a kid growing up in the '80s, Miguel thought that Michael Jackson was the *apotheosis* of cool.

belie v. (bee LIY)—to misrepresent; expose as false
The low grade *belied* all of the time Matt had spent studying for the test, so Ms. Vasquez promised to help him better structure his time.

endure v. (en DOOR)—carry on despite hardships
Peg *endured* the flu and gave a tremendous solo during the piano recital.

ensemble n. (on SOM buhl)—group of parts that contribute to a whole single effect
Louis's string *ensemble* was hired to play at the Garrison wedding and soon had gigs every weekend.

exorbitant adj. (eg ZOR bih tant)—extravagant, greater than reasonable
The artist charged *exorbitant* prices for his paintings, but gave one to the high school for free since he so appreciated the training he'd received there.

gourmand n. (goor MOND)—glutton; lover of fine food
As a boy, Robert was an admitted *gourmand*, so no one was surprised when he made it as a chef on the Food Network.

garish adj. (GAHR ish)—gaudy, glaring
Sandra thought the costumes too *garish* for the low-key school play.

grandiose adj. (GRAN dee ohs)—magnificent and imposing; exaggerated and pretentious
The architect agreed that the high school should have a *grandiose* façade so that the students would feel important every time they entered the building.

hackneyed adj. (HAK need)—clichéd, worn out by overuse
The comedian's *hackneyed* routine sent audience members running for the door.

lavish adj. (LAH vish)—extravagant, profuse
The *lavish* feast for Hispanic Heritage Month drew a photographer from the *New York Times*.

matriarch n. (MAY tree ark)—woman who rules a family or clan
Deborah Stone had been principal for over 20 years, running the school as a *matriarch* with the students' best interests at heart.

mimic v. (MIM ihk)—copy, imitate.
Henrietta asked the principal if the way Lea *mimicked* her movements could be considered bullying.

nonchalant adj. (non shuh LAHNT)—calm, casual, seemingly unexcited
Rick was very *nonchalant* when he won the art scholarship, but inside his heart was bursting with joy!

Practice 1

The key to memorization is testing yourself in as many different formats as possible. Here's one exercise that will help reinforce the words you learned in this section.

DIRECTIONS: Read the three possible synonyms, then circle the word you think best defines the word in bold.

1. **abnegate:**	portray	deny	celebrate
2. **allusiveness:**	evading	hinting	protruding
3. **endure:**	persevere	celebrate	concede
4. **exorbitant:**	reasonable	content	extravagant
5. **garish:**	gaudy	humble	simple
6. **grandiose:**	modest	magnificent	humble
7. **hackneyed:**	clichéd	original	creative
8. **lavish:**	extravagant	saccharine	modest
9. **mimic:**	imitate	rhapsody	compliment
10. **nonchalant:**	nonsense	casual	nonplussed

Your Words, Your World

Don't have time to sit around repeating these words to yourself, over and over again, in order to remember them? Well, you don't have to! The following exercise tests your knowledge of the material . . . without requiring that you take a test! So your job now is to really *think* about what you read, and to really cement an image in your mind. You never know when you'll need that image to pop up again.

apotheosis—Rather than visualizing your hero, think of someone who has been *glorified* to a degree that really annoys you. Who is the one person everybody always speaks so highly of and who you just don't think deserves the praise? *Theos* is Greek for "God" (think theology) and not many people out there deserve to be elevated to god status.

belie—To **belie** is to *misrepresent*, and usually on purpose. Think of something you were given or bought in recent months that didn't work as advertised. Maybe it was a CD, a video game, a part for your car, an article of clothing, a magazine, or even a movie you rented. Recall this thing that made you mad because it fell short of expectations. Turn this anger into something positive: use it to remember that sometimes, advertising **belies** what you're really getting.

ensemble—French for "together," an **ensemble** is a group of people working toward a *common* goal. Think, for example, of your favorite *band*. Four or five folks—maybe even a whole orchestra!—gathered on a stage or in a studio, making the kind of music you absolutely love. It doesn't matter if it's hard rock, hip hop, choral, gospel, or international. What matters is this: when a group of people can get *together* and produce something enjoyable, it is to be appreciated. Imagine your favorite **ensemble** and you'll be all set.

gourmand—If you made the observation that **gourmand** shares a resemblance with *gourmet*, then you hit the nail on the head. A **gourmand** is a *gourmet*, a person who *loves food and drink*, and who knows a lot about it. Picture Emeril Lagasse or another famous chef from the Food Network. Make this person your spokesman for **gourmands**, for *connoisseurs*, for *epicureans* everywhere.

matriarch—Matriarch is a noun, representing the *woman in charge* of the household. Who runs the show in your household or family? Find someone who fits the bill and picture her whenever the word **matriarch** comes up. And as a further reminder, think of the Latin *arch*, which means "ruler" (as in monarch).

PART TWO

ablution v. (ahb LOO shun)—act of cleansing
Taking off her makeup was the last step in Minnie's nightly *ablutions*.

aesthetic adj. (aas THEH tik)—pertaining to beauty or art
The museum curator, with her fine *aesthetic* sense, created an exhibit that crowds lined up for hours to see.

artisan n. (ar tih SAN)—craftsperson; expert
Not surprisingly, the local *artisans* were among the most popular guests at the Career Fair.

novel adj. (NOH vuhl)—new and not resembling anything formerly known
Piercing any part of the body other than the earlobes was *novel* in the 1950s, but now it is quite common.

opulence n. (AH pyoo lehns)—wealth
Mr. Livingston knew that being a teacher meant he'd never have a life of *opulence*, but told his students that it was rewarding nonetheless.

ornate adj. (ohr NAYT)—elaborately ornamented
The *ornate* stained glass looked wonderful above the entrance to the auditorium.

ostentatious adj. (ah sten TAY shuhs)—showy
Many people found the movie star's abundant gold and diamond jewelry to be beyond *ostentatious*—it was downright obnoxious!

pretense n. (PRE tens)—false appearance or action
The three students snuck into the art gallery's grand opening under the *pretense* that they were caterers.

promulgate v. (PROM ul gayt)—to make known publicly
The publicist *promulgated* the news of the rock star's "secret" wedding through one of his anonymous sources.

repose n. (ree POHZ)—relaxation, leisure
A week after wrapping up the film, the director found *repose* in the Caribbean with his wife and kids.

sinecure n. (SIN ih kyoor)—a well-paying job or office that requires little or no work
After using his connections to get a *sinecure* in marketing, Adam was able to use his free time to write poetry.

solitary adj. (SOL ih ter ee)—alone; remote, secluded
Melody found that the only way she could finish her novel was by retreating to a *solitary* cabin in the woods.

MEMORY TIP

Have you ever played the card game Solitaire? If not, it is a way to play cards when there is no one around to play with. Picture someone at a table, all alone, with the cards spread out before him. This will help you to memorize **solitary**, which is a word to describe any activity or *solo* endeavor.

---

stoic adj. (STOH ihk)—indifferent to or unaffected by emotions
His friends couldn't believe that a *stoic* man like Alonzo was capable of writing such emotionally charged plays.

sully v. (SUH lee)—to tarnish, taint
Voluntarily doing community service around town helped Gary to restore his *sullied* reputation.

vernacular n. (vuhr NAA kyoo luhr)—everyday language used by ordinary people; specialized language of a profession
Francine tried to capture the *vernacular* of her new high school, but after a few weeks decided to just speak like herself.

Practice 2

DIRECTIONS: Read the three choices, then circle the *antonym* of the word in bold.

11. **novel:**   new   hackneyed   original
12. **sinecure:**   easy   difficult   manageable
13. **sully:**   tainted   muddied   clean
14. **ablution:**   cleansing   sullied   purified
15. **pretense:**   façade   legitimate   charade
16. **promulgate:** conceal   disseminate   broadcast
17. **repose:**   toil   relax   rest
18. **solitary:**   alone   sociable   unaccompanied
19. **stoic:**   impervious   emotional   impassive
20. **vernacular:** colloquialisms   specialized   jargon

Your Words, Your World

Don't have time to sit around repeating these words to yourself, over and over again, in order to remember them? Well, you don't have to! The following exercise tests your knowledge of the material . . . without requiring that you take a test! You will find that each of these words can be used in a wide variety of conversations (not just concerning the arts).

Aesthetic—One of the joys in life is finding what is **aesthetically** appealing to you. Actually, the joy is making sure that this thing—music, paintings, drawings, flowers, candles, whatever—is readily available throughout your day. Whether in a locker, dorm room, or cubicle at work, often having something **aesthetically** pleasing at hand can make a bad day good.

Artisan—In order to decorate to taste, you'll have to figure out who your favorite **artisans** are. Whether it's a *poet* or a *pianist*, a *trumpet player* or a *tap dancer*, an **artisan** is someone who creates art. Ask your friends which **artisans** they like, and you may get yourself a new favorite.

Ornate—You may use it to criticize something that is overly complicated, but most often, **ornate**, or *elaborately decorated*, is a compliment. Beautiful tile work in a mansion, layers of stringed instruments in an orchestra, 3-D scenes from a video game, all of these can be **ornate**! A synonym of *lavish* and *opulent*, **ornate** is a vocab word that makes one feel artistic just using it.

Opulence—**Opulence** is one step up from ornate. Whereas ornate is an adjective, **opulence** is a noun, used more to describe a *state of being* than a work of art. It usually involves wealth. A successful artist might end up living in **opulence**, a welcome change after her formative years in poverty. But if this artist falls out of touch and becomes too egotistical, **opulence** may very well be used as a criticism.

Ostentatious—So, you want to criticize something *overly complicated* and *showy*, but don't want to use ornate or opulence in a negative sense? Well, there's always **ostentatious**. *Loud*, *obnoxious*, *pretentious*, and *flamboyant* are all synonyms for **ostentatious**.

PART THREE

callow adj. (CAL oh)—immature, lacking sophistication
Because the *callow* students ruined the first act of *Hamlet* for everybody else, there was a standing ovation when security escorted them from the theater.

caustic adj. (KAW stihk)—biting, sarcastic; able to burn
Walt gained his reputation as a *caustic* comedian because of his cutting commentary.

censure v. (SEHN sher)—to find fault with and condemn as wrong; blame
Rather than leave it up to the administrators, the student council decided to *censure* the students who had covered the building with graffiti.

defamatory adj. (dih FAAM uh tohr ee)—injurious to the reputation
The famous actress decided to sue the tabloid for making *defamatory* statements about her romantic relationships.

fodder n. (FOH duhr)—raw materials (as for artistic creation), readily abundant ideas or images
Mrs. Lorens asked her students to try to make a real social statement when choosing the *fodder* for their collages.

interlude n. (IN ter lood)—an intervening period of time
Willy was happy to get up and stretch his legs during the opera's *interlude*.

iridescent adj. (ir ih DEH sihnt)—showing many colors
The photography students quickly snapped as many pictures as they could before the *iridescent* butterfly flew away.

libertine n. (LIH buhr teen)—a free thinker, usually used disparagingly, one without moral restraint
Ursula lost her position as art critic for the school paper when a minister complained that having a *libertine* on staff was immoral.

MEMORY TIP

Can you see the *liberty* in **libertine**? That *liberty* equals *freedom* and somebody who is classified as a **libertine** feels tremendous *freedom* when he or she speaks. This kind of person often gets criticized for taking too many *liberties*.

licentious adj. (lih SEHN shuhs)—immoral; unrestrained by society
In an open letter, Kelly asked the town's older citizens to stop accusing her generation of *licentious* behavior and realize that the world had changed.

melee n. (MAY lay)—tumultuous free-for-all
The red carpet became slippery in the rain, causing a sloppy *melee* at the Oscars.

mellifluous adj. (mehl IH floo uhs)—having a smooth, rich flow
Betsy was such a talented flutist that her *mellifluous* playing transported the audience to another world.

mundane adj. (muhn DAYN)—ordinary, commonplace
The plot of the detective story was completely *mundane*, and the book even ended with the line, "The butler did it."

nostalgic adj. (nah STAHL jik)—longing for things of the past
After his ten-year high school reunion, Brad became *nostalgic* for the good old days.

paean n. (PEE uhn)—a tribute, a song or expression of praise
Marcus told the reporter that the painting was a *paean* to his late wife.

pariah n. (puh RIY uh)—an outcast
When Anna used racial slurs in her campaign speech, she immediately became a *pariah* among her fellow students.

pigment n. (PIG ment)—substance used for coloring
Bella wasn't surprised to learn that each person's skin and hair pigment is directly tied to his or her DNA.

rhapsody n. (RAHP suh dee)—emotional literary or musical work
In defending the music to his father, Marvin said that the name "rap" was based on *rhapsody* because the songs were so emotional.

vicariously adv. (viy KAAR ee uhs lee)—felt or undergone as if one were taking part in the experience or feelings of another
Elena loved to read because she lived *vicariously* through the characters in her books.

vilify v. (vihl ih FIE)—to slander, defame
Since gossip columnists make money from *vilifying* celebrities, they're often held in low regard.

whimsical adj. (wihm sih KUHL)—playful or fanciful idea
The ballet was *whimsical*, delighting the children with its colorful
costumes and upbeat music.

Practice 3

DIRECTIONS: Fill in the blanks, using 15 of the 20 words provided
below.

defamatory	callow	whimsical	melee	gourmand
mellifluous	libertines	licentious	interlude	mundane
nostalgic	fodder	caustic	vicariously	vilified
censured	iridescent	paean	pigment	rhapsody

21. David was pleased when one review called his
    film _____, proving that he had, indeed,
    captured the feel of being homesick for a time
    and place that no longer exists.

22. Known as a moody actor, Larry fit the bill per-
    fectly whenever a _____ criminal was
    needed.

23. Having his statues _____ by the Family
    Values Committee for being offensive was the
    best publicity break Tyshaun could have
    hoped for.

24. Mr. Olson found Eli's voice to be angelic, but
    had to be honest with him about his _____
    lyrics that made him seem young.

25. Although the film was R-rated and deemed
    _____ by many, it led all movies in
    ticket sales for the weekend.

26. Gail earned critical acclaim for her
    _____ paintings of tropical fish.

27. Paula was fond of artists who were
    _____; they had subtly rebelled against
    current culture and then subtly reshaped it.

28. In 1913, on the streets of Paris, a _____
    followed the first-ever performance of
    Stravinsky's "Rite of Spring."

29. Keith thought that writing the novel was easy,
    but that the long _____ before it was
    published was very difficult.

30. Going to the opera put Melanie in a state of
    pure _____.

31. Jesse considered himself an organic artist, right
    down to the fact that all of his colors came
    from the _____ of berries.

32. Victor realized that he was living _____
    through the successes of Tom, the lead singer,
    and so he quit the band to pursue a solo project.

33. Leslie loved the CD, while Harry disappointed
    her by yawning dramatically and calling the
    singer a _____ teeny bopper.

34. After his arrest, DJ Spinster was _____
    by the media but embraced by his fans.

35. Aiming for heart-wrenching, Carly was upset
    when her own mother called her piano concerto
    uplifting and _____.

Your Words, Your World

Don't have time to sit around repeating these words to yourself, over and over again, in order to remember them? Well, you don't have to! The following exercise tests your knowledge of the material . . . without requiring that you take a test! So your job now is to really *think* about what you read, and to really think about the questions that follow.

Defamatory—To **defame** is to *injure* someone's *reputation* or, in a sense, to take from that person's fame. This is literally the Latin root of the word as *fama* means fame and *dis* means take. Who knew that today's popular phrase for **defamation**, "dissed," came from Latin? Think of the last time you saw someone get dissed (disrespected). Or maybe you yourself got dissed. Thinking of the verb dissed should help you to remember the definition for **defamatory**.

Fodder—The German word *futter* and the Middle English *fodor* both refer to food, and **fodder** originally referred to the feed for farm animals. Later, the word was expanded to include not just objects (like scrap metal jammed into cannons by desperate troops when the supply of cannon balls had run low) but also words themselves. For example, an actor's defamatory quote about a costar may become **fodder** for the rumor mill. But the easiest way to remember **fodder** is to picture feed for farm animals. Once again, alliteration comes in handy: farm, feed, and **fodder**.

Mellifluous—*Smooth* and *honeyed* phrases are considered **mellifluous**—and doesn't the word sound like what it describes? Rather than picturing an image as you've done in other exercises, this time, use your ears rather than your inner eye. *Mel* is Latin for honey while *fluere* means to flow. Words that are **mellifluous** *flow* in a *rich*, *smooth* way.

Paean—Who would you pay *tribute* to if you were given the chance? Who would you most like to sit down and say thank you to? Imagine this actor or actress, this singer, this writer, this doctor, this family member, this dancer, this painter, this philanthropist, or this politician. Choose one person and imagine being able to not only create but deliver a **paean** to him or her. In ancient Greece, a *paian* was a hymn of praise for any of the gods, but especially for Apollo, god of the arts. Who is your Apollo?

PRACTICE ANSWERS AND EXPLANATIONS

Practice 1

1. To **abnegate** is to deny, not to portray or celebrate.

2. Someone with **allusiveness** is hinting at something, not evading something or protruding (sticking out).

3. To **endure** is to persevere and not to concede (give in) or celebrate.

4. Something **exorbitant** is extravagant. It is not content and it is far from reasonable.

5. Something **garish** is gaudy and the opposite of something humble or simple.

6. Something that is **grandiose** is magnificent, and an antonym to something modest and humble.

7. **Hackneyed** is clichéd, and the opposite of original and creative.

8. **Lavish** is extravagant and not saccharine (emotionally sweet and sappy) or modest.

9. To **mimic** is to imitate and usually not in a complimentary way. Rhapsody is a state of ecstasy and does not fit.

10. **Nonchalant** is casual. Nonsense and nonplussed (confused) may share the root of **non**, but they are both non-answers!

Practice 2

11. **Novel** is something new and original, thus hackneyed (old and clichéd) is the antonym.

12. A **sinecure** is an easy, or manageable, job. Difficult is the antonym.

13. To **sully** can be to taint or muddy something, so the antonym is clean.

14. **Ablution** can be the act of cleansing or purifying, so sullied (something tainted or muddied) is the antonym.

15. **Pretense** is a charade or façade, so legitimate (legal and honest) is the antonym.

16. To **promulgate** is to disseminate or broadcast. So to conceal (hide) is the antonym.

17. To be in a state of **repose** is to get some R 'n R (rest and relaxation!), therefore toil (hard work) is the antonym.

18. **Solitary** is alone, or unaccompanied, so sociable (outgoing and fun) is the antonym.

19. **Stoic** is impervious and impassive. To be emotional (demonstrative and dramatic) is the antonym.

20. **Vernacular** is the collection of common words also known as colloquialisms and jargon. So, to use a specialized vocabulary would be the opposite of using the vernacular.

Practice 3

21. **Nostalgic** is an adjective, and apparently that is exactly how David wanted his film to be described.

22. **Caustic** is sarcastic and edgy—an entertaining way for criminals to act, according to many of today's shows!

23. To be **censured** is to be criticized, as Tyshaun's statues were.

24. **Callow** is inexperienced and immature, and is an adjective most often used to describe people.

25. To be **licentious** is to be immoral and depraved; that's just the thing many people seem to enjoy in a movie.

26. Fish do look **iridescent** in real life, so that must have been Gail's goal.

27. **Libertines** are free thinkers thought of as immoral by certain segments of society.

28. There really was a **melee**, as people rioted in the streets.

29. An **interlude** is an interval or pause, and Keith had a hard time with this break.

30. **Rhapsody** is so often used to describe music—and the reaction to that music—that at one point it even described a type of music (such as Gershwin's "Rhapsody in Blue").

31. Ancient native peoples first used the **pigment** of berries in their artwork and Jesse is continuing that tradition.

32. Vicariously means to get enjoyment through somebody else's experiences and accomplishments, so hurray for Victor for deciding to strike out on his own.

33. Harry thought the music is boring and **mundane**, even if Leslie liked it.

34. Part of being famous is being notorious, especially in modern music, so DJ Spinster probably appreciated the free advertising he received when the media **vilified** him.

35. Whimsical is joyous in a lighthearted way; apparently this was not the way Carly wanted her audience to feel.

CHAPTER 6 TEST

Okay, it's time to put your memory to the test! Take your time not only with the questions but in reading the answer explanations that follow. Set a goal for yourself—80% (24 correct answers) is recommended— and if you don't reach that goal, go back and read through the chapter again. Good luck!

DIRECTIONS: For questions 1–15, circle T for True or F for False. For questions 16–30, circle the synonym.

1.	T	F	**mundane**—extraordinary
2.	T	F	**licentious**—moral
3.	T	F	**interlude**—interval
4.	T	F	**censure**—blameless
5.	T	F	**caustic**—sarcastic
6.	T	F	**stoic**—unaffected by emotions
7.	T	F	**solitary**—alone
8.	T	F	**promulgate**—to announce
9.	T	F	**aesthetic**—artistic
10.	T	F	**lavish**—insufficient
11.	T	F	**grandiose**—extravagant
12.	T	F	**mimic**—imitate
13.	T	F	**matriarch**—a statue or arch
14.	T	F	**nonchalant**—cowardly
15.	T	F	**novel**—traditional

16. **hackneyed:**	cut up	extraordinary	clichéd
17. **exorbitant:**	extravagant	celestial	plain
18. **endure:**	estimate	persevere	consider
19. **allusiveness:**	inclusive	mention	avoidance
20. **abnegate:**	deny	allude	contemplate
21. **ablution:**	sully	cleanse	curse
22. **ostentatious:**	gaudy	plain	earthy

23. **vernacular:**	colloquial	atypical	specialized
24. **iridescent:**	plain	earthy	colorful
25. **pigment:**	dye	density	dark
26. **belie:**	misrepresent	represent	lay down
27. **sully:**	clean	endure	tarnish
28. **callow:**	immature	sophisticated	iridescent
29. **pariah:**	hero	fish	outcast
30. **vilify:**	defame	celebrate	paean

Answers and Explanations

1. **False.** **Mundane** is ordinary, not strange or unusual.

2. **False.** **Licentious** is immoral, not honest or ethical.

3. **True.** An **interlude** is an interval.

4. **False.** To **censure** is to blame, not blameless.

5. **True.** **Caustic** is sarcastic.

6. **True.** To be **stoic** is to be unaffected by emotions.

7. **True.** **Solitary** is to be alone.

8. **True.** To **promulgate** is to announce.

9. **True.** Something **aesthetic** is something artistic and appealing.

10. **False.** **Lavish** is extravagant, not scarce or inadequate.

11. **True.** **Grandiose** is extravagant, in an ostentatious way.

12. **True.** To **mimic** is to imitate.

13. **False.** A **matriarch** is a woman who runs her family and not an arch or statue.

14. **False.** To be **nonchalant** is to be casual, while cowardly is to be scared and not courageous.

15. **False.** **Novel** is not something traditional. It is something new and interesting.

16. **Hackneyed** is clichéd and not cut up or extraordinary.

17. **Exorbitant** is extravagant and not celestial or plain.

18. To **endure** is to persevere; it has nothing to do with estimate and consider.

19. **Allusiveness** is closest to mention (as it refers to indirect references), not inclusive or avoidance.

20. **Abnegate** is to deny, but not to allude or contemplate.

21. **Ablution** is not to sully or curse. It is to cleanse, usually in a religious sense.

22. **Ostentatious** is synonymous with gaudy and the opposite of plain and earthy.

23. **Vernacular** is colloquial and not specialized or atypical.

24. Iridescent is not plain and earthy, but colorful.

25. Pigment is more associated with dye than density or dark.

26. Belie is to lie or misrepresent something. Represent is the opposite, and lay down is irrelevant.

27. To **sully** is to tarnish or dishonor. To clean is an antonym, and to endure (survive) is irrelevant.

28. Callow is immature and usually describes a person. Sophisticated is the opposite: worldly and mature. Iridescent (shimmering) is an adjective for describing objects, and does not fit either.

29. A **pariah** is an outcast, so hero is incorrect. And although pariah may sound like piranha, fish is incorrect.

30. To **vilify** is to defame or publicly insult somebody. Celebrate and paean (an artistic tribute) are its antonyms.

Literature

Words to help in your reading, your book club, and in English class

BUILDING BLOCK QUIZ

This "building block" quiz samples the information that you will learn in this chapter, plus two words from the previous chapter. By answering the questions below, you will get a sense of how closely you should study this chapter in order to master the vocabulary you need to speak knowledgeably about books, magazines, and the menu options on your new DVD! And if you choose incorrect answers for the final two questions, you'll want to go back to chapter 6 for some review.

DIRECTIONS: Fill in the blanks, using the most appropriate of the four multiple-choice answers. The correct answer will always fit into the sentence grammatically.

1. Some English teachers like Hemingway's books, while others think he benefits from undeserving _____.

   (A) archipelagos (B) adulation

   (C) scrupulous (D) naïve

2. Mrs. Lowenstein argued that Shakespeare and Dickens are not _____ because Dickens wrote stories about the poor while Shakespeare wrote plays about the powerful.

   (A) debunk (B) abridge

   (C) analogous (D) accolade

3. All of the students appreciated Ms. Hollingsworth's _____ when it came to discussing grades.

   (A) candor (B) denizen

   (C) epitaph (D) egregious

4. The low-rent apartment building was inhabited by twelve artists, and each _____ was committed to the idea of supporting the creativity of the others.

   (A) illegible (B) humane

   (C) dentistry (D) denizen

5. Lenny was planning to _____ his big plot twist in the first chapter of his novel.

   (A) lexicon (B) missive

   (C) foreshadow (D) quandary

6. Jenna liked to _____ desire in her stories without being obvious about it.

   (A) pseudonym (B) imply

   (C) tutelage (D) vignette

7. As their first bookmaking project, the students had to construct a _____ of the school's most popular words.

   (A) elegy (B) lexicon

   (C) rhetoric (D) profound

8. Elena was presented with a tough _____,
as she had to choose between writing for the
school paper and the school literary magazine.

   (A) quandary (B) prediction

   (C) figurative (D) irony

9. Under the _____ of the professors at
The Word Institute, Gary's poems went from
greeting-card rhymes to true art.

   (A) censure (B) cosmopolitan

   (C) tutelage (D) denizen

10. Wendell wanted his short stories to be
_____, but was constantly disappointed
by how simplistic they seemed.

    (A) illegible (B) epilogue

    (C) pigment (D) profound

11. Although it was the 21st century, Adriana liked
to use natural _____ when painting her
book covers.

    (A) pigment (B) bard

    (C) cogent (D) uranium

12. When the superintendent decided to
_____ the student literary magazine, a
local printer offered to publish it and sales
were fantastic!

    (A) astute (B) censure

    (C) antagonist (D) adage

Answers and Explanations

1. B. As **adulation** is undeserved praise, this is the answer. Archipelagos are strings of islands, so this word does not fit. Scrupulous (careful) and naïve (immature and innocent) are adjectives, and the sentence requires a noun.

2. C. Analogous means comparable, and as Mrs. Lowenstein was arguing against comparing Dickens and Shakespeare too closely, this is the correct answer. An accolade is a form of praise and does not fit. Debunk (expose) and abridge (shorten) are out, based on their definitions and the fact that they are verbs.

3. A. People always appreciate the truth, especially when presented in a tactful manner, so the answer is **candor** (honesty of expression). Denizen (an inhabitant or resident) and egregious (obvious) do not fit grammatically. As an epitaph is something written on a gravestone, that couldn't be right (or one would hope not!).

4. D. Another word for inhabitants, or residents, is **denizen**. Dentistry is just a silly answer that sounds like denizen, while illegible means unreadable (as in poor handwriting), and humane means caring. Humane is an adjective, so it is grammatically incorrect.

5. C. To **foreshadow** is to provide a hint or clue, so this is the answer. Lexicon (dictionary) and missive (note or letter) are both nouns indicating a form of communication, while a quandary is a problem.

6. B. The verb **imply** (suggest) is the correct answer as Jenna attempted to be subtle with her art. A pseudonym (fake name) and a vignette (short piece of literature) are inappropriate, as is tutelage (support or guidance).

7. B. A **lexicon** is a dictionary, so this is the best choice. An elegy is a poem or song at a funeral, so it is not the best choice. Rhetoric is the art of speaking or writing effectively, and profound is an adjective meaning deep or meaningful.

8. A. Elena had a problem, which is synonymous with **quandary**. Prediction is a trick answer as it sounds like predicament (which is also synonymous with problem and quandary). Figurative (symbolic language) and irony (insincere satire) are both nouns, but they don't describe a problem or choice.

9. C. **Tutelage** (guidance) is the right answer, while censure (to criticize) is not. Cosmopolitan means sophisticated and worldly, and denizen means citizen or resident, so neither of these choices works.

10. D. Whereas Wendell wanted to be **profound** (deep, meaningful), he felt his writing was coming closer to illegible (unreadable from sloppiness and not poor writing). An epilogue is a section of writing that comes at the end and pigment is a color or dye.

11. A. Adriana used natural **pigment** or coloring—berries, perhaps—to make paint for her covers. She did not use uranium! A bard is a poet and to be cogent is to be convincing, so those answers are incorrect. If you answered this question incorrectly, you might want to go back to chapter 6 for some review.

12. B. To **censure** is to criticize and show disapproval. When writers' works are censured by important public figures, the writers often get a lot of free publicity. To be astute is to be smart and although the superintendent may be smart, that's not the focus of the sentence. An antagonist is an opponent and an adage is an old saying. If you answered this question incorrectly, you might want to go back to chapter 6 for some review.

PART ONE

abridge v. (ah BRIJ)—to condense, shorten
Mrs. Gonzalez assigned an *abridged* version of *Tristram Shandy* to her class, as the original was very long.

accolade n. (AH ko lade)—praise, distinction
After Sarah won the national spelling bee, *accolades* were heaped upon her.

adage n. (ah DAJ)—old saying or proverb
Benjamin Franklin's "A penny saved is a penny earned" is a popular *adage*.

adulation n. (AAH juh la shuhn)—excessive flattery or admiration
The *adulation* Leslie showed for her professor's novel seemed insincere.

allegory n. (AL la gory)—symbolic representation
The story of Rip Van Winkle is an *allegory* for the way life changed after the Industrial Revolution.

alliteration n. (ah lit er A shun)—repetition of the beginning sounds of words
Mrs. Graves told Becky she'd never be a real poet if she continued to rely on *alliteration*.

MEMORY TIP

Analytically analogous… Pretty practical presentation…
Having the same first letters in each group of words is the basis for **alliteration**.

---

analogous adj. (uh NAL oh guhs)—comparable, parallel
"In terms of creating characters," Professor White told his class, "the writer is *analogous* to God and this is a great responsibility."

antagonist n. (an TAG on ist)—foe, opponent, adversary
Quintasia based her paper around the theory that every great story has a strong *antagonist*.

antecedent adj. (an tea SEE dent)—coming before in place or time
Dr. Baylor challenged the class to uncover the *antecedents* to Dean's erratic behavior in *On the Road*.

antidote n. (an tuh DOTE)—a remedy, an agent used to counteract
Jessica was of the opinion that books were the *antidote* to ignorance.

assertion n. (uh SIR shun)—declaration, usually without proof
"Hillary's *assertion* that Shakespeare was a woman is totally false!" Gail argued.

astute adj. (ah STOOT)—having good judgment
Judy Blume is an *astute* writer of books for children and teens.

bard n. (bard)—lyrical poet
Shakespeare is one of the most famous *bards* in English literature.

bibliophile n. (bib lee uh FIL)—book lover
Mr. Vicks was a self-proclaimed *bibliophile* and everybody's choice for school librarian.

candor n. (KAN der)—honesty of expression
The *candor* of Mike's writing impressed Mr. Wright and earned him a B+.

Practice 1

DIRECTIONS: In completing the sentences, use 10 of the 12 words below. Use each of the words just once.

antagonist	assertion	bard	astute
allegory	candor	accolade	antidote
antecedent	adage	alliteration	abridge

1. Mr. Kweller always said that a good book must include a main character and his or her

   _____.

2. Due to budget cuts, the editors had to
   _____ the yearbook.

3. Carmen spoke with such _____ that her teacher suggested she be a peer counselor for troubled classmates.

4. "If the shoe fits, wear it," is a well-known _____.

5. Danny's research paper argued that *Huckleberry Finn* was the _____ to all great American novels of the 20th century.

6. Dr. Hart warned the students against too much _____ and too little research in their persuasive essays.

7. The talk show host convinced hundreds of thousands to read more when she declared that books are the _____ to ignorance.

8. Luisa was proud of the _____ awarded her by the governor, that of State Poet.

9. "The Ant and the Grasshopper" is a(n) _____ intended to warn against laziness.

10. Mrs. Hodge was a(n) _____ judge of musical talent and gave the school's talent contest an air of legitimacy.

Your Words, Your World

Don't have time to sit around repeating these words to yourself, over and over again, in order to remember them? Well, you don't have to! The following exercise tests your knowledge of the material . . . without requiring that you take a test! So your job now is to really *think* about what you read, and to really think about the questions that follow.

Bibliophile—Do you just *love books*? Ever work in a library? Or participate in one of those summer reading clubs when you were a kid? Well, if your night table is full of books just waiting to be read, you qualify as a **bibliophile**. Yes, you are a *book lover*!

Candor—Who in your group of friends is always willing to say what everyone else is thinking? Who is the *straightforward* friend that asks, "What the heck are you wearing?" Who is most willing to tell the teacher, "Look, Mr. Whatever, this is just too much homework for spring break." Sometimes, candor is nice (if it gets you out of homework during a vacation) and sometimes it can be hurtful.

Antecedent—What was it that *came before this* memorization activity? Throughout the book, the **antecedent** to the list of words that the chapter is based on is a Building Block Quiz. In turn, the **antecedent** to these Your Words, Your World activities is a Practice. What's the **antecedent** to a baseball game? That's right, it's "The Star-Spangled Banner." The **antecedent** to a wedding is an engagement, and the **antecedent** to an engagement is a proposal. In fact, almost everything has an **antecedent**.

Analogous—Analogous is similar to the word *similar*, isn't it? And isn't **analogous** like the word *like*: as in a Coke is like a Pepsi? And don't you think that **analogous** is comparable to the word *comparable*? Indeed, it is. They all are. As with siblings who look somewhat alike, **analogous** is related to the word . . . *related*.

Adage—What is your favorite *saying*? Is there a certain *quote, proverb, maxim,* or *motto* that appeals to you? **Adages** can even be so old, and so well known, that no one can claim to have written them. For example: "Better safe than sorry."

PART TWO

cogent adj. (KOH juhnt)—logically forceful; compelling, convincing
Felix's *cogent* defense of Stephen King gained credit when King won the National Book Award for Distinguished Contribution to American Letters.

colloquial adj. (kuh LOH kwee uhl)—characteristic of informal speech
Mrs. Halloway's class enjoyed *The Outsiders*, in part because it was written in a *colloquial* style.

contradiction n. (kon tra DIK shun)—statement opposite to what was already said
Sherman liked to read books where there was a *contradiction* between what the main character said and what he or she did.

cosmopolitan adj. (kos muh POL ih tun)—pertinent or common to the whole world
The ten people gathered for the dinner party considered themselves quite *cosmopolitan* as they discussed the different museums they'd been to around the world.

debunk v. (dee BUNK)—to expose the falseness of
Dr. Louis was such a good professor because he invited students to *debunk* his theories.

denizen n. (dehn IH zihn)—an inhabitant, a resident
The *denizens* of the writing program all hoped to earn their master's degrees, but more than that, to get published.

egregious adj. (i GREE jiss)—conspicuously bad
The textbook contained several *egregious* errors, including "gramer" instead of "grammar."

elegy n. (eh luh jee)—a mournful poem, usually about the dead
Kevin's *elegy*, published on the five-year anniversary of the Columbine shootings, really captured the public's mood.

epilogue n. (EH puh log)—concluding section of a literary work
In the *epilogue* of his novel, Mike described how the characters carried on with their lives after surviving the hurricane.

epitaph n. (EH pih taf)—engraving on a tombstone, literary piece for a dead person
Upon George Washington's death, Henry Lee uttered the fitting *epitaph*: "First in war, first in peace, and first in the hearts of his countrymen."

eponymous adj. (ih PAHN uh muhs)—giving one's name to a place, book, restaurant, etc.
Macbeth is the *eponymous* protagonist of Shakespeare's play.

figurative adj. (FIG yur uh tiv)—metaphorical, symbolic
"You're driving me up the wall," is a *figurative* saying and not meant to be taken literally!

foreshadow v. (for shah dow)—to indicate beforehand
In Lynn's memoir, her mother's visit to the asylum *foreshadowed* her mother's descent into madness.

MEMORY TIP

When the sun is behind you, what comes before you? Your shadow. And this is how you can remember the word **foreshadow**. Break it down into parts: *fore* indicates something that is up front or that comes before, while *shadow* is not a thing itself but a representation of the thing. In a mystery novel, that representation might be a look at a murder weapon long before the reader learns about the murder itself.

---

humane adj. (HYOO mayn)—merciful, kindly
Writers love to create *humane* characters as they usually win the hearts of readers.

illegible adj. (ih LEJ ih bul)—unreadable, indecipherable
Robert's handwriting was so utterly *illegible* that his teacher jokingly suggested he become a doctor.

Practice 2

DIRECTIONS: Match the word (left column) with its definition (right column).

11. **debunk**		worldly
12. **cogent**		conflicting statement
13. **contradiction**		expose
14. **cosmopolitan**		informal words
15. **colloquial**		convincing
16. **figurative**		indicate beforehand
17. **denizen**		clearly bad
18. **humane**		resident
19. **egregious**		a thing named after oneself
20. **illegible**		symbolic
21. **eponymous**		kind
22. **foreshadow**		unreadable

Your Words, Your World

Don't have time to sit around repeating these words to yourself, over and over again, in order to remember them? Well, you don't have to! The following memorization exercise tests your knowledge of the material . . . without requiring that you take a test! So your job now is to really *think* about what you read, and to really cement an image in your mind. You never know when you'll need that image to pop up again.

Epitaph—Just as an adage is an old saying, often people will ask that a *quote* or *short statement* be engraved on their gravestone. When words other than the name, birth date, and other such facts, are included, they are considered an **epitaph**. If you can imagine the lettering, carved with care into the granite or marble, you will be able to remember that an epitaph is a written tribute.

Elegy—While an epitaph is usually engraved on someone's tombstone, an **elegy** is a *mournful poem* read at a funeral. An **elegy** also may just be a statement, summing up the person's life and all that was good about him or her. Picture the people smiling as they recall the life that was, remembering all that was good about their loved one.

Epilogue—An **epilogue** appears *at the end of a story.* **Epilogues** are often used to *sum up a story* by showing what becomes of an important character. Perhaps the main character was in her teens throughout the story, but the **epilogue** lets the reader know what she was like as an old woman.

PART THREE

insinuate v. (in SIN yoo ayt)—to suggest, say indirectly, imply
Brenda *insinuated* that the character's name, JC, was a reference to Jesus Christ.

irony n. (IY ur nee)—incongruity between expectations and actualities
Mr. Vonblonk often reminded his students that *irony*, even more than plot twists, makes a story more interesting.

lexicon n. (LEHK sih kahn)—a dictionary; a stock of terms pertaining to a particular subject or vocabulary
Terms like "Gen X" and "catch-22" have entered the American *lexicon* through books.

missive n. (MIHS ihv)—a written note or letter
Priscilla spent hours composing a romantic *missive* for Elvis.

naïve adj. (niy EEV)—lacking experience and understanding; French for "natural."
Nandi was *naïve* about the self-serving motives of the character.

paradox n. (PAR uh doks)—contradiction, incongruity; dilemma, puzzle
The class discussed the *paradox* of the traditional Christian idea of God's being both one and three entities.

paragon n. (PAAR uh gon)—a model of excellence or perfection; an exemplar
As far as novelists go, Philip Roth is a *paragon* of caring about every word.

profound adj. (pro FOWND)—deep, meaningful; far-reaching
The entire school listened carefully to the *profound* ideas of Toni Morrison.

MEMORY TIP

Learning a new concept that has a real impact on you and your life is basically the same as finding something, like $20 or a message in a bottle from a long-lost friend. In trying to remember what **profound** means, break the word in two: *pro found*. You found out something deep and meaningful. To make it even easier, consider the fact that the word root **pro** means *much* or *a lot*. You sure did learn a lot!

---

prosaic adj. (proh SAY ihk)—relating to prose (as opposed to poetry); dull, ordinary
Simon's *prosaic* writing took away from the effectiveness of his story.

protagonist n. (pro TAG uh nist)—main character in a play or story; hero
Charles Dickens created some of the world's more memorable *protagonists*.

protégé n. (PRO tuh zhay)—one receiving personal direction and care from a mentor
Although David was once a *protégé* of Tobias Wolf's, he'd quit the writing program and developed his own style of writing.

pseudonym n. (SOO duh nihm)—a fictitious name, used particularly by writers to conceal identity
George Eliot was the *pseudonym* that Marian Evans used when she published her classic novel *Middlemarch*.

quandary n. (KWAN du ree)—predicament, dilemma
John recognized his *quandary* as both editors informed him of their due dates, which fell on the same day!

redundancy n. (ri DUN din see)—unnecessary repetition
Jamie deleted a few paragraphs to cut down on the *redundancy* in his fourth chapter.

rhetoric n. (REH tuhr ihk)—the art of speaking or writing effectively; skill in the effective use of speech
Unfortunately, Lester's talent for *rhetoric* didn't carry over into his writing.

scrupulous adj. (SKROOP yuh luhs)—acting in strict regard for what is considered proper; punctiliously exact
Miller was known as the most *scrupulous* writer in his class and the valedictorian asked for help with her speech.

tutelage n. (TOOT uh lihj)—guardianship, guidance
Under the *tutelage* of Professor McSweeney, Michelle was able to flesh out the problem haunting her main character.

vignette n. (vin YET)—decorative design; short literary composition
Jack's big break came when his *vignette* was published in a respected literary magazine.

Practice 3

DIRECTIONS: Consider the definition and then circle T for True or F for False.

23.	T	F	**insinuate**—to imply
24.	T	F	**irony**—flat and smooth
25.	T	F	**lexicon**—against literature
26.	T	F	**missive**—written note or letter
27.	T	F	**naïve**—lacking experience
28.	T	F	**paradox**—religious
29.	T	F	**paragon**—a model of excellence or perfection
30.	T	F	**protagonist**—the main character
31.	T	F	**pseudonym**—a fake name
32.	T	F	**quandary**—a solution
33.	T	F	**redundancy**—a necessary repetition
34.	T	F	**rhetoric**—using words effectively
35.	T	F	**scrupulous**—thorough
36.	T	F	**vignette**—writing about wine

Your Words, Your World

Don't have time to sit around repeating these words to yourself, over and over again, in order to remember them? Well, you don't have to! The following exercise tests your knowledge of the material . . . without requiring that you take a test! So your job now is to really *think* about what you read, and to really think about the questions that follow.

Tutelage and **Protégé**—While **tutelage** is what the teacher or coach provides, the student who is learning is the **protégé**. You have obviously played the role of **protégé**. Just think of the teacher you have admired most; the person who had the most influence on you and on where you think you might head in life. You surely benefited under his or her **tutelage**. Take a moment to think, now, about whether or not *you* have ever had a **protégé**. . . .

Prosaic and **Profound**—Whereas **prosaic** is defined as writing that is boring and ordinary, a story that is **profound** has deep meaning. It is interesting, it evokes emotion, and it leaves an impression on you when you're done reading it. When you open a book or begin reading a magazine article, you, like everyone else, hope that the writer has put together something **profound**. Nobody ever hopes to read something **prosaic**.

PRACTICE ANSWERS AND EXPLANATIONS

Practice 1

1. An **antagonist** is a foe, and Mr. Kweller felt that each book should have a main character and somebody who causes him or her problems.

2. To **abridge** is to shorten and because they lacked funding, the editors had to condense the yearbook.

3. To speak with **candor** is to speak with meaning and heartfelt honesty; this would make someone a good peer counselor.

4. An **adage** is often metaphoric for a common observation. It's usually a familiar saying.

5. Danny is not alone in believing that Mark Twain's novel is an **antecedent** to many other books, as they followed his use of the journey as a theme.

6. An **assertion** is a declaration lacking in proof. Research provides proof!

7. Books are the **antidote** that helps fight off ignorance.

8. An **accolade** is an honor or tribute, in this case an honorary post named by the governor.

9. The story is an **allegory** because the characters are symbolic of real life.

10. To be **astute** is to be a good judge: in this case, of talent.

Practice 2

11. Debunk is synonymous with expose, as in exposing what is believed to be true but is really false.

12. When something is **cogent** it is convincing, as in a **cogent** argument or theory.

13. A **contradiction** is a conflicting statement. It is a word or set of words that goes against what was said before.

14. When something or somebody is **cosmopolitan** that thing or person is worldly.

15. When somebody says something that is considered **colloquial**, it is slang or a statement consisting of informal words.

16. When an aspect of a story is **figurative** it is symbolic, meaning that the writer is choosing to send a message indirectly. The opposite of **figurative** is literal.

17. A **denizen** is a resident.

18. To be **humane** is to be compassionate and kind.

19. When a statement, object, or action is **egregious** it is clearly bad. An oft-used term is "an **egregious** error."

20. When a group of written words is **illegible**, it is unreadable. Messy handwriting often receives the comment **"illegible"** from teachers.

21. When a band names an album after the band's name—for example, Metallica's album "Metallica"—the album is considered **eponymous**. When a restaurant, store, or even a child is named after the owner or parent (in other words, a thing named after oneself) then it is **eponymous**.

22. To indicate beforehand is to **foreshadow**. It is often a hint or clue of things to come. . . .

Practice 3

23. True. To **insinuate** is to suggest, or say, something indirectly. It is to imply.

24. False. Irony is satire and insincerity—contrasting expectations and actualities—and not flat and smooth like ironing!

25. False. A **lexicon** is a dictionary and not anything that is against literature.

26. True. A **missive** is a written note or letter.

27. True. To be **naïve** is to be lacking in experience and understanding.

28. False. A **paradox** is an inconsistency or contradiction and not religious.

29. True. A **paragon** is something that is used as a model of excellence or perfection.

30. True. The **protagonist** is the main character in a story and is often considered the hero.

31. True. A **pseudonym** is a fake, or fictitious, name.

32. False. A **quandary** is a predicament, or dilemma, and not a solution. Solution is actually the antonym.

33. False. A **redundancy** is an unnecessary repetition. It is not necessary at all.

34. True. **Rhetoric** is the art, or skill, of writing or speaking effectively.

35. True. To be **scrupulous** is to act in regard for what is proper. It is to be conscientious and meticulous.

36. False. A **vignette** is a short literary composition and not writing about wine. Sometimes, the word **vignette** refers to an elaborate design.

CHAPTER 7 TEST

Okay, it's time to put your memory to the test! Take your time not only with the questions but in reading the answer explanations that follow. Set a goal for yourself—80% (24 correct answers) is recommended—and if you don't reach that goal, go back and read through the chapter again. Good luck!

DIRECTIONS: For questions 1–15, circle T for True or F for False. For questions 16–30, circle the synonym.

1.	T	F	**adulation**–unnecessary criticism
2.	T	F	**allegory**–in total
3.	T	F	**analogous**–an opponent
4.	T	F	**antagonist**–an opponent
5.	T	F	**antidote**–a remedy
6.	T	F	**assertion**–to withdraw
7.	T	F	**astute**–to have good judgment
8.	T	F	**bibliophile**–a book lover
9.	T	F	**cogent**–illogical
10.	T	F	**colloquial**–a work of art
11.	T	F	**denizen**–an inhabitant
12.	T	F	**figurative**–not literal but symbolic
13.	T	F	**humane**–kind
14.	T	F	**profound**–boring
15.	T	F	**prosaic**–deep, meaningful

16. **insinuate:**
    state   to suggest   specify

17. **protagonist:**
    main character antagonist   villain

18. **irony:** literal   mockery   sincere

19. **paragon:**
    exemplar   imperfect   paraguay

20. **naïve:** knowledgeable inexperienced   sophisticated

21. **paradox:**
    contradiction   consistency   reliability

22. **missive:** lexicon   paradox   note

23. **lexicon:** dictionary   encyclopedia   Qur'an

24. **pseudonym:**
    false name   Bob   vignette

25. **quandary:**
    solution   diorama   dilemma

26. **redundancy:**
    original   a pointless repetition   colloquial

27. **scrupulous:**
    conscientious   improper   careless

28. **rhetoric:**
    missive   lexicon   public speaking

29. **vignette:**
    vinaigrette   novel   short story

30. **accolade:**
    an honor   allegory   antidote

Answers and Explanations

1. False. Adulation is excessive, over-the-top flattery and not unnecessary criticism.

2. False. An **allegory** is a symbolic story. The definition is not in total.

3. False. To be **analogous** is to be comparable, or similar, and not to be an opponent.

4. True. An **antagonist** is an opponent or adversary. In a story, the main character is the protagonist, not to be confused with antagonist (which is his or her foe).

5. True. An **antidote** is a remedy. Sometimes, this takes the form of medicine, while other times it might mean a decision to ease people's minds or a solution to solve a problem.

6. False. An **assertion** is not to withdraw. It is actually more the opposite: a statement or declaration usually made without any proof.

7. True. To be **astute** is to have good judgment.

8. True. A **bibliophile** is a book lover.

9. False. To be **cogent** is to be convincing in a logical way, the opposite of illogical.

10. False. A **colloquial** phrase, or word, is characteristic of the informal speech of a certain era or location. It is not a work of art.

11. True. A **denizen** is an inhabitant or resident.

12. True. When something is presented in a **figurative** manner it is symbolic or metaphoric. The use of rain is often a **figurative**, or symbolic, representation of a character's sadness.

13. True. To be **humane** is to be kind. Think of the Humane Society, which does so much for needy animals.

14. False. When a book is **profound** it is meaningful and deep and not uninteresting. It is not boring, either.

15. False. Prosaic is an adjective which describes writing that is dull. Not only is it simplistic, it does not have a lasting impact on the reader.

16. To **insinuate** is to suggest. It is to hint and not to state or specify.

17. The **protagonist** is the main character in the story. Although she or he may be a villain, main character is the much more obvious answer. In addition, antagonist and villain are synonymous, or at least closely associated, as they both represent the protagonist's foe.

18. When something is **ironic**, it is done in a mocking, sarcastic fashion. So, mockery = irony. Things that are literal are sincere and therefore not a mockery.

19. A **paragon** is a model of perfection or an exemplar. If a model is imperfect it is not a **paragon**. And although there may be **paragons** in Paraguay, Paraguay is the name of a country.

20. To be **naïve** is to be inexperienced. It is not to be knowledgeable, nor sophisticated.

21. Another word for a contradiction is a **paradox. Paradox** is synonymous with inconsistency, so consistency is out, as is reliability.

22. A **missive** is a note or letter. A lexicon is a dictionary, which is close but not close enough. A paradox is a contradiction and is not close at all!

23. Another word for a dictionary is a **lexicon**. An encyclopedia is a reference book, but is not a dictionary. Nor is the religious text of Islam, the Qur'an.

24. Bob is not a false name. A **pseudonym**, however, is. A vignette is a short story.

25. Another word for dilemma, or problem, is **quandary**. So, solution is actually an antonym. Diorama doesn't work either as it is a miniaturized scene, often seen in museums.

26. A **redundancy** is a pointless repetition, so it definitely isn't original. Colloquial refers to common language, so it is also incorrect.

27. To be **scrupulous** is to be conscientious and caring. Careless and improper (rude and inappropriate) are careless choices.

28. Rhetoric is the skill of public speaking or writing. A missive (note or letter) and a lexicon (dictionary) are incorrect.

29. A **vignette** is a short story or any other short piece of literature. Vinaigrette is a salad dressing—tasty but irrelevant. A novel is just too long to be a vignette. And just too bland to be vinaigrette!

30. An **accolade** is an honor or form of praise. An allegory is a fable and an antidote is a remedy, so both of those are wrong.

CHAPTER 8

The Law

Words that will help you understand everything from "CSI" to your parking ticket

BUILDING BLOCK QUIZ

This "building block" quiz samples the information that you will learn in this chapter, plus two words from the previous chapter. By answering the 12 questions below, you will get a sense of how closely you should study this chapter in order to master all of that vocabu*law*ry! And if you choose incorrect answers for the final two questions, you'll want to go back to chapter 7 for some review.

DIRECTIONS: Fill in the blanks, using the most appropriate of the four multiple-choice answers. The correct answer will always fit into the sentence, grammatically.

1. When international news carried the story of the thief who had his hand amputated for stealing, many said it was a(n) _____ punishment.

   (A) attest (B) apposite

   (C) opposite (D) arbitrary

2. When Jim Klonberg released his legal thriller, he _____ that the details of the plot were taken from a recent celebrity court case.

   (A) averred (B) arraigned

   (C) absconded (D) paradoxed

3. All of Allen's photographs were ruined when the security guards subjected him to a random search and _____ at the airport.

(A) candor (B) substantiation
(C) conviction (D) confiscation

4. Meghan was _____ in her pursuit of justice as a public defense attorney, especially when the death penalty was involved.

(A) hazardous (B) castigated
(C) dogged (D) denizen

5. When Mr. Applebaum was told that there would be a(n) _____ involving his various bank accounts, he broke down in tears and admitted his guilt.

(A) epochal (B) inquest
(C) negligible (D) quandary

6. As soon as the police officer explained to Grandma Brown what _____ meant, she knew that Frankie had slipped back into stealing cars and racing them.

(A) recidivism (B) meticulous
(C) tutelage (D) deft

7. As the deal _____, instead of jail time the running back would serve two hundred hours of community service at area high schools.

(A) stipulated (B) exculpated
(C) confiscated (D) impugned

8. Terry was relieved to learn that his story had
   been _____ by the cashier who saw a
   man slip the CD in his bag.

   (A) purloined (B) proscribed

   (C) nullified (D) substantiated

9. If the civil suit were to be won, Jan had to find
   at least one doctor to _____ that the
   man had experienced back problems before the
   accident.

   (A) censure (B) attest

   (C) de facto (D) gravity

10. Warren finally agreed: the following day he
    would _____ control of the case to the
    junior partner and resign.

    (A) concede (B) corroborate

    (C) abscond (D) profound

11. In studying freedom of speech, students are
    always interested in debating _____ like
    banning flag burning and barring hate groups
    like the Ku Klux Klan from marching.

    (A) paradoxes (B) prosaics

    (C) protagonists (D) disputants

12. When the Supreme Court turned down the
    case, they said it would be a(n) _____ as
    Congress had already passed a law dealing with
    the voting age.

    (A) astute (B) reprieve

    (C) redundancy (D) adage

Answers and Explanations

1. B. As **apposite** means strikingly appropriate, it is the correct choice. Attest (testify) is a verb. Arbitrary (subjective) is also wrong. Opposite sounds like apposite, but it is also incorrect.

2. A. **Averred** means to vow or claim to be true. To arraign is to accuse and to abscond is to escape, so neither is appropriate. Paradox (contradiction) is a word, but paradoxed isn't.

3. D. A **confiscation** takes place when something is taken away from someone, like Allen. Substantiation is when an accusation is proven and a conviction is when you are found guilty, neither of which applies (hopefully!) to Allen. Candor is honesty and is an incorrect choice.

4. C. To be determined is to be **dogged** and Meghan was **dogged** in defending her low-income clients. Hazardous is dangerous, castigated is punished, and a denizen is a resident, so none of those fits as well as **dogged**.

5. B. An **inquest** is an investigation and in this case, the **inquest** was sure to turn up something, so Mr. Applebaum gave up. If something is epochal, it is a tremendously important moment in history. If something is negligible it is not important, so that is incorrect. A quandary is a problem and although that's not the answer, Mr. Applebaum did have problems.

6. A. **Recidivism** occurs when someone falls back into a pattern of behavior, usually criminal. To be meticulous is to be very careful and to be deft is to be highly skilled. Tutelage is incorrect, too, as it means studying under a mentor.

7. A. To make a part of a deal is to **stipulate** and in this case, community service hours were **stipulated**. Exculpated (cleared of blame), confiscated (legally taken), and impugned (questioned) are all relevant but not right.

8. D. Terry's story was **substantiated**, or verified, so he was proven innocent. Purloined means stolen and proscribed means forbidden, so those are incorrect. Nullified is close as perhaps the charges against Terry were nullified, but **substantiated** is more appropriate.

9. B. Jan needed someone to **attest**, or testify, so that her client isn't blamed for the man's bad back. To censure is to criticize, de facto is "from the fact" in Latin, and gravity describes a situation's seriousness. None of these fits as well as **attest**.

10. A. Warren was going to give in, or **concede**. Since he was resigning, he could not corroborate (support) the case. He may abscond (run away), but that only fits into the theme of the sentence and not the blank. Profound (thoughtful) is an inappropriate choice.

11. A. Paradoxes are interesting situations involving inconsistencies and contradictions, so this is the best answer. Prosaics is not a word, although prosaic means dull writing. Protagonists (main characters) and disputants (those involved in a disagreement) are close, but not close enough. If you answered this question incorrectly, you might want to go back to chapter 7 for some review.

12. C. A **redundancy** is an unnecessary repetition. In this case, the Supreme Court did not feel it necessary to revisit the voting age. If someone is astute, he or she is smart. If someone receives a reprieve, he or she is pardoned. And an adage is an old saying. To repeat . . . **redundancy** wins! If you answered this question incorrectly, you might want to go back to chapter 7 for some review.

PART ONE

abet v. (uh BEHT)—to aid; to act as an accomplice
While Dale was convicted, Malcolm was also sent to jail for aiding and *abetting* his friend.

abscond v. (aab SKAHND)—to leave quickly in secret
During the night, Sean *absconded* with all of his mother's money.

absolve v. (ahb SAHLV)—to forgive, free from blame
Although Sean's mother *absolved* him, his father did not.

adjudicate v. (uh JOOD ih kayt)—to hear and settle a matter; to act as a judge
Principal Wykowski *adjudicated* the disagreement between the two students.

annul v. (ah NULL)—to cancel, nullify, declare void, or make legally invalid
The couple asked the court to *annul* their marriage, as they both felt it was a big mistake.

MEMORY TIP

We all know what it means when someone says, "The deal is **null** and void." It's off, is what it means. And as **nul** appears at the end of **annul**, use this phrase to trigger your memory. To **annul** is to *cancel* or *nullify* something; something like a deal.

---

apposite adj. (AAP puh ziht)—strikingly appropriate or well adapted
Barry's *apposite* approach with the jury meant a life sentence instead of the death penalty.

arbitrary adj. (AR ba trer e)—depending solely on individual will; inconsistent
The panel's choices were obviously *arbitrary* as Nancy's legal brief was awarded a prize, while Fred's was not.

arbitration n. (ar bih TRAY shun)—process where a dispute is settled by an outside party
The NHL and the Players' Association tried using *arbitration* to settle the strike, but to no avail.

arraign v. (ah RAYN)—call to court to answer an indictment
Jesse was *arraigned* yesterday, but failed to show up in court.

attest v. (ah TEST)—to testify, stand as proof of, bear witness
Once Mr. Martin *attested* to the fact that Mrs. Martin was with him on the night of the murder, the jury had no choice but to acquit her of the crime.

aver v. (ah VER)—to declare to be true, affirm
The witness *averred* that Eddie had, in fact, been holding the gun.

FLASHBACK

In Latin, *"veritas"* means *true*. And as a word root, **ver** also means *true*. So, it only makes sense that **aver** means *to tell the truth*.

---

castigate v. (kas ti GAYT)—to punish, chastise, criticize severely
Authorities in Singapore harshly *castigate* people convicted of crimes that would be considered minor in the U.S.

concede v. (kon SEED)—to yield, admit
Ralph *conceded* that the case would be nearly impossible to win, but vowed to try nonetheless.

confiscation n. (kon fis KAY shun)—seizure by authorities
The *confiscation* of Bethany's cell phone was the administration's first step in stopping students from calling one another in school.

corroborate v. (ke ROB uh rayt)—to confirm, verify
Fingerprints *corroborated* Theo's testimony that he saw the defendant holding the bag.

Practice 1

DIRECTIONS: Consider the two word choices in the parentheses and circle the one that best fits in the context of the sentence.

1. Miguel was surprised to learn that jury selection was a long, thought-out process and not (arbitrary OR apposite).

2. Judge Tinsely overruled the objection, allowing the witness to (abscond OR aver) the defendant's presence at the party that night.

3. John (conceded OR arraigned) that the plea bargain was a good deal and told his lawyer he would accept.

4. Karl was nervous when his case went to (confiscation OR arbitration) as he had no idea if the mediator would be sympathetic or not.

5. Penny hoped that her history of charity work would be enough to (annul OR attest) to her innocence.

6. When Jenna was (arraigned OR averred) for her DWI, her mother came to support her, but her father did not.

7. Paul was pleased when the judged decided to (annul OR corroborate) the contract with his former partner.

8. Although the prosecution brought in a surprise witness, her testimony (absolved OR corroborated) that of the defendant, so the plan backfired.

9. Jerry couldn't believe that Michael, his partner in the restaurant for over ten years, would (adjudicate OR abscond) with the cash, the cappuccino machine, and even the CDs from the jukebox.

10. Everyone agreed that one hundred hours of community service was the (apposite OR absolve) punishment for the one hundred flowers Hank had ridden through on his bike.

Your Words, Your World

Don't have time to sit around repeating these words to yourself, over and over again, in order to remember them? Well, you don't have to! The following exercise tests your knowledge of the material . . . without requiring that you take a test! So your job now is to really *think* about what you read, and to really cement an image in your mind. You never know when you'll need that image to pop up again.

Castigate—To **castigate** is to *punish* and two images might help you to remember this definition. There is the old rule about a guilty person not casting the first stone. The casting, or throwing of the stone, was intended as a *punishment*. Second is the image of a gate swinging shut as the prisoner enters the prison. Think of cast and gate and you should remember the idea of punishment.

Absolve—One way to solve a problem is to *forgive* the person with whom you have the problem! Although this solution might not always work in real life, "solve" should help you remember the meaning of **absolve**. To **absolve** is to *forgive*, so if you just think of *solving* a problem through *forgiveness*, you will surely remember that **absolve** is the opposite of castigate. Can you think of a time when you *forgave* someone for something he or she did to you?

Abet—To *aid* and **abet**: this old phrase from cop shows means to *help* out. And never is a friend more in need of *help* than after losing a big bet. So, to remember what **abet** means, just picture the friend who lost a big bet: the sad eyes, the frown, the sagging shoulders. And even if you can't *help* your friend to pay off that bet, at least he or she *helped* you to memorize a word.

Adjudicate—*Adjudicare* is Latin for *to judge*. One way to remember a word is to think about its origins. Let the letters **jud** serve as a reminder as well. Look at those letters and think of **jud**ge. The definition of adjudicate is to hear and settle a matter. This is the main responsibility of judges, from the ancient days of Rome right up to today.

Confiscation—At the end of the movie, the detective leads the **con** artist into the police station as his partner brings in the stolen money. A con artist is a thief and another way of referring to money is with the word fiscal. Envision the criminal and the stolen money and you will be able to remember that **confiscation** is *seizure by authorities*. It involves returning something like money to its rightful owners and sending the **con** artist to jail.

PART TWO

de facto adj. (dee FAK toh)—officially recognized but not necessarily legally established. Latin for "from the fact."
Alexi was the *de facto* head of the Russian mob in town.

deft adj. (DEFT)—skillful, dexterous
From a young age, Jane had been *deft* with legal jargon, having learned from her father.

disputant n. (dis PYOO tent)—someone in an argument
As Mr. Walters broke up the fight, he saw that his son was one of the bloody *disputants*.

dogged adj. (DAW guhd)—stubbornly persevering
Detective Conrad's *dogged* investigation helped catch the stalker.

epochal adj. (EHP uh kuhl)—momentous, highly significant
The Supreme Court's *epochal* decision will no doubt affect generations to come.

exculpate v. (EK skul payt)—to clear of blame or fault, vindicate
In a system based on "innocent till proven guilty," no defense attorney should ever have to *exculpate* a client, but of course they make that their goal.

expedite v. (EK spe diyt)—to speed up the progress of
The right to a speedy trial is why Judge West tries to *expedite* the judicial process.

extirpate v. (EHK stuhr payt)—to root out, eradicate, literally or figuratively; to destroy wholly
Lawrence became a cop so as to *extirpate* crime in his beloved city.

FLASHBACK

In chapter 1: Word Roots, you learned that **ex** means *out* or *out of*. To **extirpate** is to *root something out* and destroy it. The *rooting out* is derived from the **ex**. In **exculpate**, the **ex** represents getting someone *out of trouble*. And in **expedite**, you could say that the **ex** stands for getting something like a package or message *out in a hurry*. Whatever helps you to get the definition *out* of your memory bank when you need it!

---

gravity adj. (GRAH vih tee)—importance, seriousness
Phyllis, not grasping the *gravity* of the situation, strode into the police station with a smile on her face.

hazardous adj. (HAZ er duss)—dangerous, risky, perilous
After the public learned that the Healthy Acres Condominiums had been built on a *hazardous* waste site, talk of a lawsuit began.

impugn v. (im PYOON)—to call into question, attack verbally
Harry was quite upset when the detective *impugned* his explanation.

incriminate v. (in KRIM uh nayt)—accuse of a crime, implicate
Although being found with a dead body is usually very *incriminating*, Peg's alibi was airtight.

inquest n. (IHN kwehst)—an investigation, an inquiry
Chief Masterson ordered an internal *inquest* as a means of cleaning up the police department's image.

meticulous adj. (meh TIK yoo luss)—extremely careful, painstaking
Carmine was a *meticulous* private investigator, and he charged a lot for his services.

negligible adj. (NEG lih ju bul)—not worth considering
The Freihoffs decided to move to Madison because the crime rate was so low as to be *negligible*.

Practice 2

DIRECTIONS: After reading the three choices, circle the one that you think is the *antonym*.

11. **de facto:**	untrue	proven	fact
12. **deft:**	handy	unskilled	dexterous
13. **disputant:**	fighter	combatant	ally
14. **dogged:**	stubborn	quitter	persevering
15. **exculpate:**	to pardon	to acquit	to prosecute
16. **expedite:**	to speed up	to hinder	to advance
17. **extirpate:**	to hide	to find	to root out
18. **impugn:**	to censure	to charge	to acquit
19. **incriminate:**	to implicate	to exonerate	to accuse
20. **inquest:**	to ignore	to examine	to inquire
21. **negligible:**	insignificant	noteworthy	unimportant

Your Words, Your World

Don't have time to sit around repeating these words to yourself, over and over again, in order to remember them? Well, you don't have to! The following exercise tests your knowledge of the material . . . without requiring that you take a test! So your job now is to really *think* about what you read, and to really think about the questions that follow. You'll find that each of these words can be used in many situations, not just those associated with legal matters.

Meticulous—When a person is **meticulous**, she takes great *care*, using *caution* in everything that she does. And this doesn't just apply to hazardous situations. Her desk, handbag, car, bedroom, life, is *well organized*. Are you **meticulous**? If not, can you think of someone who is? Imagine that person's face and you'll be reminded of what this word means.

Hazardous—As stated above, meticulous people are usually pretty good at avoiding **hazardous**, or *dangerous*, situations. **Hazardous** things can range from nuclear radiation to activities like roller blading. Since things that are a **hazard** are **hazardous** to *us*, why don't we all be a little more meticulous, shall we?

Gravity—A **grave** situation has an air of *seriousness* and *importance*. The noun **gravity** describes the same thing. In many a *hazardous* situation, there is **gravity** to be found. You can see the **gravity** on the newscaster's face as he or she discusses war or natural disaster. When your teacher hands back all of those failing tests, you can almost feel the **gravity** in the room. Even meticulous people cannot avoid all **grave** situations, unfortunately.

Epochal—An **epochal** situation may include the hazardous and it may be filled with gravity, but the key to this definition is *historical*. When something is **epochal**, it marks a new and important era in history. Possible examples include a world war or a global disease of epidemic proportions. What **epochal** events have happened during your lifetime?

PART THREE

nolo contendere n. (nah loh kahn TEN duh ree)—no contest; Latin for "I do not wish to contend."
Studying his bar exam flashcards, Mike used "no" to remind himself that *nolo contendere* means no contest.

nullify v. (NUL ih fiy)—to make legally invalid; to counteract the effect of
Crystal *nullified* her contract with the law firm when a better offer came along.

perjure v. (PIR joor)—to tell a lie under oath
Benson *perjured* himself to protect his son, forgetting what he'd said earlier and claiming he'd been with him on the night in question.

precedent n. (PRESS uh dent)—earlier example of a similar situation
Denise was proud when she finally unearthed the *precedent*-setting case she'd been assigned to find.

procure v. (pro KYOOR)—to acquire, obtain; to get
The evidence was inadmissible as Officer Jefferson had not *procured* it legally.

proscribe v. (proh SKRIEB)—to condemn or forbid as harmful or unlawful
During Prohibition, alcohol was *proscribed* in the U.S.

purloin v. (PUHR loyn)—to steal
Dupay *purloined* the photograph and brought it to the police department immediately.

recidivism n. (rih SIHD uh vih zihm)—a tendency to relapse into a previous behavior, especially criminal behavior
According the statistics, the *recidivism* rate for high school dropouts is tremendous.

refute v. (re FYOOT)—to contradict, discredit
Ned *refuted* the charge against his client by highlighting his positive traits with a lot of character witnesses.

relevance n. (REL uh vens)—pertinence to the matter at hand, applicability
Judge Frome demanded that all objections have *relevance* as he hated to have his time wasted.

reprieve n. (re PREEV)—postponement of a punishment; relief from danger
Stevens earned a brief *reprieve* as the governor considered the case one last time.

sedition n. (seh DIH shuhn)—behavior that promotes rebellion or civil disorder against the state
Lee was arrested for *sedition* after handing out Karl Marx's *Communist Manifesto*.

sequester v. (suh KWEH stuhr)—to set apart, seclude
When juries are *sequestered*, it can take days, even weeks, to come up with a verdict.

statute n. (STA choot)—law, edict
According to the new town *statutes*, it is illegal to throw chewed bubblegum onto the street.

stipulate v. (STIHP yuh layt)—to specify as a condition or requirement of an agreement or offer
As part of the plea bargain, the defense *stipulated* that a public apology would not be required.

substantiate v. (sub STAN she ayt)—to verify, confirm, provide supporting evidence
The ice cream cone in the garbage can *substantiated* Jill's alibi.

surrogate n. (SUR uh git)—a substitute; one filling in for someone else
The boy was assigned a *surrogate* by the state and given a court date.

verbatim adv. (ver BA tum)—word for word
A court stenographer's job is to record everything said in court, *verbatim*.

Practice 3

DIRECTIONS: Fill in the blanks, using 13 of the 15 words provided below.

sedition	proscribed	nolo contendere	relevance	verbatim
nullified	precedent	surrogate	recidivism	refute
reprieve	prescribe	sequester	stipulated	statute

22. When the _____ concerning seat belts
went into effect, police officers issued hundreds
of tickets to enforce the new law.

23. The athlete entered a plea of _____, basically admitting his guilt but hoping to avoid
more bad press and a possible civil suit.

24. The stenographer's fingers flew over the keys as
she recorded the trial _____.

25. Judge Riordan did not see the _____ of
the testimony and warned the defense to stop
wasting everyone's time.

26. As both his parents were deceased, Heather
often acted as Taylor's _____, especially
in matters at school that required signatures.

27. With only two hours to go, Benny received a
_____ from the governor and was not
put to death.

28. The principal used Mick's 66% average as a
_____ in deciding that he had cheated in
order to score a 98% on the test.

29. In times of war, the United States has strictly enforced laws of _____ so as to avoid treason and rebellion.

30. The judge warned that if Jesse showed the least bit of _____, he would be tried for all of the crimes on his record.

31. The jury feared that the judge would _____ them for the weekend and quickly decided that the murderer was guilty.

32. Prohibition was the time when the U.S. Constitution _____ the sale and consumption of alcoholic beverages.

33. The church leaders agreed to allow the king to marry again and his first marriage was _____.

34. Dr. Warner _____ that if Danielle were allowed to return, she had to promise to never again bring drugs to school.

Your Words, Your World

Don't have time to sit around repeating all these words to yourself in order to remember them? Well, you don't have to! The following exercise tests your knowledge of the material . . . without requiring that you take a test! So your job now is to really *think* about what you read, and to really think about the questions that follow.

Perjure—There are little white lies and then there is **perjury**. Have you ever told Mom or Dad you were going to the movies when, instead, you hit a party? Well, unless they had you *take an oath* on the Bible before telling them who the actors were, the basic plot, and whether or not it was R-rated, you did not **perjure** yourself.

Purloin—Admit it, at least once in your life you *stole* something. Did you *steal* a pack of gum on a dare? Did you *take* your friend's Yu-Gi-Oh or baseball trading cards? Or, is it true? Have you never, ever in your life **purloined** something?

Procure—Slightly better than *purloining* is **procuring**. Although **procurement** sometimes involves a criminal act, it is used more in reference to *obtaining* something. What was the best thing you ever *acquired*? Was it a T-shirt from a friend? A CD? A DVD?

Refute—What's the hardest you have ever had to work to *right* a wrong? Can you remember a time when you really had to put forth great effort to *discredit* someone who'd tried to discredit you? A *rebuttal* is a more official form of **refutation**; for example, in a court case or in a debate. If someone has ever accused you of perjury, purloining, or even procuring, chances are you tried to **refute** that charge.

Substantiate—Have you ever been accused of something and the only way to *prove your innocence* was by **substantiating** your story? It is an awful feeling to be threatened in this way, but at least there is an *opportunity to refute the story*. Think of how you (or if not you, a friend) **substantiated** the story. What facts did you present? Who *validated* your story for you? Were your parents convinced? The principal? The police?!?!

PRACTICE ANSWERS AND EXPLANATIONS

Practice 1

1. Lawyers care very much about their jury, thus jury selection is not an **arbitrary** process. Apposite (suitable) is the opposite.

2. To **aver** is to declare to be true and this was what Judge Tinsely wanted to hear. To abscond is to leave quickly.

3. When John **conceded** to the plea bargain, he decided to give in and agree to the terms. To arraign is to accuse someone.

4. This is not a case of confiscation, even though something may be taken from Karl after his **arbitration** hearing. **Arbitration** is a process in which a dispute is settled by an outside party (arbiter).

5. Penny was hoping her charitable ways would verify, or **attest** to, her innocence. To annul is to cancel, so this is definitely not what she was hoping for.

6. Averred is actually very close, as she could hear that the DWI was, and is, true. But the best answer is **arraigned**, which is the first step in a court case. Jenna was called in to hear the charge(s) against her.

7. As Paul wanted the contract cancelled and not corroborated (confirmed or substantiated), he was pleased when the judge decided to **annul** it.

8. To **corroborate** is to confirm, or verify, so when the witness gave her testimony, it proved that the defendant wasn't lying and he was found innocent. To absolve is to forgive, which is incorrect.

9. To **abscond** is to leave quickly and in secret, which is what Michael did. To adjudicate is to give a ruling or decision and this is incorrect.

10. A punishment that is **apposite** is appropriate and fitting. There is no such thing as an absolve (pardon or forgive) punishment as absolve is a verb and not an adjective.

Practice 2

11. De facto is Latin for "from the fact" and so untrue is not true!

12. Deft means skillful and dexterous. To be unskilled is not to be **deft**.

13. A **disputant** is someone involved in an argument. An ally is a friend and so this is the correct answer.

14. To be **dogged** is to be determined or stubbornly persevering. To be **dogged** is not to be a quitter.

15. To **exculpate** is to clear someone of fault or blame. It is to vindicate and not to prosecute.

16. To **expedite** is to speed up the progress of something. To hinder is its antonym.

17. To **extirpate** is to root out and not to hide.

18. To **impugn** is to call someone into question. At worst, it is to accuse. At best, it is to hold that person responsible for his or her actions. To acquit is the antonym.

19. To **incriminate** is to accuse someone of a crime. It is to implicate and not to exonerate.

20. An **inquest** is an investigation. To ignore would be the opposite.

21. If something is **negligible** it is not worth considering. It is insignificant and not noteworthy in the least.

Practice 3

22. A **statute** is a law and in this case, the law involves wearing a seat belt.

23. **Nolo contendere** means no contest and is Latin for "I do not wish to contend." The athlete was looking for a quick out and was obviously following his lawyer's advice.

24. **Verbatim** translates from Latin as "word for word." The stenographer, even if she was using shorthand, was recording every word from the trial.

25. Judge Riordan had deemed the testimony irrelevant, so much so that he was getting angry! **Relevance** means significance and in this case, whatever it was the witness was saying was not applicable, significant, or **relevant**.

26. A **surrogate** is a substitute and often, children who do not have family to look out for them are assigned a legal surrogate. Makes you appreciate Mom and/or Dad a little bit more, doesn't it?

27. To receive a **reprieve** is to receive a postponement of punishment. This word has crept out into the rest of the world, too, as you might hear a teacher give a class a **reprieve** when he or she delays a test till next week.

28. A **precedent** is an earlier example of a similar situation. Lawyers will use **precedent**-setting cases to try and convince a judge, and in the case of Mick's grade, an educator used past behavior as a **precedent** in making a tough decision.

29. Sedition is behavior that promotes rebellion against the state. The most famous example in U.S. history was when Abraham Lincoln enacted habeus corpus, which meant that war criminals from the Confederacy could be held without trial. This was in order to keep them from committing further acts of **sedition**.

30. Recidivism is a tendency to relapse into a previous behavior, especially criminal behavior. When a judge gives someone an ACD (Adjournment in Contemplation of Dismissal), it means that he or she will be tried for all crimes if arrested again within (usually) six months. Jesse'd better stay out of trouble!

31. When a judge **sequesters** members of a jury, it is to keep them away from all influences while they decide on a verdict. The more serious the case, the longer the **sequester** may be.

32. To **proscribe** is to condemn or ban something, in this case the sale and consumption of alcoholic beverages.

33. To **nullify** something is to virtually erase it. When the church **nullified** the king's first marriage, it was as if it had never happened.

34. To **stipulate** is to order or specify in detail. In Danielle's situation, the **stipulation** was a trade-off: a return to school for a promise.

CHAPTER 8 TEST

Okay, it's time to put your memory to the test! Take your time not only with the questions but in reading the answer explanations that follow. Set a goal for yourself—80% (24 correct answers) is recommended— and if you don't reach that goal, go back and read through the chapter again. Good luck!

DIRECTIONS: For questions 1–15, circle T for True or F for False. For questions 16–30, circle the synonym.

1.	T	F	**abet**—to aid
2.	T	F	**arraign**—to declare innocent
3.	T	F	**procure**—to acquire
4.	T	F	**de facto**—Latin for "from the fact"
5.	T	F	**incriminate**—to plead innocent
6.	T	F	**abscond**—to obtain
7.	T	F	**expedite**—to hurry
8.	T	F	**castigate**—to punish
9.	T	F	**absolve**—to forgive
10.	T	F	**gravity**—unimportance
11.	T	F	**annul**—to proceed
12.	T	F	**arbitrary**—consistent
13.	T	F	**nullify**—to cancel
14.	T	F	**concede**—to deny
15.	T	F	**corroborate**—to verify

16. **surrogate:**	substitute	substantiate	statute
17. **deft:**	deaf	skillful	dealt
18. **refute:**	to contradict	to rebate	to proscribe
19. **exculpate:**	arraign	vindicate	verify
20. **substantiate:**	verify	substitute	subject
21. **impugn:**	to implore	to question	to procure
22. **statute:**	law	refute	purloin

23. **meticulous:**	verbatim	thorough	abscond
24. **proscribe:**	forbid	permit	purloin
25. **negligible:**	stipulate	unimportant	vital
26. **sequester:**	seclude	inquest	hazardous
27. **inquest:**	incriminate	an inquiry	expedite
28. **arbitration:**	a hearing	dispute	arbitrary
29. **stipulate:**	de facto	gravity	a requirement
30. **purloin:**	steal	aver	relevance

Answers and Explanations

1. True. To **abet** is to aid.

2. False. To **arraign** is to formally charge with a crime. It is not to be acquitted (declared innocent).

3. True. To **procure** is to acquire, obtain, or get.

4. True. The Latin **de facto** means "from the fact."

5. False. When someone is implicated in a crime he or she is **incriminated**. It is not to plead innocent, although that might be what this person does.

6. False. To **abscond** is to leave quickly, often in secret, and not to obtain something.

7. True. To **expedite** is to hurry or speed up the progress of something.

8. True. To **castigate** is to punish.

9. True. To **absolve** is to forgive.

10. False. If a situation has **gravity** then it has a level of seriousness and importance.

11. False. To **annul** is to cancel and not to proceed, which is an antonym.

12. False. If something is done in an **arbitrary** fashion, it is done haphazardly. It is done purely on a whim and not in a manner consistent with anything that has been done before.

13. True. To **nullify** is to make legally invalid.

14. False. To **concede** is to yield, give up, or admit. It is not to deny.

15. True. When somebody **corroborates** a story, he or she confirms or verifies it.

16. A **surrogate** is a substitute and not a statute (law) or to substantiate (verify).

17. To be **deft** is to be skillful. It has nothing to do with being deaf or being dealt (as in dealt a hand of cards).

18. To **refute** a point (or a criminal charge) is to contradict it. It is not to proscribe (ban or bar) the point, nor is it to rebate (get a refund for) it.

19. To **exculpate** is to vindicate or clear of fault. To arraign is to charge, while to verify is to confirm.

20. To **substantiate** a story is to verify it. To substitute is to replace and to subject is to expose, so those are both incorrect.

21. To call someone into question is to **impugn** him or her. To implore is to beg and to procure is to obtain, so those could not be right.

22. Another word for a law is **statute**. To refute is to deny and to purloin is to steal and although those may be associated with a certain law, they do not work here.

23. To be very thorough and careful is to be **meticulous**. Verbatim (word for word) and abscond (to leave) are both out.

24. To **proscribe** is to forbid. To permit is the opposite while to purloin is to steal. Stealing may be forbidden, but it is still an incorrect choice.

25. When something is **negligible** it isn't worth considering. It is unimportant and so could not be vital. To stipulate is to make a demand, which may or may not be worth considering. Either way, stipulate is incorrect.

26. To **sequester** is to seclude, or separate, as often happens to an important jury. An inquest is an investigation and something hazardous is dangerous.

27. An **inquest** is an investigation or inquiry. The other possibilities—incriminate (look guilty or implicate) and expedite (to hurry)—might be associated with an **inquest**, but are not right.

28. To go to **arbitration**, or a hearing, is to have your argument heard by a third party. Although a dispute is being settled, this is incorrect, as is arbitrary (random or inconsistent).

29. To include a requirement is to **stipulate** that something has to be done or included to get a deal done. De facto (from the fact) and gravity (importance) are not correct.

30. To **purloin** is to steal. To aver is to vow (to tell the truth) and relevance means significance, which is insignificant in this case.

CHAPTER 9

Etiquette, Culture, and Religion

Build your vocabulary for everything from manners to culture and religion

BUILDING BLOCK QUIZ

This "building block" quiz samples the information that you will learn in this chapter, plus two words from the previous chapter. By answering the 12 questions below, you will get a sense of how closely you should study this chapter in order to master the vocabulary you need to speak knowledgeably about etiquette, culture, and religion. And if you choose incorrect answers for the final two questions, you'll want to go back to chapter 8 for some review.

DIRECTIONS: Fill in the blanks, using the most appropriate of the four multiple-choice answers. The correct answer will always fit into the sentence grammatically.

1. Sam told his friends that he wasn't sure how he felt about organized religion and that he was either an atheist or a(n) _____.

    (A) archipelago (B) agnostic

    (C) cherubic (D) arcane

2. Rashaad promised his mother he would
   _____ for all of his mistakes, starting
   with an apology to the principal.
   (A) adverse (B) condone
   (C) espouse (D) atone

3. Father Joseph's sermon was about the
   _____ of the government in making the
   Girl Scouts pay taxes on their cookie sales.
   (A) benign (B) avarice
   (C) anoint (D) substantiate

4. The rabbi could tell how _____ the little
   girl was, so he advised her parents to talk with
   her about right and wrong, rather than punishing her.
   (A) contrite (B) humane
   (C) adverse (D) clairvoyant

5. For Muslims, praying five times a day is a
   source of _____, giving them the
   strength to be true to their faith.
   (A) tenet (B) dissident
   (C) fortitude (D) malediction

6. As a part of her newspaper editorial, the minister thanked the congregants for their
   _____ donations to the tsunami relief
   fund.
   (A) munificent (B) avarice
   (C) contrite (D) blasphemous

7. The leaders of the commune said that organic
farming was one of its _____, along with
holistic medicine and home schooling.

   (A) impenitents (B) tenets

   (C) rhetorics (D) incantations

8. The chief of police allowed the Hare Krishnas
to walk the streets, singing their songs and
beating their drums, even though some townspeople called their behavior _____.

   (A) verbatim (B) adulterate

   (C) ethos (D) blasphemous

9. When the girls started their Secret Society of
the Tree House, they made up a whole list of
_____ rituals and passwords.

   (A) credo (B) arcane

   (C) zealot (D) perfidious

10. After surviving the _____ conditions of
war, Wilt became a regular attendee at church.

   (A) adverse (B) agnostic

   (C) sanctimonious (D) prostrate

11. Benny was so strongly against the president's
plan that he organized violent protests that
bordered on _____.

   (A) sedition (B) orthodox

   (C) gravity (D) contrite

12. Only when the figure of 6 million deaths was released did people truly begin to understand the _____ of the Holocaust.

(A) exultant (B) gravity

(C) baleful (D) apostate

Answers and Explanations

1. B. An atheist doesn't believe in God, while an **agnostic** simply questions God's existence. An archipelago is a string of islands, cherubic is to look angelic, and arcane is mysterious, so those choices are all incorrect.

2. D. To **atone** is to make amends for a mistake, or for many mistakes in Rashaad's case. To condone (overlook) and to espouse (support) are almost antonyms. Adverse means unfavorable, but it is an adjective and this sentence needs a verb.

3. B. Avarice is greed and Father Joseph felt the government was being stingy. Benign is kind, so that definitely isn't right. To anoint is to bless and to substantiate is to verify.

4. A. To be **contrite** is to be deeply sorrowful, and obviously, the girl feels regretful. Although clairvoyant (psychic) fits grammatically as an adjective, its meaning does not fit. Humane (caring) and adverse (unfavorable conditions) are both incorrect.

5. C. The praying is a source of strength, or **fortitude**. A tenet is a principle, so that is close, but not close enough. A dissident is a rebel and a malediction is a curse, so those are obviously wrong.

6. A. Munificent is an adjective used to describe generous deeds. Avarice (greed) and blasphemous (sacrilegious) are basically antonyms. To be contrite is to be full of remorse, so that is not the best option.

7. B. A **tenet** is a principle or belief; in this case, organic farming was one of the keystone beliefs of the commune. Impenitent is to not be remorseful and rhetoric is public speaking, neither of which is ever written in the plural form (with an "s" at the end). Incantations are songs or prayers, so this is incorrect.

8. D. The complainers saw the behavior as profane, irreverent, and **blasphemous**, but the police chief disagreed. Of the other three choices, verbatim means word-for-word, adulterate (a verb, while an adjective is called for here) means to contaminate, and ethos (a noun) is a group philosophy.

9. B. The girls were trying to be mysterious, so they came up with a bunch of **arcane** (secretive) rituals and passwords. A credo is a set of beliefs, a zealot is a passionate (or fanatical) believer, and perfidious means disloyal, so none of those is appropriate.

10. A. The choice is **adverse** as war is full of traumatically difficult situations. An agnostic doubts God's existence, but Wilt's faith deepened due to the war. To be sanctimonious is to make a pretense of being devout, and to be prostrate is to lie facedown in a submissive position.

11. A. Sedition is a form of rebellion against the government. Orthodox (traditional and customary) and gravity (seriousness) do not fit grammatically. To be contrite is to be sorry, so that doesn't work, either. If you answered this question incorrectly, you might want to go back to chapter 8 for some review.

12. B. Gravity means seriousness and is the only possible choice. Baleful means menacing, but the sentence needs a noun and not an adjective. An apostate is a traitor and to be exultant is to feel triumphant, so those are both wrong. If you answered this question incorrectly, you might want to go back to chapter 8 for some review.

PART ONE

abjure v. (aab JOOR)—to renounce under oath; to abandon forever; to abstain from
Although he had been a Catholic all his life, Paul *abjured* his religious beliefs and became a Buddhist.

adulterate v. (ah DULL ter ayt)—to corrupt or make impure
Father Gowen wrote a convincing sermon about television's ability to *adulterate* unsupervised children.

adverse adj. (ad VERHS)—unfavorable, unlucky; harmful
In *adverse* conditions, many people turn to religious leaders for solace.

agnostic n. (aag NAHS tik)—one who doubts that God exists
Upon telling his parents that he was an *agnostic*, Matt was surprised at their lack of anger.

anoint v. (ah NOYNT)—to apply oil to someone or something especially as a sacred rite
The ceremony required Kelly to *anoint* her daughter's head with oil.

apostate n. (uh PAHS tayt)—one who renounces a religious faith
King Charles XII declared himself an *apostate* so that he could marry out of his faith.

arcane adj. (ahr KAYN)—secret, obscure; known only to a few
Walter decided to do a research paper on the *arcane* rituals of the world's lesser-known religions.

atone v. (ah TON)—to make amends for a wrong
Rabbi Schultz was pleased to hear that the three boys wanted to *atone* for their wrongdoings.

avarice n. (AH var iss)—greed
Rebecca told her brother, "You'd be hard-pressed to find a faith that doesn't warn against *avarice*."

baleful adj. (BAYL ful)—harmful, with evil intentions
Mishka worried that her son was turning *baleful* as a result of the divorce.

benign adj. (buh NIYN)—kindly, gentle, or harmless
Sully was relieved to learn that the reverend was *benign* and not cruel or judgmental in the least.

blasphemous adj. (BLAS fuh muhs)—cursing, profane, irreverent
Jack had a long conversation with his daughters about avoiding *blasphemous* behavior and was pleased that they seemed to understand.

canonize v. (KAN on iyz)—to declare a person a saint; raise to highest honors
Everyone in the city was excited to learn that the nun from St. Francis would be *canonized* in Rome.

cherubic adj. (CHAR ub ik)—sweet, innocent, resembling a cherub (type of angel)
Isadoro's *cherubic* appearance was only enhanced by his role as an altar boy.

clairvoyant adj., n. (klayr VOY nt)—exceptionally insightful, able to foresee the future; a person with those abilities
Having tried organized religion, Nancy turned to a *clairvoyant* for guidance.

Practice 1

DIRECTIONS: Match the word (left column) with its definition (right column).

1. **avarice:**	obscure
2. **arcane:**	one who doubts God's existence
3. **abjure:**	to renounce a religious faith
4. **baleful:**	one who renounces a religious faith
5. **adulterate:**	to apply oil in a sacred rite
6. **apostate:**	unfavorable
7. **anoint:**	to corrupt
8. **blasphemous:**	harmful
9. **agnostic:**	to be irreverent
10. **adverse:**	greed

Your Words, Your World

Don't have time to sit around repeating these words to yourself, over and over again, in order to remember them? Well, you don't have to! The following exercise tests your knowledge of the material . . . without requiring that you take a test! So your job now is to really *think* about what you read, and to really think about the questions that follow.

Cherubic—When you were a *baby*, did everyone say you were **cherubic**? Did you have those big *rosy cheeks* that old folks just love to pinch? Did you have that *sweet, innocent* look associated with cherub *angels*?

Clairvoyant—There's nothing like a Ouija board when it comes to *supernatural* party games. It's probably all silliness, but some people do claim to be **clairvoyant**. And even more people believe in **clairvoyance**, or the *skills of insight* that are associated with *psychics* and *mystics*.

Benign—Has anyone ever called you **benign**? If so, did you know you were being complimented? To be called *gentle* and *kind* may not be what you're aiming for (especially if you're a teenage boy or a business executive), but it's nice to hear, nonetheless.

Canonize—Maybe you've surpassed benign and gone straight to **canonization**! If so, this means that somebody has noticed your good deeds and *declared you a saint*. Of course, chances are they are just being figurative, but it is a great *accolade* nonetheless. Does benign describe you? Should you be *praised*, if not **canonized**?

Atone—Have you been shaking your head as you read the last two paragraphs? Are you wondering if perhaps, since neither benign nor canonize applies to you, it's time to *right your wrongs*? To *make amends* to those you've hurt? If so, you are ready to **atone** for your mistakes. The first step towards *forgiveness* is **atonement**.

PART TWO

condone v. (kon DOHN)—to pardon or forgive; overlook, justify, or excuse a fault
Despite being Muslim, Shef could not *condone* the suicide bombings in Israel.

consecrate v. (KON si krayt)—to declare sacred; dedicate to a goal
Father Mike *consecrated* the rings and Ben and Wendy were married!

contrite adj. (kon TRYT)—deeply sorrowful and repentant for a wrong
Ted seemed *contrite*, but his family was slow to forgive him as he had apologized for his drunk driving many times before.

credo n. (KREE doh)—system of principles or beliefs
Taylor knew that if she chose a virtuous *credo* to live by, she could be spiritual without necessarily being religious.

dissident adj., n. (DIHS ih duhnt)—disagreeing with an established religious or political system; the person who disagrees in this way
Everyone suspected Gene cared more about being a *dissident* than about the actual issues.

espouse v. (ih SPOWZ)—to take up and support as a cause
Because of his religious beliefs, Karl could not *espouse* the family-planning curriculum at the high school.

ethos n. (EE thohs)—beliefs or character of a group
In accordance with the *ethos* of the Quakers, Lowell did not have to serve in the military.

exalt v. (eg ZAHLT)—to glorify or honor
Easter is a glorious celebration; it is a day for Christians all over the world to *exalt* the resurrection of Jesus.

expound v. (ehk SPOWND)—to explain or describe in detail
To the point of being distasteful, the minister liked to *expound* the sins that haunt mankind.

exultant adj. (eg ZUHL tent)—triumphant
The Dalai Llama was *exultant* in his own peaceful way.

fidelity n. (fih DEL ih tee)—loyalty, faithfulness
During their marriage counseling sessions, the priest constantly reminded Frank and Heather of the importance of *fidelity*.

fortitude n. (FOHR tih tood)—strength of mind that allows one to face danger or trouble with courage
In order to maintain his "internal *fortitude*," as he called it, Justin would kneel five times a day and pray facing east.

heretical adj. (huh REH tih kuhl)—departing from accepted beliefs or standards, oppositional
Throughout history, the actions of many spiritual leaders have been called *heretical*.

impenitent adj. (im PEN ih tent)—not remorseful
David was so *impenitent* that his outraged father put the boy in the back of the car and drove straight to the synagogue.

incantation n. (in kan TAY shun)—a verbal spell
Speaking in tongues is a form of *incantation*.

Practice 2

DIRECTIONS: Consider the definition and then circle T for True or F for False.

11.	T	F	**contrite**—regretful
12.	T	F	**exultant**—triumphant
13.	T	F	**impenitent**—remorseful
14.	T	F	**heretical**—deeply religious
15.	T	F	**credo**—system of beliefs
16.	T	F	**ethos**—to glorify
17.	T	F	**condone**—to condemn
18.	T	F	**consecrate**—to declare sacred
19.	T	F	**fidelity**—loyalty
20.	T	F	**exalt**—to honor

Your Words, Your World

Don't have time to sit around repeating these words to yourself, over and over again, in order to remember them? Well, you don't have to! The following exercise tests your knowledge of the material . . . without requiring that you take a test! So your job now is to really *think* about what you read, and to really cement an image in your mind. You never know when you'll need that image to pop up again.

Fortitude—Is there any greater image of *strength* than a well-guarded fort? Put this image in your mind: tall walls of five-foot thick stone, a moat a half-mile wide and filled with crocodiles and piranha. Since fortitude means the *strength of mind to encounter adversity with courage*, the image of the fort will be a helpful reminder.

Incantation—In Spanish, cantar means to sing. Imagine the sound of singing coming from a church, synagogue, mosque, or any other sort of spiritual gathering. An incantation is a *chant, prayer,* or *song*.

Dissident—History is full of people who have **dissed** religions, and if you can picture one of them, Martin Luther, making a **dent** while posting his "95 Theses" on the door of the Castle Church, you will be able to remember that a **dissident** is *one who disagrees with an established religion or system*.

Expound—Like the pounding of Luther's hammer, many a leader has gotten dramatic while **expounding**—or *explaining and describing in detail*—this or that point. In 1960, Soviet leader Nikita Khrushchev reportedly pounded his shoe on the table to get the attention of the United Nations as he **expounded** his disapproval. If you can picture this, if you can hear it, you will remember it!

Espouse—Another word for husband or wife is spouse. And no one is more *supportive* than a spouse. So, as you are trying to remember that to **espouse** is to *support*, and in particular to support a cause, just think of the right-hand man or woman. It's hard to make it in this world without a *supportive* spouse.

PART THREE

intrapersonal adj. (in trah PER sah nul)—occurring within one person's mind or self
As Jane matured, her *intrapersonal* strengths grew.

FLASHBACK

In chapter 1: Word Roots, you learned that **intra** means *within*. Not to be confused with **inter** (between), **intra** has a personal, individual aspect to it. As in **intrapersonal**, which means *occurring within one's mind*, when a word includes the root **intra** it refers to a private occurrence.

---

malediction n. (maal ih DIHK shun)—a curse, a wish of evil upon another
The frog prince needed a princess to kiss him and put an end to the witch's *malediction*.

mea culpa n. (me ah KUL puh)—my fault; Latin for "my fault"
Meghan's mother always blamed herself for everything, muttering *mea culpas* constantly.

medium n. (MEE dee um)—psychic
Carla was so upset about the death of her grandmother that she decided to use a *medium* to contact her and say a proper goodbye.

munificent adj. (myoo NIF ih sint)—generous
After the Wilsons made their *munificent* donation, the church finally was able to build a rectory.

omniscient adj. (ahm NISH ent)—having knowledge of all things
Marty questioned whether it was rational to believe in an *omniscient* God.

orthodox adj. (OR thu doks)—adhering to what is customary or traditional
Robert wanted to continue going to church, but knew he needed a congregation that was a little less *orthodox*.

penitent adj. (PEH nih tehnt)—expressing sorrow for sins or offenses, repentant
Manson's eyes were more crazed than *penitent*, and everybody was relieved to hear that he'd been convicted.

perfidious adj. (pir FID ee uss)—faithless, disloyal, untrustworthy
Martha was upset to learn that her daughter was *perfidious*, and she longed to get the girl some spiritual counseling.

prostrate adj. (PRAH strayt)—lying facedown in submission
During the ceremony, the young priests lay *prostrate* as they named all the saints.

repentant adj. (re PEN tant)—apologetic, remorseful, guilty
After stealing from the collection plate, Ralph was so *repentant* that he offered to do everything from lawn work to carpentry for the church.

sanctimonious adj. (SAANGK tih MOH nee uhs)—hypocritically devout; acting morally superior to another
Father Chris's *sanctimonious* tone drove many parishioners away.

secular adj. (SEH kyoo luhr)—not specifically pertaining to religion, relating to the world
In addition to the Bible, Reverend Sheila had a copy of the Qur'an, Friday's *New York Times*, and several **secular** novels by her bed.

serendipity n. (se ren DIP ih tee)—habit of making fortunate discoveries by chance
Rosemary would tell anyone willing to listen that her *serendipity* was a sure sign of God's presence.

stringent adj. (STRIHN juhnt)—imposing severe, rigorous standards
The class debated whether the Pilgrims' *stringent* ways were a help or a hindrance in the New World.

talisman n. (TAL iss man)—magic object that offers supernatural protection
Greg counted on the little bobble-head *talisman* on the dashboard to keep his old Toyota running.

tenet n. (teh niht)—a principle, belief, or doctrine accepted by members of a group
One of the *tenets* of Islam is that it is not acceptable to eat pork.

zealot n. (zel UHT)—someone passionately devoted to a cause, a fanatic
Zealots have given organized religion a bad name since the beginning of recorded history.

Practice 3

DIRECTIONS: Read the three possible synonyms, then circle the word you think best defines the word in bold.

21. **penitent:**	sorrowful	joyous	munificent
22. **repentant:**	refusing	apologetic	sanctimonious
23. **mea culpa:**	"my bad"	"my, oh my"	"Mama mia"
24. **intrapersonal:**	introspective	interactive	international
25. **orthodox:**	paradox	traditional	serendipity
26. **secular:**	worldly	separate	religious
27. **munificent:**	municipal	medium	generous
28. **tenet:**	a principle	a principal	to be principled
29. **omniscient:**	all-knowing	zealot	unapologetic
30. **medium:**	heretic	physician	psychic
31. **perfidious:**	disloyal	nice	trustworthy
32. **prostrate:**	submissive	dissident	zealot
33. **malediction:**	a hymn	a curse	a bad book

Your Words, Your World

Don't have time to sit around repeating these words to yourself, over and over again, in order to remember them? Well, you don't have to! The following exercise tests your knowledge of the material . . . without requiring that you take a test! So your job now is to really *think* about what you read, and to really think about the questions that follow.

Sanctimonious—In a nonreligious sense, to be **sanctimonious** is to be *critical* in a *hypocritical* way. All people at one time or another *criticize* others for doing things that they themselves have done (or wished they could do). Everybody has had a **sanctimonious** moment. Can you remember one of yours, or a time when you felt someone was being **sanctimonious** with you?

Serendipity—**Serendipity** is good fortune. When something nice happens by chance to you, it is **serendipitous**. Have you ever had a great week? Perhaps a want ad for the perfect job landed in your lap, a check arrived from a long-lost relative, or you randomly found a friend from childhood while surfing the Internet.

Stringent—But luck changes . . . sometimes serendipity disappears and you have to face a **stringent** new teacher or manager. His *severe rules* and his *rigorous standards* bring everyone down. Can you think of someone you know who is **stringent**?

Talisman—In a secular, nonreligious sense, this could be a *good-luck charm*. It could be that rabbit's foot you carry around. When everybody crowds in to take the SAT, GRE, or any standardized test, no doubt there will be some **talismans** coming along for the ride.

Zealot—In a spiritual sense, a **zealot** is someone *passionately devoted to a cause*. With this *passion*, the **zealot** may or may not become stringent. He or she may or may not act in a sanctimonious manner, in the opinion of those who knew that person before he or she became a **zealot**. Do you know anyone who went through a change and was suddenly *highly devoted to a cause*?

PRACTICE ANSWERS AND EXPLANATIONS

Practice 1

1. Avarice is greed.

2. If something is **arcane** it is obscure, or vague.

3. To **abjure** is to renounce a religious faith.

4. If something, or someone, is **baleful** it is menacing and harmful.

5. To **adulterate** is to corrupt, spoil, or make impure.

6. An **apostate** is one who renounces his or her religious faith.

7. To **anoint** is to apply oil in a sacred rite or ceremony.

8. If someone is acting in a **blasphemous** manner, that person is being irreverent and, more specifically, sacrilegious.

9. An **agnostic** is one who doubts the existence of God.

10. If conditions are **adverse**, then they are unfavorable.

Practice 2

11. True. To be **contrite** is to be regretful and repentant for doing wrong.

12. True. To feel **exultant** is to feel triumphant.

13. False. **Impenitent** is the opposite of remorseful.

14. False. To be **heretical**, one must depart from accepted beliefs. Heretical does not mean deeply religious.

15. True. A **credo** is the system of beliefs of a person or group.

16. False. An **ethos** is the beliefs or character of a group. It is not to glorify.

17. False. To **condone** is not to condemn. It is to pardon or permit.

18. True. To **consecrate** is to declare sacred.

19. True. **Fidelity** is loyalty and faithfulness.

20. True. To **exalt** is to glorify or honor.

Practice 3

21. To be **penitent** is to be sorrowful and full of remorse. Joyous is basically the opposite, while munificent means generous.

22. To be **repentant** is to be penitent and apologetic. Refusing is incorrect as is sanctimonious (self-righteous).

23. A **mea culpa** is a term for "my fault," as translated from Latin, or "my bad."

24. When something is **intrapersonal**, usually it means that the person is being introspective. She or he is thinking about things and working them out. Interactive involves doing things with other people, while international involves other countries.

25. If something (or someone), is **orthodox**, it is not a paradox. It is traditional and conformist. Serendipity refers to the chance occurrence of good fortune.

26. When something (or someone) is considered **secular**, it is worldly and not religious or spiritual. For example, the U.S. government is supposed to be **secular**, through the doctrine of "separation of church and state." But neither separate nor religious is the right answer.

27. The adjective **munificent** is used to describe a generous act or person. Municipal is a distracter based on a similar prefix, and a medium is a psychic or clairvoyant.

28. A **tenet** is a principle, as in a theory or doctrine. A principal runs a school, and to be principled, or honorable, is nice but not the correct answer.

29. To be **omniscient** is to be all-knowing. If you were **omniscient**, you wouldn't need this book. A zealot is an intense believer, and to be unapologetic has nothing to do with **omniscience**.

30. A **medium** is a psychic with supposed supernatural powers. Although religious leaders may call a **medium** a heretic, this is an incorrect answer, as is physician (doctor).

31. To be **perfidious** is to be disloyal. Nice is clearly wrong while trustworthy is a near-antonym.

32. To be **prostrate** is to be submissive and usually involves laying facedown on the floor, as in a religious ceremony. A dissident is a rebel and a zealot is a passionate believer (who may, at times, lie prostrate).

33. A **malediction** is a curse. Many baseball fans believe the Boston Red Sox had been cursed not to win the World Series, but in 2004 the supposed "curse" was broken. While the prefix **mal-** means bad, a bad book is not the answer. A hymn is a religious song.

CHAPTER 9 TEST

Okay, it's time to put your memory to the test! Take your time not only with the questions but in reading the answer explanations that follow. Set a goal for yourself—80% (24 correct answers) is recommended—and if you don't reach that goal, go back and read through the chapter again. Good luck!

DIRECTIONS: For questions 1–15, circle T for True or F for False. For questions 16–30, circle the synonym.

1.	T	F	mea culpa—Latin for "my cup"
2.	T	F	adverse—favorable
3.	T	F	medium—psychic
4.	T	F	anoint—to apply oil as a sacred rite
5.	T	F	expound—to describe in detail
6.	T	F	atone—noise
7.	T	F	repentant—remorseful
8.	T	F	avarice—greed
9.	T	F	clairvoyant—exceptionally insightful
10.	T	F	baleful—full of love
11.	T	F	incantation—a hymn, chant, or prayer
12.	T	F	benign—obscure
13.	T	F	blasphemous—reverent
14.	T	F	cherubic—sweet and innocent
15.	T	F	consecrate—to declare sacred

16. **contrite:**
    gleeful   contrasting   repentant

17. **credo:**
    system of beliefs   statement of disbelief   nonbeliever

18. **exalt:** to upstage   to ridicule   to honor

19. **penitent:**
    repentant   offensive   facedown

20. **exultant:**
    orthodox   talisman   triumphant
21. **fidelity:**
    unfaithful   stringent   loyalty
22. **impenitent:**
    remorseless   without debt   with hope
23. **prostrate:**
    subjective   submissive   sacrilegious
24. **arcane:**
    secret   well known   prehistoric
25. **malediction:**
    a foolish notion a lexicon   a curse
26. **munificent:**
    glorious   affable   generous
27. **abjure:**
    to reject   to accept   to be official
28. **orthodox:**
    traditional   clean   adverse
29. **perfidious:**
    faithless   loyal   trusting
30. **condone:**
    to renounce   to forgive   to anoint

Answers and Explanations

1. False. Mea culpa is Latin for "my fault."

2. False. If a situation is **adverse**, then the conditions are unfavorable.

3. True. A **medium** is a psychic.

4. True. To **anoint** is to apply oil, especially as a part of a religious ceremony.

5. True. To **expound** is to explain or describe in detail.

6. False. To **atone** is to make amends for a wrong and has nothing to do with sound!

7. True. To be **repentant** is to be apologetic and remorseful. It is to admit guilt and ask for forgiveness.

8. True. **Avarice** means greed.

9. True. To be **clairvoyant** is to be, in the least, exceptionally insightful. Usually it means that a person is psychic.

10. False. To be **baleful** is not to be full of love and joy. It is the opposite: to have evil intentions and to be harmful.

11. True. An **incantation** is a hymn, chant, or prayer. Remember the Spanish cantar (to sing or chant)?

12. False. To be **benign** is to be kindly and gentle. It is not to be obscure.

13. False. To be **blasphemous** is to be disrespectful and irreverent, not reverent.

14. True. If someone is called **cherubic**, he or she looks sweet and innocent.

15. True. To **consecrate** is to declare sacred.

16. To be **contrite** is to be repentant for a wrong. It is the opposite of gleeful and has nothing to do with contrasting.

17. A **credo** is a system of beliefs. It isn't a statement of disbelief, nor is it a person who is a nonbeliever.

18. To **exalt** is to honor or glorify. To upstage (embarrass publicly) and to ridicule (criticize) are incorrect.

19. To be **penitent** is to be repentant. It is to express sorrow for your misdeeds. To be prostrate is to lie facedown on the ground, and one might be **penitent** after committing an offensive act.

20. To be **exultant** is to be triumphant. Orthodox (traditional) and talisman (a sacred object that supposedly brings good luck) are both irrelevant.

21. To have **fidelity** is to have loyalty: to be faithful. So unfaithful doesn't fit. Stringent, which means strict, may seem close, but isn't close enough.

22. To be **impenitent** is to not be penitent. It is to be remorseless and not without debt or with hope.

23. To be **prostrate** is to be submissive, usually while lying facedown in adoration. It is certainly not sacrilegious, nor is it subjective (biased).

24. If something is **arcane**, it is secret or obscure (thus ruling out well known). The choice of prehistoric is irrelevant.

25. A **malediction** is a curse and not a foolish notion, although you might find the notion of curses to be foolish. A lexicon is a dictionary.

26. To be **munificent** is to be generous. And although generosity can be glorious and affable (pleasant), those are incorrect choices.

27. To **abjure** is to officially reject something or to renounce under oath. It is not to be official or to accept.

28. **Orthodox** means traditional. It has nothing to do with being clean. Adverse refers to unfavorable conditions.

29. To be **perfidious** is to be faithless. It is not to be loyal, nor is it to be trusting.

30. To **condone** is to pardon or forgive. It isn't to renounce (reject) and it isn't to anoint (apply oil in a religious ceremony).

CHAPTER 10

The Five Senses

Descriptive words for a world worth describing

BUILDING BLOCK QUIZ

This "building block" quiz samples the information that you will learn in this chapter, plus two words from the previous chapter. By answering the 12 questions below, you will get a sense of how closely you should study this chapter in order to master the vocabulary you need to speak knowledgeably about the sights, sounds, smells, touches, and tastes of the world around you. Should you happen to choose incorrect answers for the final two questions, you'll want to go back to chapter 9 for some review.

DIRECTIONS: Fill in the blanks, using the most appropriate of the four multiple-choice answers. The correct answer will always fit into the sentence grammatically.

1. The point of the science experiment was to show that light without water would cause the plants to _____.

   (A) parch (B) onerous

   (C) delectable (D) munificent

2. As the odor in the science lab might have indicated a(n) _____ situation, Mr. Bryant should have evacuated the building and alerted the principal.

   (A) incandescent (B) stringent

   (C) deleterious (D) vapid

3. The _____ from the landfill smelled so strongly that homeowners in the area didn't want to open their windows.

   (A) effervescence (B) effluvia
   (C) effort (D) efficacious

4. When Mrs. Bailey told Jenna about her failing grade in front of the whole class, she lived up to her reputation as the most _____ teacher in the school.

   (A) nocturnal (B) communicable
   (C) agile (D) nefarious

5. Professor Traylor refused to move the April 1st deadline, despite complaints that the assignment was long and _____.

   (A) onerous (B) calculated
   (C) ersatz (D) palpable

6. Charlie was excited about his Home Economics project, but the brownies came out thin and _____.

   (A) raucous (B) vapid
   (C) reprehensible (D) resolute

7. The Children's Museum was full of _____ items that kids could easily touch and understand.

   (A) venerable (B) nefarious
   (C) palpable (D) jagged

8. Dean Jobey had no patience for the _____ behavior of the school's trouble-makers.

   (A) wanton (B) mature

   (C) destitute (D) blanch

9. Gail's _____ efforts were inspiring and soon everyone at the church was raising money for the hurricane victims.

   (A) stringent (B) heckler

   (C) olfactory (D) resolute

10. Before the divorce, Teddy's house was full of _____, so he spent many nights with his grandmother.

    (A) visceral (B) acrimony

    (C) astringent (D) askance

11. Kate proved how _____ she could be as she told another girl one of Terrica's secret fears.

    (A) tactile (B) resplendent

    (C) chromatic (D) perfidious

12. The school's _____ leader, Principal Fontaine, was highly respected and praised by students, staff, and parents.

    (A) jeopardize (B) declaiming

    (C) avuncular (D) exalted

Answers and Explanations

1. **A.** To **parch** is to dry out and shrivel. Onerous (burdensome), delectable (delicious), and munificent (generous) do not apply here.

2. **C. Deleterious** is the best answer as it means harmful or destructive. Incandescent (shining brightly) and vapid (tame and uninspiring) are incorrect and although stringent (severe) might work here, it does not fit as well as **deleterious**.

3. **B. Effluvia** is the odor given off by waste. Effervescence is fizz or sparkle, and efficacious means effective. Effort means exertion or attempt. You'll notice the wrong answers all sound like the correct answer—don't let that confuse you.

4. **D.** To be **nefarious** is to be wicked or vicious and Mrs. Bailey was just that. To be nocturnal is to live at night, to be communicable is to be infectious, and to be agile is to be flexible and athletic.

5. **A.** Although Professor Traylor disagreed, the class thought that the assignment was **onerous**, or burdensome, much more so than being calculated (planned out), ersatz (fake), or palpable (obvious).

6. **B.** Unfortunately, Charlie's brownies were **vapid**, or dull and tasteless. They were not raucous (harsh sounding), nor were they resolute (determined). And although you could argue that they were reprehensible (worthy of public scorn), **vapid** is still the best choice.

7. **C. Palpable** has two definitions and both work here: touchable and understandable. Venerable (respected), nefarious (wicked), and jagged (sharp) are all incorrect.

8. **A. Wanton** behavior is reckless. **Wanton** students are undisciplined and apparently unappreciated by the dean! Although destitute may sound right, it means impoverished. To blanch is to become pale, and the students' behavior was the opposite of mature.

9. **D.** It was Gail's firm determination that earned everyone's respect, so **resolute** is the answer. Stringent could work in the sentence, but it seems less likely that strict, rigid efforts would gather a following. Heckler (obnoxious critic) and olfactory (relating to the sense of smell) are incorrect.

10. B. Acrimony describes bitterness and hostility, so it's no wonder Teddy didn't want to be around. Visceral describes an instinctive feeling or reaction, while astringent describes something harsh or severe (close, but not quite right here). Note that both of those are adjectives and the sentence requires a noun. Askance is an adverb that means doubtfully or suspiciously.

11. D. Perfidious means disloyal and untrustworthy. Tactile (creating the sensation of touch), resplendent (splendid), and chromatic (relating to color) clearly are incorrect choices. If you answered this question incorrectly, you might want to go back to chapter 9 for some review.

12. D. To be **exalted** is to be glorified and honored. To jeopardize is to endanger, declaiming is speech making, and avuncular refers to warmth and kindness, but the sort one would receive informally from an uncle. If you answered this question incorrectly, you might want to go back to chapter 9 for some review.

PART ONE

acrid adj. (AHK rid)—harsh, bitter
The *acrid* smell of the vinegar drove Janet from the kitchen.

acrimony n. (AK ri MOH nee)—bitterness, animosity
The game ended in *acrimony* after the pitcher hit three successive batters.

MEMORY TIP

Acrid rhymes with acid, so when you see words that begin with "acri", like **acrid** and **acrimony**, think of the harsh, bitter taste of acid.

---

agile adj. (AH jil), (ah JIYL)—well coordinated, nimble
Ned was *agile* enough to talk on the phone, peel a banana, and nudge the cat away from the dog's food, all at the same time.

askance adv. (uh SKAANS)—with disapproval; with a skeptical sideways glance
Freida looked *askance* at her son's awful report card.

astringent adj. (ahs STRING eynt)—harsh, severe, stern
The cheese tasted much too *astringent* for Jon.

avuncular adj. (ah VUHNG kyuh luhr)—like an uncle in behavior, especially in kindness and warmth
Coach Williams's *avuncular* style made him well liked.

blanch v. (BLAHNCH)—to pale; take the color out of
Ward's face turned red, but quickly *blanched* as the hot sauce worked its way down to his stomach.

cacophony n. (kuh KAH fuh nee)—a jarring, unpleasant noise
Kelly didn't know how her husband could stand the *cacophony* of Pearl Jam.

> **FLASHBACK**
>
> You'll remember from chapter 1: Word Roots that **phon** means *sound*. Let this be a reminder that **cacophony** is *an unpleasant, usually loud, sound*.

cadence n. (KAYD ns)—rhythmic flow; marching beat
All of the reviews complimented P Nice's original style, the *cadence* he used when he rapped.

calamity n. (ka LAM uh tee)—disaster, catastrophe
The earthquake was a *calamity* that claimed hundreds of lives.

chromatic n. (kro MA tik)—relating to color; colorful
The interior designer presented a bright *chromatic* scheme that was exactly what Matt and Deborah wanted.

clamor n. (KLAH mor)—noisy outcry
The *clamor* of band practice was so bad that Principal Howell personally raised money for soundproof walls.

communicable adj. (ka MUN ihk ka bul)—transmittable
Universal protection includes rubber gloves to help caregivers avoid *communicable* diseases.

declaim v. (dih KLAYM)—to speak loudly and vehemently
Grandpa Myers always *declaims* at Thanksgiving grace, using it as an opportunity to criticize everyone from liberals to foreigners to his neighbors.

deleterious adj. (de le TEER ee us)—harmful, destructive, detrimental
In order to protect Mother Earth, environmentalists are constantly lobbying to outlaw *deleterious* substances.

destitution n. (des tih TOO shun)—complete poverty
The *destitution* that prevailed during the Great Depression left many Americans without the means even to buy bread.

Practice 1

DIRECTIONS: In completing the sentences, use 10 of the 11 words below. Use each of the words just once.

clamor	cadence	cacophony	askance
declaimed	acrid	deranged	avuncular
agile	blanched	deleterious	

1. Julia always enjoyed the measured _____ of marching bands, so halftime was her favorite part of every football game.

2. Miss Mayall looked _____ at the boys who were chewing gum.

3. It wasn't until he'd been sent to the emergency room that Jerry realized how _____ alcohol was to his body.

4. Coach Dennis's _____ style might not have won the team many games, but his players really liked playing for him.

5. The candidates for class president _____ their positions at a schoolwide assembly.

6. Robert _____ when the teacher asked him to remove the frog's lungs.

7. The supervising teacher, Mr. Wells, ran into the cafeteria as soon as the _____ began.

8. Deon was the most _____ of the gymnasts and received a college scholarship.

9. The birdwatchers listened to the _____ of the baby robins as they waited for food from their mother.

10. When the lunch lady found the month-old milk, she knew immediately what was causing the _____ smell.

Your Words, Your World

Don't have time to sit around repeating these words to yourself, over and over again, in order to remember them? Well, you don't have to! The following exercise tests your knowledge of the material . . . without requiring that you take a test! So your job now is to really *think* about what you read, and to really think about the questions that follow.

Destitution—This word is used to describe the condition of not just someone on *welfare*, but a person living in complete *poverty*. Have you ever seen a homeless person? If you've never seen a *homeless* person, think of the *starving* children who live in places like Ethiopia.

Communicable—Have you ever been confused by this word, thinking that it has something to do with "communications" and "cable?" Instead of text or images, **communicable** refers to the *transmission of diseases*. A disease that is **communicable** is one that people can pass to one another.

Acrimony—Is there a friend or family member whom you love dearly, but *fight* with constantly? You could almost say that **acrimony** is the opposite of matrimony: rather than a happy "marriage," **acrimony** describes *bitterness* and *animosity*. Hopefully, none of your friendships are **acrimonious** and *hostile*.

Chromatic—Are you considered a good dresser? Or do your friends say you're a disaster when it comes to fashion? Some sloppy dressers fall into the monochromatic category: the only way these people can match is by wearing clothes that are all the same *color*. Others wear clothes that are overly **chromatic**, trying to cover all the *colors* of the rainbow in a single outfit. Where do you fall in the **chromatic** scheme?

PART TWO

discern v. (dih SUHRN)—to perceive something obscure
It is easy to *discern* the difference between real butter and margarine.

effluvia n. (ih FLOO vee uh)—waste; odorous fumes given off by waste
The *effluvia* coming off the river was so bad that Jen and Harrison
considered moving.

ersatz adj. (uhr SAHTZ)—being an artificial and inferior imitation
The *ersatz* strawberry shortcake tasted more like plastic than real cake.

espy v. (ehs PEYE)—to catch sight of, glimpse
Marshall was pleased to *espy* Barry Bonds after years of being a Giants fan.

heckler n. (HEH kler)—someone who tries to embarrass and annoy
others
The comedian was unable to continue his act when the *heckler* started
shouting insulting remarks.

incandescent adj. (ihn kahn DEHS uhnt)—shining brightly
The *incandescent* glow of the moon forced Tate to pull down her
shade.

incongruous adj. (in KONG roo us)—inappropriate, incompatible
Tracy found the explanation to be *incongruous* because she already
knew the facts.

insidious adj. (in SIHD ee uhs)—subtly harmful, beguiling, alluring
Professor Coleman's reputation was destroyed by the *insidious* rumors
that spread like wildfire through the campus.

jeopardize v. (JEH pehr diyz)—endanger, expose to injury
The frostbite *jeopardized* three of Erin's fingers.

nefarious adj. (nih FAHR ee uhs)—intensively wicked or vicious
Nefarious deeds were the Wicked Witch's trademark.

olfactory adj. (ohl FAAK tuh ree)—relating to the sense of smell
After years of coffee and cigarettes, BJ's *olfactory* abilities were gone.

onerous adj. (OH ne rus)—burdensome
Having a bad back made even walking an *onerous* task for Jeffrey.

palpable adj. (PAHLP uh buhl)—capable of being touched or felt; easily perceived
The students were excited to learn that heartbeats and pulses are both *palpable*.

parch adj. (PARCHt)—dried up, shriveled
The pile of mail, not to mention the *parched* plants, indicated to Renee that her housesitter hadn't once entered the house.

raucous adj. (RAW kus)—harsh sounding; boisterous
The middle school cafeteria was a *raucous* place at lunchtime.

Practice 2

DIRECTIONS: After reading the three choices, circle the one that you think is the *antonym*.

11. **discern:**	to perceive	to overlook	to describe
12. **effluvia:**	fragrant`	odoriferous	air pollution
13. **ersatz:**	artificial	fascinating	genuine
14. **espy:**	to glimpse	to attempt	to miss
15. **incandescent:**	dull	shining	decent
16. **incongruous:**	contemptuous	incompatible	fitting
17. **insidious:**	harmful	considerate	within
18. **jeopardize:**	protect	endanger	expose
19. **nefarious:**	vicious	decent	descent
20. **onerous:**	burdensome	errorless	inspiring

Your Words, Your World

Don't have time to sit around repeating these words to yourself, over and over again, in order to remember them? Well, you don't have to! The following memorization exercise tests your knowledge of the material . . . without requiring that you take a test! So your job now is to really *think* about what you read, and to really cement an image in your mind. Actually, not just an image: the following five words make use of—you guessed it—all five senses.

Heckler—Picture the *obnoxious* **heckler**: mouth wide open, red in the face, fists clenched, struggling to come up with the next *rude* sentence. Imagine all of these things as you recall that a **heckler** is someone who tries to *embarrass others*.

Olfactory—What are your favorite *smells*: chocolate-chip cookies fresh out of the oven, a bouquet of flowers, a baby's hair, perfume or cologne? Take one of these or one of your own, and think of it when you think of **olfactory**.

Palpable—Almost as easy as picturing your prized possessions is remembering how they *feel* in your *hands*. Think of one of those. Whether it's the *feel* of *hard* metal, *polished* wood, *soft* cotton, or a *rubbery* toy, as long as you associate *physical contact* with the word **palpable**, you'll be able to define it.

Parch—If you've ever played a sport in hundred-degree weather, hiked through a desert, or drank caffeine all day without having a glass of water, then you know what it means to be **parched**. When your body is crying out for water, you are *dehydrated* or at least close to it.

Raucous—Almost as easy as picturing the *loudest* place you've ever been—a stadium, the tarmac of an airport, beneath a waterfall, or maybe a dance club—is *hearing* it. Whether it was a crowd, an engine, water, or a DJ, the **raucous** noise was *boisterous*, animated and *loud*.

PART THREE

reprehensible adj. (rehp ree HEHN suh buhl)—blameworthy, disreputable
Lenny was disliked around the neighborhood for his *reprehensible* behavior.

resolute adj. (REH suh LOOT)—marked by firm determination
Louise was *resolute*, she would get into medical school no matter what.

resplendent adj. (ree SPLEHN dehnt)—splendid, brilliant, dazzling
As a bride, Marian looked *resplendent* in her long train and gentle veil.

MEMORY TIP

Whenever you see the prefix **re-** some sort of emphasis is being placed on the word's meaning. Take **reprehensible**, for example: there is an emphasis being put on someone's *bad behavior*. If a person is **resolute**, she or he is *firmly determined*. And if something can be described as **resplendent**, it is *dazzling*.

---

sophomoric adj. (sahf MOHR ihk)—exhibiting great immaturity and lack of judgment
After Sean's *sophomoric* behavior, he was grounded for weeks.

squalid adj. (SKWA lihd)—filthy and degraded as the result of neglect or poverty
Karl hated his family's *squalid* living conditions and resolved to move out of the apartment building as soon as possible.

strident adj. (STRIY dehnt)—loud, harsh, unpleasantly noisy
The school choir sang "Jingle Bell Rock" in a humorously *strident* manner.

tactile adj. (TAAK tihl)—producing a sensation of touch
As opposed to reading and taking tests, it is easier for many people to learn new subject matter through *tactile* activities.

turpitude n. (TUHR pi tood)—inherent vileness, foulness, depravity
Lord of the Flies provides insight into the *turpitude* of life without societal constraints.

vapid adj. (VAH pid) (VAY pid)—tasteless, dull
Todd found his blind date so *vapid* and boring that he couldn't wait to get away from her.

venerable adj. (VEN erh ah bul)—respected because of age
Noelle often sought the advice of her *venerable* grandfather.

vestige n. (VES tij)—trace, remnant
Three years after the accident, *vestiges* still marked the crossroads.

visceral adj. (VIHS urh uhl)—instinctive, not intellectual; deep, emotional
When Joseph's twin was wounded in the war, he had a *visceral* reaction, suddenly crying out at the dinner table.

vociferous adj. (voh SIH fuhr uhs)—loud, noisy
There is still debate about whether or not Khrushchev banged his shoe on the table in *vociferous* protest at the UN.

unobtrusive adj. (uhn ob TROO siv)—modest, unassuming
The countess demanded that her servants be *unobtrusive* and that they carry out their duties quietly and efficiently.

vindictive adj. (vin DIK tiv)—spiteful, vengeful, unforgiving
After Clarice's husband left her for a younger woman, she dreamed up all sorts of *vindictive* plans.

virulent adj. (VEER uh lint)—extremely poisonous; malignant; hateful
Alarmed at the *virulent* hate mail she was receiving, Sheryl decided to stop protesting the war.

wanton adj. (WAHN tuhn)—undisciplined, unrestrained; reckless
The townspeople were outraged by the *wanton* disrespect shown by the graffiti on the town hall.

Practice 3

DIRECTIONS: Consider the two word choices in the parentheses and circle the one that best fits in the context of the sentence.

21. The sound in the gym during Battle of the Bands was so (visceral OR vociferous) that half of the teachers left early.

22. Due to his (reprehensible OR reputable) behavior, Clyde was given a three-day suspension.

23. Meghan had such a (visceral OR superficial) reaction to the poem that she couldn't sleep that night.

24. Decorated for the dance, the common area was (resolute OR resplendent) with lights.

25. Principal Brown called the local paper to complain that a harsh criticism like (vapid OR vestige) did not belong in a review of a school play.

26. As Tim's three older brothers had a reputation for (tenet OR turpitude), the teachers were surprised to find him a polite and caring young man.

27. Regina's parents were (resolute OR ersatz) about her punishment, and so she could not go to the homecoming game.

28. Without knowing about the long, slow death of Gerry's grandfather, his teachers mistakenly complained that he was (tactile OR wanton).

29. Empty popcorn bags and tire tracks in the mud were the last (vestiges OR vindictives) of the carnival.

30. Although she'd been teaching for thirty-one
    years, Greta Gonzalez still wasn't used to the
    (visceral OR strident) sounds of dismissal.

31. (Virulent OR Unobtrusive) rumors of
    corruption in the administration eventually
    forced the mayor to hold a press conference.

32. Teachers and parents agreed the elementary
    school needed a modern facility, although they
    loved its (wanton OR venerable) prewar
    building.

Your Words, Your World

Don't have time to sit around repeating these words to yourself, over
and over again, in order to remember them? Well, you don't have to!
The following exercise tests your knowledge of the material . . . without
requiring that you take a test! You will find that each of the following
words can be used in school, at home, and in the workplace. Read on
to learn how.

Sophomoric—This word should probably be "freshmanic," as most
students know. If someone you know is behaving in a **sophomoric**
manner, he or she is being *immature* and *unsophisticated*. And
actually, one of **sophomoric's** synonyms is *collegiate*, so the word has
less to do with tenth graders and more to do with young adults who
are a bit *too confident* in their *uninformed opinions*.

Unobtrusive—To be obtrusive is to be flashy and meddlesome, so it
only makes sense that **unobtrusive** people are *shy, modest,* and
unassuming. Obtrusive people often like to have **unobtrusive** people
as friends, as they tend to be good (and patient) listeners. Are you
more obtrusive or **unobtrusive**?

Vindictive—There is no getting along with the **vindictive** person.
Perhaps you know one or two of these spiteful, *unforgiving, vengeful*
people. If you make the slightest error around these people, they never
let you forget it. Offend them at your own risk!

Tactile—In your day-to-day life, what are the things you come into *contact* with most often? Your list might include one or two faucets in the bathroom, the car door and steering wheel, your bag, pens, the computer keyboard, or the remote control. You get a **tactile** response from each of the things in the aforementioned list. Come up with the two or three things you *touch* most often and this will help you to remember that tactile means *producing a sensation of touch*.

Squalid—Whether it was on TV, on the Internet, in the newspaper, or in a magazine, you probably recently have seen people across the world living in **squalid**, or *unclean*, conditions. This is the unfortunate truth because so many of the world's people are living in *poverty*. Maybe there's something you can do to help. . . .

PRACTICE ANSWERS AND EXPLANATIONS

Practice 1

1. Julia liked the **cadence**, or rhythmic flow, of the marching band.

2. Miss Mayall disapproved of the gum chewing, so she looked **askance** at the boys.

3. Jerry had to get sick before realizing how **deleterious**, or harmful, alcohol can be to the body.

4. Coach Dennis was **avuncular** in that he was kind to his players.

5. Like professional politicians, the candidates gave speeches about, or **declaimed**, their positions before the election.

6. Robert **blanched**, or turned pale, because dissecting the frog sickened him.

7. Mr. Wells was supposed to keep the cafeteria quiet, so he reacted as soon as he heard the **cacophony** (jarring noise).

8. To be **agile** is to be well coordinated as Deon clearly is.

9. The **clamor** of the robins was a cry for the food their mother had brought back.

10. Sour milk has a harsh, **acrid** smell.

Practice 2

11. To **discern** is to perceive, or notice, and not to overlook. It isn't to describe, either, although this is not an antonym.

12. **Effluvia** is odoriferous and **air** pollution may qualify as such. Fragrant is the antonym.

13. If something is described as **ersatz** it is artificial and fake and certainly not genuine. Fascinating is not an opposite.

14. To **espy** is to glimpse. The antonym is to miss (noticing something), while to attempt is irrelevant.

15. When something is **incandescent** it is glowing or shining brightly. If an object is dull it is not incandescent. Decent is a just a distracter.

16. To be **incongruous** is to be inappropriate or incompatible, like a penguin in the desert. Fitting is the antonym. Contemptuous means disapproving, so is neither a synonym nor an antonym.

17. **Insidious** means harmful. When you think of harmful villains, they are rarely considerate. Within is a distracter based on the possible "inside" root of this word.

18. To **jeopardize** is to endanger: to expose to danger. To jeopardize is definitely not to protect.

19. Much like insidious, to be **nefarious** is to be vicious. It is the opposite of being decent and kind. Descent means going down and is incorrect.

20. When a situation is **onerous** it is burdensome, so inspiring is the correct answer. Errorless is irrelevant.

Practice 3

21. Although visceral fits grammatically, **vociferous** (loud) is the better answer.

22. Reputable, or trustworthy, behavior doesn't get you suspended. Behavior that is disreputable, **reprehensible**, and blameworthy does.

23. **Visceral** means deeply emotional, whereas superficial means the opposite. Obviously, this poem made quite an impact on Meghan.

24. Resolute means firmly determined, so that's not the answer. You could say, however, that the dance committee was obviously determined to make the common area look brilliant and **resplendent**.

25. As **vapid** means tasteless and dull, Principal Brown took offense. Needless to say, the use of the word vestige (trace or mark) would not garner such a reaction!

26. A tenet is a principle and it sounds like Tim, unlike his brothers, was pretty principled. So **turpitude** (vulgarity) is the correct choice.

27. Regina's parents were **resolute**, or firmly determined, about grounding her. Their reaction was anything but fake (ersatz).

28. Gerry wasn't **wanton** (undisciplined and reckless) as his teachers suspected. Tactile relates to the sense of touch.

29. Vindictives is not a word, but **vestiges** is: traces or remnants were all that was left of the carnival.

30. Visceral means intuitive and is incorrect. Dismissal may be **strident** (loud, harsh, and unpleasantly noisy), but shouldn't Greta have been used to it?

31. Virulent means extremely poisonous, malignant, and hateful. Unobtrusive means modest and unassuming, so it does not describe the rumors.

32. Wanton means undisciplined while **venerable** is used to describe something—or somebody—respected because of age. A teacher may be venerable just as a building may be.

CHAPTER 10 TEST

Okay, it's time to put your memory to the test! Take your time not only with the questions but in reading the answer explanations that follow. Set a goal for yourself—80% (24 correct answers) is recommended—and if you don't reach that goal, go back and read through the chapter again. Good luck!

DIRECTIONS: For questions 1–15, circle T for True or F for False. For questions 16–30, circle the synonym.

1.	T	F	**onerous**—easy
2.	T	F	**vapid**—dull
3.	T	F	**vociferous**—loud
4.	T	F	**strident**—unpleasantly noisy
5.	T	F	**wanton**—disciplined
6.	T	F	**resolute**—lazy
7.	T	F	**nefarious**—wicked
8.	T	F	**incandescent**—vapid
9.	T	F	**vindictive**—vengeful
10.	T	F	**ersatz**—legitimate
11.	T	F	**declaim**—to speak loudly
12.	T	F	**deleterious**—harmful
13.	T	F	**clamor**—gear for mountain climbing
14.	T	F	**blanch**—to belch
15.	T	F	**acrid**—harsh

16. **askance:**	disapprovingly	approvingly	questioningly
17. **cacophony:**	a cell phone	unpleasant music	unpleasant noise
18. **discern:**	act sincerely	differentiate	act vengefully
19. **espy:**	to glimpse	to excel	to ask
20. **visceral:**	instinctive	dull	naïve
21. **incongruous:**	compatible	inappropriate	pathetic
22. **olfactory:**	taste	touch	smell

23. **cadence:**   nefarious   lexicon   rhythm
24. **palpable:**   fleeting   doubtful   substantial
25. **raucous:**   smooth   harsh   placid
26. **reprehensible:** disreputable   reputable   scrupulous
27. **resplendent:**   improper   brilliant   uninteresting
28. **turpitude:**   pleasantness   vileness   decency
29. **venerable:**   esteemed   reviled   ventilated
30. **insidious:**   unappealing   blatant   harmful

Answers and Explanations

1. **False.** **Onerous** means burdensome and not easy.

2. **True.** **Vapid** is synonymous with dull.

3. **True.** To be **vociferous** is to be noisy and overly enthusiastic.

4. **True.** To be **strident** is to be unpleasantly noisy.

5. **False.** To be **wanton** is to be reckless and definitely not disciplined.

6. **False.** To be **resolute** is not to be lazy or wanton. It is to be firmly determined.

7. **True.** To be **nefarious** is to be wickedly vicious.

8. **False.** If an object is **incandescent** it shines brightly. It is not vapid or dull.

9. **True.** To be **vindictive** is to be vengeful, spiteful, and unforgiving.

10. **False.** If something is described as **ersatz** it isn't legitimate, but artificial to the point of being an inferior substitute or imitation.

11. **True.** To **declaim** is to speak loudly.

12. **True.** To be **deleterious** is to be harmful.

13. **False.** A **clamor** is not mountain-climbing gear, but a noisy outcry.

14. **False.** To **blanch** is not to belch, but to turn pale.

15. **True.** If something is **acrid** it is harsh or bitter.

16. **Askance** is synonymous with disapprovingly. Approvingly is an antonym and questioningly is incorrect.

17. **Cacophony** is unpleasant noise. It is not unpleasant music, nor is it a cell phone.

18. To **discern** is to differentiate. It has nothing to do with acting sincerely (honestly) or vengefully.

19. To **espy** is to glimpse. To excel and to ask are both irrelevant.

20. If something can be considered **visceral**, then it has happened instinctively. It took place on a deep, emotional level. It is not something dull or naïve.

21. If something is **incongruous**, it is inappropriate. Compatible (well matched) and pathetic (sad) are incorrect.

22. **Olfactory** relates to the sense of smell and not the senses of taste or touch.

23. If music has **cadence** it has a certain rhythm and tempo. A lexicon is a dictionary and nefarious is wicked.

24. Something **palpable** is substantial; one can touch it or at least understand it. Fleeting and doubtful are near-antonyms.

25. If a sound is **raucous,** it is harsh and neither smooth nor placid.

26. To be **reprehensible** is to be disreputable. Obviously, reputable is the opposite, as is scrupulous (conscientious).

27. **Resplendent** is synonymous with brilliant. Uninteresting is an antonym and improper is inappropriate.

28. **Turpitude** is a noun meaning inherent vileness. Pleasantness and decency are near-antonyms.

29. To be **venerable** is to be esteemed; it is to have earned respect over the years. It is not to be reviled. And ventilated (allowing air in and out) is a trick answer based on the ven- prefix.

30. To be **insidious** is to be sneakily harmful. Although this kind of behavior may be unappealing and blatantly wrong, neither of those words is the best answer.

CHAPTER 11

Positive Emotions

Vocabulary that falls on the sunny side of the street

BUILDING BLOCK QUIZ

This "building block" quiz samples the information that you will learn in this chapter, plus two words from the previous chapter. By answering the 12 questions below, you will get a sense of how closely you should study this chapter in order to master all of that vocabulary! And if you choose incorrect answers for the final two questions, you'll want to go back to chapter 10 for some review.

DIRECTIONS: Fill in the blanks, using the most appropriate of the four multiple-choice answers. The correct answer will always fit into the sentence grammatically.

1. There's just something about a _____ child actor that makes for a good uplifting movie.

   (A) vindictive (B) plucky
   (C) becalm (D) wanton

2. When Carrie was able to walk just two weeks after the accident, everybody credited her athleticism and _____ nature.

   (A) resilient (B) amorous
   (C) virulent (D) consummate

3. When Marquis _____ his love for
   Tamara with an engagement ring, both families
   immediately began to talk about the wedding.
   (A) alleviated (B) cavorted
   (C) avowed (D) confiscated

4. Miya pursued her college degree with
   _____ and was able to graduate within
   four years.
   (A) vim (B) approbation
   (C) turpitude (D) lethargy

5. Jake's mother always said that the difference
   between a job and a career comes from the
   _____ with which you work.
   (A) synergy (B) parch
   (C) chortle (D) ardor

6. As Mrs. Harris was _____ to a transfer,
   the whole family would be moving to Japan for
   a year.
   (A) amenable (B) wry
   (C) sportive (D) obstructive

7. Matt's fingers were _____ and this
   helped to make him an excellent typist and
   guitar player.
   (A) tout (B) lithe
   (C) winsome (D) appalling

8. Miss Eggert was a school-wide favorite because she was never hesitant to _____ her students.

   (A) surmount (B) proscribe

   (C) nullify (D) extol

9. Although Mr. Helene wasn't yet tenured, he was _____ in his requests for funding for a school photography club.

   (A) intrepid (B) solicitous

   (C) amenable (D) tactile

10. Mrs. Unger took the student council to the outdoor education center for an afternoon of teamwork training, in hopes that this would lead them to _____ and become more productive.

    (A) alleviate (B) contradict

    (C) coalesce (D) salvage

11. The athletic director decided that the pressure-filled tournament would be _____ to the young team and turned down the invitation.

    (A) deleterious (B) resilient

    (C) facetious (D) squalid

12. Everyone liked the fact that the new science teacher was so _____, despite having already published two books.

    (A) olfactory (B) saccharine

    (C) mawkish (D) unobtrusive

Answers and Explanations

1. B. A **plucky** (spunky and courageous) child actor is sure to sell out theaters. Vindictive (vengeful) and wanton (undisciplined and reckless) actors probably make bad movies, as they are difficult to work with. To becalm is to rest or stop.

2. A. Carrie is **resilient**, which means she is able to recover quickly. She may be amorous (passionate) and virulent (dangerous), but neither explains her ability to recuperate. Consummate (accomplished) doesn't really make sense before "nature."

3. C. To **avow** is to state openly or declare, so this is correct. Alleviated (relieved), cavorted (frolicked), and confiscated (took) do not fit in the context of the sentence.

4. A. To pursue something with **vim** is to pursue it with great energy. Lethargy is the opposite, meaning laziness and lack of energy. Approbation (approval) and turpitude (moral depravity) are both incorrect.

5. D. The difference Jake's mother was referring to was passion or **ardor**. Synergy (cooperation) sounds right but doesn't really make sense, nor do parch (dry out) and chortle (laugh).

6. A. When her company asked about a transfer, Mrs. Harris was **amenable** (agreeable and cooperative). She was neither wry (sarcastic) nor obstructive (unhelpful). And although the move might have made her happy, she wasn't sportive (playful) about it, either.

7. B. **Lithe** means bending with ease and describes Matt's fingers perfectly. To tout is to hype, winsome is charming, and appalling is frightful, so all three of those are out.

8. D. The correct answer is **extol** as it means to praise. The other three words are too negative: to surmount is to conquer, to proscribe is to forbid, and to nullify is to cancel.

9. A. In the context of the sentence, only **intrepid** (meaning fearless) fits perfectly. The key to this question is the contrast, indicated by "Although," between Mr. Helene's lack of tenure and his efforts to start a new club. Amenable is too friendly and agreeable, while solicitous is too considerate. Tactile refers to the sensation of touch.

10. C. The student council has to **coalesce**; to unite and band together so as to be more productive. Although alleviate (ease or lessen) and salvage (save) are close, they aren't close enough. And the last thing Mrs. Unger wants is for members of the student council to contradict (disagree with) one another.

11. A. The pressure would be **deleterious**, or harmful, to the team. It would not be resilient (flexible and hardy), facetious (joking), or squalid (filthy). If you answered this question incorrectly, you might want to go back to chapter 10 for some review.

12. D. Despite having published three books, the teacher was **unobtrusive**, which means modest and unassuming. Saccharine and mawkish both mean sickeningly sweet or sentimental. Olfactory relates to the sense of smell, so it's completely irrelevant here. If you answered this question incorrectly, you might want to go back to chapter 10 for some review.

PART ONE

affable adj. (AH fah buhl)—friendly, easy to approach, fun
Since she was so *affable*, Jessie was named "Most Huggable" in the yearbook, to nobody's surprise.

affinity n. (ah FIN ih tee)—fondness, liking; similarity
George felt an instant *affinity* for his new neighbor when he realized that the neighbor was also a Yankees fan.

> **MEMORY TIP**
>
> When you think of "aff," think of the three Fs: fondness, friendly, and fun! **Affable** means *friendly* and *fun*, while **affinity** means *fondness*.

alacrity n. (ah LAK rah tee)—cheerful willingness, eagerness; speed
Mancha jumped for the Frisbee with agility and *alacrity* that Dave had never before seen in a dog.

alleviate v. (ah LEEV ee ayt)—to relieve, improve partially
For Isabelle, nothing *alleviated* the stress of teaching like seeing a student improve.

amenable adj. (ah MEHN ah buhl)—agreeable, cooperative
Hector's reputation wasn't good, but by the end of the first week, everybody at the radio station found him to be *amenable*.

amorous adj. (AH mehr uhs)—strongly attracted to love; showing love
All of the greetings cards were way too *amorous* for Glenn, so he just wrote his own.

approbation n. (ah pro BAY shun)—praise, official approval
Approbation came for Billy in the form of a college recommendation from Principal Unger.

ardor n. (AHR dur)—great emotion or passion
Beth's *ardor* for gardening was evident in the colorful spread of her yard.

assignation n. (ah sihg NAY shun)—appointment for lovers' meeting; assignment
Juliet and Romeo had many secret *assignations*.

avow v. (ah VOW)—to state openly or declare
In speaking their vows, Neil and Macy publicly *avowed* their love for one another.

blithe adj. (BLIYTH)—joyful, cheerful, carefree
Michelle *blithely* assumed that her coworkers would be as happy as she was about the promotion.

cavalier adj. (kah vuh LEER)—carefree, happy; with lordly disdain
Vin's *cavalier* attitude made him the life of the party, but he had few good friends.

cavort v. (ka VOHRT)—to frolic, frisk, play
The puppies looked adorable as they *cavorted* in the grass.

chortle v. (CHOR tuhl)—to chuckle
Santa *chortled* as Rudolph led the team of reindeer through the clouds.

Practice 1

DIRECTIONS: Match the word (left column) with its definition (right column).

1. **approbation**	loving
2. **affinity**	great passion
3. **amenable**	rendezvous
4. **affable**	praise
5. **ardor**	friendly
6. **cavalier**	carefree
7. **alacrity**	disdainful
8. **blithe**	enthusiasm
9. **amorous**	fondness
10. **assignation**	agreeable

Your Words, Your World

Don't have time to sit around repeating these words to yourself, over and over again, in order to remember them? Well, you don't have to! The following exercise tests your knowledge of the material . . . without requiring that you take a test! So your job now is to really *think* about the following verbs and how they apply to your everyday life.

Alleviate—If you think about what it is you want to do most this weekend, about what it is that *improves* your mood, you will be thinking of how you **alleviate** your stress. You will be *relieving* yourself of the tension and pressure that comes with school and/or work.

Avow—Pick a friend and *state openly* how much he or she means to you. To **avow** is to *confirm* and *acknowledge* how you are feeling or what you are thinking.

Cavort—Maybe you want to **cavort** with some friends after a long, hard week. That paper has been turned in, the project is finished, so now it's time to *play* and *frolic*. Everybody likes to **cavort** in one way or another.

Chortle—Think of what makes you laugh. Maybe it's a movie or maybe it's one of your friends. Remember these things—and also the fact that **chortle** and *chuckle* both begin with "ch"—and you'll surely remember that to **chortle** is to *laugh*, *chuckle*, or *giggle*.

PART TWO

cloying adj. (KLOY ing)—overly sweet
Kids today enjoy making fun of the *cloying* TV shows of previous decades.

coalesce v. (KOH ah less)—to grow together or cause to unite as one
Both sides of the family *coalesced* to celebrate Wendy's sixteenth birthday.

consummate adj. (KON suh mit)—accomplished, complete, perfect
Karen skated a *consummate* routine, winning the gold medal with ease.

cordial adj. (KOR juhl)—warm and sincere, friendly, polite; from Latin "cord" or "cor" meaning heart
Before getting down to business, Matthew extended his hand in a *cordial* manner.

elate v. (ee LAYT)—to make joyful; exhilarate
Nothing *elates* children like the announcement of a snow day.

euphoria n. (yoo FOR ee uh)—great happiness or well-being
Euphoria swept through the crowd as Oprah handed out the car keys.

extol v. (ehk STOL)—to praise
The salesman *extolled* the virtues of the used car.

facetious adj. (fuh SEE shuhs)—witty, humorous, in jest
Quinn's *facetious* remarks made the meeting more lively and interesting.

frolicsome adj. (FRO lihk sum)—frisky, playful
The *frolicsome* kitten entertained them for hours.

gregarious adj. (greh GAAR ee uhs)—outgoing, sociable
Unlike her introverted friends, Susan was very *gregarious*.

indefatigable adj. (in de FAH tee gu buhl)—never tired
Theresa seemed *indefatigable*, running from one meeting to another.

intrepid adj. (in TREH pid)—fearless
The *intrepid* kayak team went into the rapids and over the waterfall.

jocular adj. (JAH kyoo luhr)—playful, humorous
Ever *jocular*, Grandpa Hughes told stories for hours that night.

lithe adj. (LIYTH)—moving and bending with ease; marked by grace
Edy's *lithe* movements led her parents to believe that she would be a dancer.

mawkish adj. (MAW kihsh)—sickeningly sentimental
Mr. Goldberg let Myles know, as gently as possible, that his poem was more *mawkish* than romantic.

Practice 2

DIRECTIONS: Consider the definition and then circle T for True or F for False.

11.	T	F	**cloying**—overly sweet
12.	T	F	**coalesce**—to break apart
13.	T	F	**consummate**—accomplished
14.	T	F	**elate**—to make joyful
15.	T	F	**euphoria**—unhappiness
16.	T	F	**extol**—to criticize
17.	T	F	**frolicsome**—playful
18.	T	F	**indefatigable**—never tired
19.	T	F	**intrepid**—fearful
20.	T	F	**lithe**—moving with ease
21.	T	F	**mawkish**—hawkish

Your Words, Your World

Don't have time to sit around repeating these words to yourself, over and over again, in order to remember them? Well, you don't have to! The following exercise tests your knowledge of the material . . . without requiring that you take a test! So your job now is to really *think* about what you read, and to really think about the questions that follow.

Jocular—Although you may have athletic friends called "jocks," to be **jocular** has nothing to do with sports. It is to be *playful* or *humorous*. Who is the most **jocular** person you know?

Gregarious—And who is the most **gregarious** person you know? To be **gregarious** is to be *extroverted* and *outgoing*, so think of the most *sociable* person you know.

Facetious—The most **facetious** person you know probably isn't the most jocular. Do you know someone who is *funny*, but in a *witty*, *teasing* sort of way? Someone who is pleasantly *sarcastic*? These folks tend to make life a lot more *fun*, don't they?

Cordial—**Cordial** means *friendly*. In most high school yearbooks, one of the Senior Superlatives is "Most Friendly." If you're a student, who do you think will win this when you graduate? Or, if you've graduated from high school already, do you remember who this person was? If you can associate this person with the word **cordial**, you will remember that to be cordial is to be *pleasant*, *warm*, and *genial*.

PART THREE

plucky adj. (PLUH kee)—courageous; spunky
Nurse Rose was *plucky* and just what the cancer patients needed when they were feeling depressed.

prospect n. (PRAH spehkt)—possibility, a chance
The *prospect* of making the team caused Stephon to practice eight to ten hours every day.

purport v. (puhr POHRT)—to profess, suppose, claim
Brad *purported* to be an opera lover, but he fell asleep when Francine took him to see "The Barber of Seville."

resilient adj. (rih SIHL ee uhnt)—able to recover quickly after illness or bad luck; able to bounce back
Psychologists say that being *resilient* is one of the keys to happiness.

saccharine adj. (SAA kuh ruhn)—excessively sweet or sentimental
Lucy loved *saccharine* movies, so at least once a month Paul had to watch one.

salvage v. (SAHL vij)—to recover, save from loss
Terry sent the letter in hopes of *salvaging* their friendship.

solicitous adj. (suh LIH sih tuhs)—concerned, caring, eager
Dory's overly *solicitous* questions made her father wonder what she wanted.

sportive adj. (SPOHR tihv)—frolicsome, playful
Because they wanted a more *sportive* vacation, the Hendersons decided to visit Disney World instead of going antiquing in Vermont.

surmount v. (suhr MOWNT)—to conquer, overcome
The blind woman *surmounted* great obstacles to become a well-known trial lawyer.

synergy adj. (SIN ehr jee)—cooperative interaction producing greater results
Improving creative *synergy* among the team was Jennifer's goal.

tenacious adj. (ten AY shuhs)—determined, keeping a firm grip on
Becky was *tenacious* when it came to determining a budget for the school's art programs.

tout v. (TOWT)—to praise or publicize loudly or extravagantly
Principal Velanueva *touted* his choice of assistant principal, discussing the man's background as a police officer.

vim n. (VIHM)—vitality and energy
The *vim* with which Andy worked was awe-inspiring.

vindicate v. (vihn dih KAYT)—to clear of blame; support a claim
Tess felt *vindicated* when the newspaper reported a rise in unemployment.

winsome adj. (WIHN suhm)—charming, happily engaging
Dawn gave the police officer a *winsome* smile, and he let her go without writing a speeding ticket.

Practice 3

DIRECTIONS: Read the three possible synonyms, then circle the one you think best defines the word in bold.

22. **plucky:**	lucky	spunky	portly
23. **purport:**	to claim	insignificant	to frolic
24. **resilient:**	to recover	to be quiet	to review
25. **saccharine:**	merciless	wanton	sentimental
26. **solicitous:**	begging	considerate	uncaring
27. **sportive:**	playful	jocular	athletic
28. **synergy:**	energy	solitude	cooperation
29. **tenacious:**	indeterminate	infirm	determined
30. **vim:**	vitality	mellow	whim
31. **winsome:**	charming	losing	victorious

Your Words, Your World

Don't have time to sit around repeating these words to yourself, over and over again, in order to remember them? Well, you don't have to! The following exercise tests your knowledge of the material . . . without requiring that you take a test! So your job now is to really *think* about what you read, and to really cement an image in your mind. You never know when you'll need that image to pop up again.

Vindicate—Picture a shady-looking guy named Vin, sitting up on the stand during the trial of the century. Fortunately for Vin, there isn't any evidence against him, and this is because Vin is *innocent*. Imagine the look on his face when he is found *not guilty* and he is *cleared of all blame*. He has been **vindicated**.

Prospect—Anyone who is a sports fan knows that a new **prospect** symbolizes *hope* . . . a *possibility* . . . a chance for a brighter future. Imagine the young smiling face on a trading card or in a magazine. To think of a **prospect** is to think of *potential greatness*.

Salvage—**Salvage** teams will raise ships from the bottom of the ocean, in an attempt to find great wealth. **Salvage** teams have tried several times to *retrieve* the *SS Titanic*, but they have been unsuccessful. However, if you can remind yourself that to **salvage** means *to recover* or *save* just by imagining the *Titanic*, all will not be lost.

Surmount—To *conquer* a mountain is a tremendous feat. As the second syllable of **surmount** is "mount," picture yourself atop Mt. Everest, the world's highest peak. To **surmount** is to *overcome*.

Tout—As **tout** rhymes with *shout*, think of someone shouting your *praises* in public. Imagine your mother or father standing on a street corner, *yelling* about your good grades or good job to anyone who'll listen! When something is **touted**, it must be praised *loudly* and *extravagantly*.

PRACTICE ANSWERS AND EXPLANATIONS

Practice 1

1. **Approbation** is praise or official approval.

2. To have an **affinity** for something is to have a fondness or liking.

3. To be **amenable** is to be agreeable and cooperative.

4. If someone is **affable**, he or she is friendly and approachable.

5. **Ardor** is a noun that means great emotion and passion.

6. To be **cavalier** is to be disdainful. (NOTE: Carefree also is acceptable.)

7. **Alacrity** is defined as enthusiasm.

8. To be **blithe** is to be carefree.

9. When a person is **amorous**, he or she is loving and affectionate.

10. An **assignation** is a rendezvous or a meeting of lovers, like Romeo and Juliet.

Practice 2

11. **True.** To be **cloying** is to be overly sweet.

12. **False.** To **coalesce** is to grow together and not to break apart.

13. **True.** If someone is considered **consummate**, he or she is skilled and highly accomplished in his or her field.

14. **True.** To **elate** is to make joyful, to thrill, to exhilarate.

15. **False.** **Euphoria** is a great feeling of happiness.

16. **False.** To **extol** is not to criticize; it is to praise.

17. **True.** If someone is **frolicsome**, then he or she is frisky and playful.

18. **True.** To be **indefatigable** is to never be tired.

19. **False.** To be **intrepid** is to be fearless. It is not to be fearful.

20. **True.** To be **lithe** is to be able to move with ease.

21. **False.** To be **mawkish** is to be sickeningly sentimental. The only connection to hawkish is that it rhymes!

Practice 3

22. To be **plucky** is to be courageous and spunky. To be lucky is to be fortunate and to be portly is to be overweight.

23. To **purport** is to claim or profess. It is not to frolic (play) or be insignificant (unimportant).

24. To be **resilient** is to be able to recover quickly. To review and to be quiet are both incorrect.

25. If someone is **saccharine**, he or she is excessively sweet or sentimental. He or she is not wanton (reckless) or merciless (without sympathy).

26. To be **solicitous** is to be caring and considerate. Begging is a trick answer, playing off of the word soliciting (begging for business). Uncaring is an antonym.

27. The adjective **sportive** describes someone who is playful. Jocular means humorous and is a bad choice, as is athletic.

28. **Synergy** is the kind of cooperation that leads to great results. Energy is a distracter in that it sounds the same, while solitude is basically an antonym.

29. To be **tenacious** is to be determined. On the other hand, infirm means to be sickly, while indeterminate means undefined.

30. **Vim** is a noun synonymous with vitality and energy. A whim is an impulse. To be mellow is to be calm.

31. To be **winsome** is to be charming. Victorious is irrelevant, as is losing.

CHAPTER 11 TEST

Okay, it's time to put your memory to the test! Take your time not only with the questions but in reading the answer explanations that follow. Set a goal for yourself—80% (24 correct answers) is recommended—and if you don't reach that goal, go back and read through the chapter again. Good luck!

DIRECTIONS: For questions 1–15, circle T for True or F for False. For questions 16–30, circle the synonym.

1.	T	F	**consummate**—incomplete
2.	T	F	**vindicate**—persecute
3.	T	F	**tout**—praise
4.	T	F	**resilient**—unable to recover
5.	T	F	**purport**—claim
6.	T	F	**intrepid**—fearless
7.	T	F	**gregarious**—outgoing
8.	T	F	**cloying**—without fragrance
9.	T	F	**cavalier**—unhappy
10.	T	F	**ardor**—great passion
11.	T	F	**sportive**—playful
12.	T	F	**affinity**—near-allergic
13.	T	F	**prospect**—an impossibility
14.	T	F	**solicitous**—concerned
15.	T	F	**euphoria**—happiness

16. **salvage:**	immerse	recover	surmount
17. **cavort:**	to frolic	to drive	to devise
18. **amenable:**	stubborn	winsome	cooperative
19. **blithe:**	cheerful	lithe	cynical
20. **chortle:**	to gag	to praise	to chuckle
21. **elate:**	to alleviate	to elevate	to exhilarate
22. **extol:**	to criticize	to praise	to withdraw

23. **facetious:**	witty	honest	pious
24. **alleviate:**	to raise	to confound	to relieve
25. **frolicsome:**	gathering	playful	exhausted
26. **winsome:**	charming	victorious	elated
27. **avow:**	to shock	to declare	to be friendly
28. **tenacious:**	to be vicious	to be lonely	to be determined
29. **surmount:**	to overcome	to praise	to bemuse
30. **affable:**	laughable	euphoric	friendly

Answers and Explanations

1. False. If a person is considered **consummate**, he or she is accomplished and in no way incomplete.

2. False. To **vindicate** is to clear of blame, which is the opposite of persecute.

3. True. To **tout** is to praise extravagantly.

4. False. To be **resilient** is actually to be able to recover quickly.

5. True. To **purport** is to claim, profess, or suppose.

6. True. To be considered **intrepid** one must be fearless.

7. True. If a person is **gregarious**, he or she is outgoing and sociable.

8. False. To be **cloying** is to be overly sweet. It is not to be without fragrance.

9. False. To be **cavalier** is to be carefree and happy—definitely not unhappy.

10. True. To do something with **ardor** is to do it with great emotion or passion.

11. True. People who are **sportive** are playful and fun.

12. False. To have an **affinity** for something is to be quite fond of it— the opposite of feeling near-allergic to it!

13. False. **Prospect** is a noun that means a possibility or a chance. Impossibility is an antonym of **prospect**.

14. True. To be **solicitous** is to be anxious and concerned.

15. True. The state of **euphoria** is one of great happiness!

16. To **salvage** is to recover. Although immerse (submerge) and surmount (overcome) are words that may be used when discussing a salvage mission, they are both incorrect.

17. To **cavort** is to frolic and have fun. This has nothing to do with driving or devising.

18. To be **amenable** is to be cooperative. Stubborn is an antonym and winsome means charming, but not necessarily cooperative.

19. To be **blithe** is to be cheerful, which is nearly the opposite of cynical. And although lithe rhymes, it is a distracter and means flexible.

20. To **chortle** is to chuckle. It is not to gag or praise.

21. To **elate** is to exhilarate or make joyful. The other two answers sound similar, but are not. To alleviate is to relieve, while to elevate means to raise.

22. To **extol** is to praise, while criticize is its antonym. To withdraw is also incorrect.

23. To be **facetious** is to be witty in a tongue-in-cheek sort of way. It is definitely not to be honest or pious (religious).

24. To **alleviate** is to relieve (think of the similar sound). To raise and to confound (baffle) are both incorrect.

25. Although one might be exhausted after being **frolicsome**, the answer is playful. Gathering is irrelevant.

26. To be **winsome** is to be charming. To be elated is to be overjoyed and to be victorious is to be the winner.

27. To **avow** is to declare. It is neither to shock nor to be friendly.

28. To be **tenacious** is to be determined. It should not be confused with vicious and it is not to be lonely.

29. To **surmount** is to overcome: to conquer, prevail, and triumph. It is not to praise or to bemuse (confuse).

30. To be **affable** is simply to be friendly. Euphoric means overjoyed while laughable means funny in a somewhat critical way.

CHAPTER 12

Grumpy, Crabby, Mean

Words to describe the down, depressed, and degraded

BUILDING BLOCK QUIZ

This "building block" quiz samples the information that you will learn in this chapter, plus two words from the previous chapter. By answering the 12 questions below, you will get a sense of how closely you should study this chapter in order to be able to recall all of these negative words. Keep in mind, should you happen to choose incorrect answers for the final two questions, you'll want to go back to chapter 11 for some review.

DIRECTIONS: Fill in the blanks, using the most appropriate of the four multiple-choice answers. The correct answer will always fit into the sentence, grammatically.

1. Rebecca's poor report card was _____ as she was usually an A student.

   (A) plaintive (B) jaded
   (C) enigmatic (D) torpid

2. Mr. Walters knew that the surprise quiz would _____ his class, but gave it anyway.

   (A) pique (B) alleviate
   (C) bellicose (D) brandish

3. Nurse Greene noted how _____ Peter's face was and called his mother.

   (A) austere (B) wan

   (C) contentious (D) choleric

4. Alex treated all of his teachers with _____ and so none of them were shocked, or sad, to hear that he'd been expelled.

   (A) respect (B) disconcert

   (C) malaise (D) disdain

5. Over the year, Kelly became more and more _____ until finally her guidance counselor called her parents in for a meeting.

   (A) morose (B) gregarious

   (C) sportive (D) winsome

6. The entire school was _____ upon learning of the student's death in that morning's accident.

   (A) elated (B) plaintive

   (C) flagrant (D) oscillate

7. Usually cheerful and energetic, Natalie felt _____ because of her flu.

   (A) torpid (B) plucky

   (C) jocular (D) indefatigable

8. A(n) _____ person and a by-the-book
teacher, Miss Lopez taught the least popular
class in school.

(A) saccharine (B) ignoble

(C) bilious (D) opprobrious

9. The class stared in awe as Mike's mother
_____ him in front of everybody for his
rude remarks.

(A) chided (B) extolled

(C) baned (D) brandished

10. Mr. Tompkins had a talent for _____
upset students and getting to the heart of the
matter.

(A) counteracting (B) demeaning

(C) beleaguering (D) mollifying

11. Javier painted the homecoming float with
_____ and before long, he was done!

(A) misanthrope (B) alacrity

(C) lampoon (D) contemptuous

12. Nothing could _____ Monique like
putting on her earphones and cranking her
music.

(A) disparage (B) demean

(C) rankle (D) elate

Answers and Explanations

1. C. Rebecca's report card was not the usual, so it was **enigmatic**, or puzzling. Plaintive (expressing woe) is incorrect as are jaded (weary) and torpid (lazy).

2. A. The quiz would **pique** (arouse anger, or at least interest) the class and this seems to be, at least in part, what Mr. Walters wanted. Although it was an aggressive move, bellicose (warlike) is not the answer. Nor is it alleviate (ease or lessen) or brandish (wield or wave).

3. B. Peter was sickly pale (**wan**) and not angry, so contentious (quarrelsome) and choleric (easily angered) are ruled out, as is austere (strict).

4. D. Alex treated his teachers with **disdain**, which is to say with scorn and contempt. It was definitely not with respect. Disconcert (ruffle or upset) and malaise (depression or unease) are also incorrect.

5. A. The guidance counselor wouldn't have called home if Kelly were gregarious (outgoing), sportive (frolicsome), or winsome (charming). It was because she was **morose** (gloomy or sullen) that the guidance counselor called for a meeting.

6. B. The entire school was feeling **plaintive** in that students and staff were expressing their woe and suffering. They certainly weren't elated (ecstatic). Flagrant (blatant) and oscillate (swing back and forth, physically or emotionally) are both incorrect as well.

7. A. Natalie was feeling **torpid**, or lethargic (lacking energy). The other three choices are near-antonyms: plucky (spunky), jocular (playful), and indefatigable (never tired). The word "usually" sets up a contrast with Natalie's typical "energetic" behavior, and **torpid** is the only choice that has this meaning.

8. C. Miss Lopez was **bilious** (bad-tempered) and this was, in part, why students didn't like her. Although ignoble (having low moral standards), opprobrious (disgraceful, shameful), and saccharine (excessively sentimental) all fit—the first two better than the third—the most likely choice remains **bilious**.

9. A. Mike's mother **chided**, or scolded, him in front of everybody. Although she may have brandished something (waved something menacingly) while doing this, **chided** is the better choice. Extolled (praised) doesn't make sense. Bane (nuisance) is a word but "baned" is not.

10. D. The best choice is **mollifying**, which means soothing in temper or disposition. Demeaning (humiliating) and beleaguering (harassing) are the opposite. Counteracting (offsetting) has a similar meaning, but doesn't really make sense here (how do you "offset" a student?).

11. B. Javier took to the job with **alacrity**, which is cheerful willingness or eagerness. He was not a misanthrope (a person who distrusts humanity), nor did he seem to be contemptuous (scornful). Lampoon (to ridicule with satire) does not fit, either. If you answered this question incorrectly, you might want to go back to chapter 11 for some review.

12. D. To **elate** is to exhilarate or make joyful and this is what music did for Monique. The other words are negative and therefore inappropriate: disparage (belittle), demean (humiliate), and rankle (anger or irritate). If you answered this question incorrectly, you might want to go back to chapter 11 for some review.

PART ONE

adversarial adj. (ahd ver SAR ee uhl)—competitive or antagonistic
The brothers' *adversarial* relationship made it impossible for their
parents to enjoy a meal.

affront n. (ah FRONT)—personal offense, insult
Clyde took the waiter's insulting remark as an *affront* to his family.

appalling adj. (uh PAW lihng)—causing dismay, frightful
Fern argued that the amount of cheating in today's high schools was
absolutely *appalling*.

aversion n. (ah VER shun)—intense dislike
Laura had an instant *aversion* to Mike because of his obnoxious
personality.

bane n. (BAYN)—cause of harm or ruin; source of annoyance
Traffic was the *bane* of Tori's existence; she couldn't stand all that
wasted time in her car.

beleaguer v. (bee LEE guhr)—to harass, plague
Mickey's *beleaguered* parents finally gave in to his request for a Nintendo.

bellicose adj. (BELL uh kohs)—warlike, aggressive
The *bellicose* Chief Eaglehawk surprised everyone when he called for a
truce.

> ### FLASHBACK
>
> In the first chapter, you learned that the word root **bell** means
> *war*. **Belligerent** and **bellicose** both mean *aggressive*, but
> **bellicose** goes a step further, meaning *warlike*.

bemuse v. (bee MUZ)—to confuse, stupefy; plunge deep into thought
Helen was *bemused* and certainly not amused at the computer problems.

berate v. (bee RAYT)—to scold harshly
When Coach Reed got his team into the locker room, he *berated* them
for their sloppy playing.

bilious adj. (bihl EE uhs)—ill-tempered; sickly, ailing
Uncle Jack's *bilious* complaining about his health ruined every holiday.

brandish v. (BRAN dish)—wave menacingly
Wyatt Earp could make outlaws surrender by simply *brandishing* his revolver.

cantankerous adj. (kaan TAANG kuhr uhs)—having a difficult, uncooperative, or stubborn disposition
Haley couldn't stand to be around Wendall when he was being *cantankerous*.

chide v. (CHIYD)—to scold, express disapproval
Florence *chided* her poodle for licking the icing off of the birthday cake.

choleric adj. (KOL er ik), (koh LEER ik)—easily angered, short-tempered
Ms. West was *choleric* and her students quickly figured out when to keep quiet.

confound v. (kuhn FOWND)—to baffle, perplex
Vince, *confounded* by the difficult algebra problems, threw his math book at the wall and stormed out.

Practice 1

DIRECTIONS: After reading the three choices, circle the one that you think is the *antonym*.

1. **affront:**	behind	compliment	insult
2. **bane:**	annoyance	banter	assistance
3. **beleaguer:**	harass	delight	ignore
4. **bellicose:**	passive	warlike	progressive
5. **berate:**	scold	tardy	praise
6. **bilious:**	odoriferous	companionable	crabby
7. **cantankerous:**	stubborn	accommodating	fantastic
8. **choleric:**	easygoing	gabby	short-tempered
9. **appalling:**	appealing	frightful	scolding

Your Words, Your World

Don't have time to sit around repeating these words to yourself, over and over again, in order to remember them? Well, you don't have to! The following exercise tests your knowledge of the material . . . without requiring that you take a test! So your job now is to really *think* about what you read, and to really cement an image in your mind. You never know when you'll need that image to pop up again.

Bemuse—**Bemused** is often used to describe the look on a person's face. Not to be *confused* with amused, **bemused** means to be *confused*. Although this definition—and the preceding sentence—may be tough to remember, just picture your own face as you're *thinking hard* about it.

Confound—Picture the lost and found at the gym, movie theater, or local swimming pool. Someone is standing there with a *baffled, perplexed* look on her face. She's **confounded** because she can't find what she's lost. She is *puzzled, frustrated,* and not happy about it.

Adversarial—If you are taking a class in which the students are always *fighting* with the teacher, or vice versa, then that class is an **adversarial** situation. Or maybe when you think of *antagonistic* situations you think of arguing with family and even friends. Hopefully not, because whatever situation comes to mind, nobody likes **adversarial** situations.

Chide—To **chide** is to *scold* or to *express disapproval*. If you have a teacher, manager, or parent who does this to you, you will surely remember what **chide** means.

Brandish—Movies, music videos, and video games often show people **brandishing** weapons. To **brandish** is to *wave menacingly,* so if you picture a gun the hands of a gangster or a gangsta rapper, you will be able to recall this definition.

Aversion—Think of your *least favorite* thing, activity, or person and you will remember what **aversion** means. If you have an *intense dislike* for anchovy pizza, for example, you have an **aversion** to it.

PART TWO

consternation n. (KAHN stuhr nay shuhn)—intense fear or dismay
Tony, a seasoned hunter, showed a surprising amount of *consternation*
when the black bear lumbered too close to camp.

contemptuous adj. (kuhn TEHMP choo uhs)—scornful; expressing
contempt
Unfortunately, Clara served a cold clam chowder to the food critic, and
his review of her restaurant was critical and *contemptuous*.

contentious adj. (kuhn TEHN shuhs)—controversial, always ready to
argue, quarrelsome
Jay was known to be *contentious* and after a while nobody bothered to
argue with him anymore.

counteract v. (kown ter ACT)—to oppose the effects by contrary action
Dr. Byron started administering antibiotics to *counteract* the sickness.

demean v. (dee MEEN)—to degrade, humiliate, humble
The editor constantly tried to *demean* Betsy and her writing, but Betsy
stuck with her job as a reporter.

disconcert adj. (dis kuhn SURT)—ruffle; distress; disturb; disappoint
David was *disconcerted* to find his locker left open after class.

disdain v. (diss DAYN)—to regard with scorn or contempt
Colonel Bennet's approach to commanding respect was to show
disdain for his troops.

disparage v. (diss PAHR ij)—to belittle, speak disrespectfully about
Gregorio loved to *disparage* his brother's dancing skills, pointing out
every mistake he made on the floor.

doleful adj. (DOHL fuhl)—sad, mournful
Looking into the *doleful* eyes of the lonely puppy, Lynn yearned to take
him home.

enigmatic adj. (en ihg MA tik)—puzzling
The class was even more confused after Professor Noble's *enigmatic*
answers about his final exam.

flagrant adj. (FLAY grent)—outrageous, shameless
Joan's *flagrant* disregard for the rules led to her eventual removal from
the ethics commission.

frenetic adj. (freh NEH tihk)—frantic, frenzied
The *frenetic* schedule of the school day suited some of the teachers'
personalities just fine, while other teachers would have preferred a
more relaxed pace.

ignoble adj. (IHG noh buhl)—having low moral standards, not noble in
character; mean
Tabloids like *The National Enquirer* may have an *ignoble* reputation,
but their sales numbers couldn't be better.

irascible adj. (ih RAA suh buhl)—easily angered, hot-tempered
One of the most *irascible* barbarians in history, Attila the Hun ravaged
much of Europe during his time.

irreverent adj. (ir REHV er ehnt)—disrespectful, gently or humorously
mocking
Kevin's *irreverent* attitude in Sunday school annoyed the priest, but it
amused the other children.

Practice 2

DIRECTIONS: In completing the sentences, use 11 of the 12 words
below. Use each of the words just once.

contemptuous	irreverently	consternation	demeaning
flagrant	contentious	doleful	disparage
irascible	decorative	disdain	ignoble

10. Mrs. Penders became _____ whenever a
    student asked to go to the bathroom.

11. It seemed that everyone in town was down-
    right _____ upon hearing that the diner
    had closed.

12. Although she was often too argumentative,
    being _____ made Mrs. Bishop a good
    choice as advisor to the debate club.

13. Willie's _____ violations of his parole led
    to yet another arrest.

14. Tim was so _____ towards everyone that
    Linda found it easy to ignore his taunts.

15. Kenneth's parents were in such a state of
    _____ about his weight loss and drop in
    grades that they brought him to see a psychol-
    ogist.

16. The math professor accused the science depart-
    ment of being _____ after three of his
    missing laptops were found in a science lab.

17. After the third suspension, Melinda decided
    that she'd had enough of her son acting so
    _____ towards his teachers.

18. Sure now that his teacher was out to get him,
    Joe threw the failed exam into the trash with
    great _____ and left the room.

19. Peter's parents had always told him it was
    wrong to _____ others, and he passed
    the lesson on to his own children.

20. Although Freda had cancer, she was never con-
    tentious or _____ with family or friends
    and they were all amazed by her patience.

Your Words, Your World

Don't have time to sit around repeating these words to yourself, over
and over again, in order to remember them? Well, you don't have to!
The following exercise tests your knowledge of the material . . . without
requiring that you take a test! So your job now is to really *think* about
the following words and how annoying it is when they are a part of your
life!

Counteract—Think of something that is a part of your daily life that you
have an aversion to. Maybe it's hearing your alarm clock in the
morning. Now think of a way to **counteract** this thing. Can you *undo*
the annoyance of your alarm clock by setting your stereo to turn on first
thing in the morning?

Disconcert—Imagine paying $40 to see your favorite band, only to have the band not show up, or leave after playing for just one hour. Imagine how *distressed, disturbed,* and *displeased* you would be. You probably would feel **disconcerted** about this *disappointing concert.*

Enigmatic—Picture a puzzle, plain and simple. As **enigmatic** means *puzzling* (as well as *mysterious* and *unfathomable*), the image of a puzzle should trigger your memory.

Frenetic—**Frenetic** shares the same root with *frantic* and *frenzied,* which also happen to be synonyms. And if that trick doesn't work, you can always picture a *frantic, frenzied,* **frenetic** cartoon character—one like the Tasmanian Devil, perhaps.

PART THREE

jaded adj. (JAY dehd)—tired by excess or overuse; slightly cynical
The musician played more than twenty *jaded* love songs, and scowled the whole time, making it hard to enjoy the show.

lampoon v. (laam POON)—to ridicule with satire
Mayor McNichols hated being *lampooned* by the press for trying to improve people's manners.

malaise n. (MAA layz)—a feeling of unease or depression
During his presidency, Jimmy Carter spoke of a "national *malaise*" and was subsequently criticized for being too negative.

malevolent adj. (mah LEH vuhl ehnt)—exhibiting ill will; wishing harm to others
Vicky was a *malevolent* gossip, and soon no one trusted her.

misanthrope n. (MIHS ahn throhp)—a person who hates or distrusts humankind
Scrooge was such a *misanthrope* that even the sight of children singing made him angry.

mollify v. (MAAL uh fiy)—to soothe in temper or disposition
A small raise and an extra vacation day *mollified* Mickey after he failed to get the promotion.

morose adj. (muh ROHS)—gloomy, sullen
After hearing that the internship had been given to someone else, Lenny was *morose* for days.

obfuscate v. (AHB fyoo skayt)—to confuse, make obscure
Benny tends to *obfuscate* his own point by bringing in irrelevant facts.

MEMORY TIP

To remember **obfuscate**, think of the "ob" and associate it with obscure; and also, think of the "fus" and associate it with confuse. To **obfuscate** is to *make obscure* and to *confuse*.

---

opprobrious adj. (uh PROH bree uhs)—disgraceful, shameful
The singer's new song was an *opprobrious* plea for money and record sales were disappointing.

oscillate v. (AH sih layt)—to swing back and forth like a pendulum; to vary between opposing beliefs or feelings
Because they are out of touch with young people, politicians tend to *oscillate* on education legislation.

ostracize v. (ah struh SIYZE)—to exclude from a group
Feeling *ostracized* by her friends, Tabitha couldn't figure out what she had done.

pique v. (PEEK)—to arouse anger in; to arouse interest in; provoke
It seemed that Farley's one joy in life was *piquing* his father's anger.

plaintive adj. (playn TIHV)—expressive of suffering or woe, melancholy
The *plaintive* cries of the girl trapped in the well quickly drew a team of rescuers.

precarious adj. (prih CAA ree uhs)—lacking in security or stability; dependent on chance or uncertain conditions
War is always a *precarious* time, at home and abroad.

rancor n. (RAAN kuhr)—bitter hatred
Having been teased for years, Hal was filled with *rancor* for his classmates.

rankle v. (RAANG kuhl)—to cause anger and irritation
At first the babysitter found the children's television show adorable, but after half an hour it began to *rankle*.

saturnine adj. (saat uhr NIYN)—cold and steady in mood; slow to act
Tim's *saturnine* responses made him seem unapproachable.

skepticism n. (SKEP tih sizm)—doubt, disbelief; uncertainty
Despite widespread *skepticism*, the Wright Brothers built a functional airplane.

torpid adj. (TOR pid)—lethargic; unable to move; dormant
After surgery, Allen was *torpid* until the anesthesia wore off.

truculent adj. (truhk YUH lehnt)—disposed to fight, belligerent
Quentin was *truculent* when he first enrolled at Washington High, but
quickly realized he didn't need to be so defensive.

vex v. (VEHKS)—to irritate, annoy; confuse, puzzle
Herbert, who loved his peace and quiet, was *vexed* by his neighbor's
loud music.

vitriolic adj. (VIH tree AH lik)—spiteful; caustic; bitter
It had been a long time since anyone had seen such a *vitriolic* review
of a Julia Roberts film.

vituperate v. (VIY TUP er ayt)—to abuse verbally
Leonard *vituperated* his wife one too many times; no one was
surprised when she left him.

wan adj. (WAHN)—sickly pale
In the midst of her cold, Melody's usually rosy cheeks looked *wan*.

Practice 3

DIRECTIONS: Consider the two word choices in the parentheses and
circle the one that best fits in the context of the sentence.

21. In trying to (chide OR mollify) the seniors
    with a test exemption, Mr. Glenridge just made
    all of the underclassmen angry.

22. Melanie's (vitriolic OR bemused) words
    made it impossible for Eleanor to ever think of
    her as a friend again.

23. Theo's behavior was (wan OR opprobrious),
    but his apology was heartfelt and soon all was
    forgotten.

24. After students started referring to "(Morose
    OR Misanthrope) Mondays," the staff used
    the nickname as well.

25. Miss Westerville was (colossal OR saturnine),
    yet all of the students really liked her.

26. Wrestling was a good way for Troy to make use of his (truculent OR torpid) urges.

27. Tiffany always looked (wan OR effervescent) and people wondered if she was anorexic.

28. Coach Forde complained to the referees about the other team's (malevolent OR plucky) fouls and they issued the other coach a warning.

29. One newspaper called Ian a(n) (amenity OR misanthrope) after his plot to blow up the school was revealed.

30. The team's lead was (contemptuous OR precarious) as they entered the final minute of play up by just one point.

31. No one could believe the (rancor OR surmount) with which Mr. DeLeon gave his resignation.

32. Kevin enjoyed philosophy class because he was able to make good use of his (skepticism OR malaise).

33. After weeks of feeling (flagrant OR torpid), Lisa was finally diagnosed with Lyme Disease.

34. Ginny's (plaintive OR cantankerous) cries were so heart wrenching that her parents agreed to get her another cat the very next day.

35. Norm (disparaged OR lampooned) the school's staff and students in his weekly cartoon, but he did it so well that nobody seemed to mind!

36. The students knew they could (burgeon OR pique) Mrs. Lowenstein's interest in politics by mentioning the president and did so whenever they wanted to get out of doing class work.

37. The group of friends was so well liked because they never tried to (oscillate OR ostracize) anybody.

38. By the time Jan was a senior, she was extremely (wan OR jaded) with school life and never went to a party or dance.

39. The entire school was in a state of deep (malaise OR morose) until that first nice day of spring, when everyone instantly cheered up.

40. All too often, Mr. Thyme tried to (obfuscate OR vituperate) his students with impossible test questions and none of them appreciated it.

Your Words, Your World

Don't have time to sit around repeating these words to yourself, over and over again, in order to remember them? Well, you don't have to! The following exercise tests your knowledge of the material . . . without requiring that you take a test! So instead of memorizing, your job now is to really *think* about what you read, and to really think about the questions that follow.

Vituperate—Have you ever known a victim of verbal *abuse*, who has no bruises, but is still injured on the *inside*? In some relationships, one person will frequently **vituperate**, or *verbally abuse*, the other. Have you ever been around a couple like this?

Vex—Does it seem like life was better when you were a kid, with no *worries*? Well, that's because life's questions really begin to **vex** people once they become teenagers, and it only continues into adulthood. People are constantly *perplexed* and *irritated* by those questions they just can't answer.

Rankle—What really **rankles** you? What really gets your *blood boiling*? Is it people who cheat? What is it that causes *anger* and *irritation*?

Oscillate—If you imagine a *rotating* fan on a hot summer day, you can remember that to **oscillate** is to *swing back and forth*. In addition to physical *motion*, **oscillate** can also be used in reference to *changing positions, beliefs, and feelings*.

PRACTICE ANSWERS AND EXPLANATIONS

Practice 1

1. An **affront** is an insult, so the antonym is compliment. Behind is an irrelevant distracter.

2. **Bane** is a noun that means annoyance, so the answer is assistance. Banter means conversation and is incorrect.

3. To **beleaguer** is to harass. Delight is the correct choice. Ignore is unrelated.

4. To be **bellicose** is to be warlike and not to be passive. Progressive (modern and forward thinking) is incorrect.

5. To **berate** is to scold while praise is the antonym. Tardy means late and is neither the antonym nor the synonym.

6. If someone is **bilious**, he or she is crabby, making companionable the antonym. Odoriferous relates to the sense of smell and is irrelevant.

7. To be **cantankerous** is to be stubborn and not accommodating. Fantastic is unrelated.

8. A person who is **choleric** has a short temper. Choleric people definitely are not easygoing. Nor are they gabby, but easygoing is the antonym.

9. To be **appalling** is to be frightful, so appealing is the antonym. Scolding (punishing and criticizing) is incorrect.

Practice 2

10. Mrs. Penders disapproved of the request, so she was **contemptuous** of it.

11. Everybody felt **doleful**, or sad, upon hearing the news.

12. Mrs. Bishop was **contentious**, meaning she was quick to debate or argue.

13. Willie's violations were **flagrant**, which means outrageous or shameless.

14. To **demean** is to degrade and humiliate.

15. To be in a state of **consternation** is to feel intense fear or dismay.

16. The math professor accused the members of the science department of being **ignoble**, or of having low moral standards.

17. Her son was acting **irreverently**, or disrespectfully, towards his teachers.

18. Joe threw his paper out with great **disdain**, which means great scorn and contempt.

19. The lesson relates to the importance of not belittling others, as such **disparaging** is hurtful and not nice.

20. Freda was still a positive person and never acted in an **irascible** (irritable) manner.

Practice 3

21. **Mollify** is the choice as it means to soothe. Chide, on the other hand, means to reprimand.

22. Melanie's **vitriolic** (spiteful) words did not amuse her friend although they might have bemused (confused) her.

23. Theo's behavior was not wan (sickly pale), but **opprobrious**, which means disgraceful and shameful.

24. "**Morose** Mondays" is a nickname for gloomiest day of the week. A misanthrope is a person who hates humanity.

25. The affection for Miss Westerville was surprising because she was **saturnine**, or cold. Colossal means large and is an inappropriate choice.

26. To be **truculent** is to be disposed to fight, making it a better choice than torpid, which means lethargic.

27. Tiffany looked **wan**, which means sickly pale. Effervescent (sparkly or bubbly) doesn't work in the context of the sentence.

28. **Malevolent** fits best as it means exhibiting ill will or wishing harm to others. Plucky means courageous and spunky, and Coach Forde wouldn't have much of a case if he used that word!

29. A **misanthrope** is a person who hates or distrusts mankind. An amenity is something that increases comfort or pleasantness.

30. The team's one-point lead was unstable, or **precarious**. It was not contemptuous, which means disapproving or scornful.

31. The answer is **rancor**, which means bitter hatred. Surmount is not the answer as it is grammatically incorrect and means to overcome.

32. **Skepticism** can be useful when questioning things as it means doubt, disbelief, and uncertainty. Malaise is a feeling of depression and is an inappropriate choice.

33. To feel **torpid** is to feel lethargic and unable to move. People don't feel flagrant (outrageous) so much as act in a flagrant manner.

34. A **plaintive** (expressive of suffering or woe) cry is much more likely to bring Ginny a new cat than one that is cantankerous (crabby, ill-tempered, or argumentative).

35. If Norm were to disparage (belittle) everyone, they certainly would mind. To be **lampooned** (ridiculed in a humorous way) on the other hand, might be acceptable to students and maybe even staff.

36. To **pique** is to arouse anger, while to burgeon is to flourish. By getting their teacher upset, the students knew they could avoid doing their work!

37. They never tried to **ostracize**, or exclude, anybody. To oscillate is to swing back and forth, which is irrelevant.

38. Jan was **jaded**, or fed up with school life. She was not wan, which means sickly pale.

39. Morose is incorrect because it is an adjective. **Malaise** is a noun and means a feeling of depression, gloom, or unease.

40. Mr. Thyme tried to confuse, or **obfuscate**, his students, but did not go so far as to vituperate them (abuse them verbally).

CHAPTER 12 TEST

Okay, it's time to put your memory to the test! Take your time not only with the questions but in reading the answer explanations that follow. Set a goal for yourself—80% (24 correct answers) is recommended—and if you don't reach that goal, go back and read through the chapter again. Good luck!

DIRECTIONS: For questions 1–15, circle T for True or F for False. For questions 16–30, circle the synonym.

1.	T	F	**misanthrope**—distrusting
2.	T	F	**counteract**—to pretend
3.	T	F	**ignoble**—immoral
4.	T	F	**precarious**—insecure
5.	T	F	**ostracize**—to exclude
6.	T	F	**bane**—source of joy
7.	T	F	**malaise**—a joyful feeling
8.	T	F	**consternation**—state of fear
9.	T	F	**disconcert**—to upset
10.	T	F	**affront**—an insult
11.	T	F	**lampoon**—to ridicule with satire
12.	T	F	**vituperate**—to recuperate
13.	T	F	**jaded**—fed up
14.	T	F	**malevolent**—compassionate
15.	T	F	**vitriolic**—kind

16. **vex:**	pacify	annoy	invigorate
17. **beleaguer:**	harass	crescendo	accretion
18. **saturnine:**	aloof	friendly	resilient
19. **demean:**	augment	humiliate	abate
20. **contentious:**	disagreeable	contestant	agreeable
21. **brandish:**	to brand	to abuse	to wield
22. **bellicose:**	veins	aggressive	sickly pale

23. **aversion:**	dislike	penchant	fondness
24. **morose:**	gloomy	cheerful	rancor
25. **confound:**	to find	to soothe	to baffle
26. **bemuse:**	to amuse	to regret	to confound
27. **appalling:**	awful	legion	vex
28. **opprobrious:**	joyful	shameful	full
29. **doleful:**	sad	glad	lampoon
30. **choleric:**	irreverent	irritable	cantankerous

Answers and Explanations

1. **True.** A **misanthrope** is a person who hates or distrusts mankind.

2. **False.** To **counteract** is to oppose by contrary action and not to pretend.

3. **True.** To be **ignoble** is to have low moral standards or to be immoral.

4. **True.** If something is in a **precarious** position it is lacking in security and stability.

5. **True.** To **ostracize** is to exclude from a group by common consent.

6. **False.** A **bane** is a nuisance or source of annoyance and not a source of joy.

7. **False.** A **malaise** is a feeling of unease or depression and not a joyful feeling.

8. **True.** A feeling of **consternation** is an intense state of fear or dismay.

9. **True.** To **disconcert** is to ruffle or upset.

10. **True.** An **affront** is a personal offense or insult.

11. **True.** To **lampoon** is to ridicule with satire, to mock in a good-natured way.

12. **False.** To **vituperate** is not to recuperate, but to abuse verbally.

13. **True.** To feel **jaded** is to be tired of something because of its excess or overuse. It is to be fed up.

14. **False.** **Malevolent** means exhibiting ill will and wishing harm to others. It is the opposite of compassionate.

15. **False.** To be **vitriolic** is to be spiteful, caustic, and bitter. It is definitely not to be kind.

16. To **vex** is to irritate or annoy. It is not to pacify (calm someone down) or invigorate.

17. To **beleaguer** is to harass. To crescendo is to increase and an accretion is an accumulation.

18. To be **saturnine** is to be aloof and cold toward others. It is neither friendly nor resilient.

19. To **demean** is to degrade or humiliate. To augment is to supplement and to abate is to decrease, both of which are incorrect.

20. To be **contentious** is to be disagreeable. The antonym is agreeable. Contestant is also incorrect.

21. To **brandish** is to wield (wave menacingly). It is neither to brand nor to abuse.

22. To be **bellicose** is to be aggressive. Veins is a distracter intended to make you think of "varicose" veins, and sickly pale is the definition of wan.

23. An **aversion** is an intense dislike of something. Penchant and fondness are synonyms of one another, but antonyms of aversion as they mean a liking for something.

24. To be **morose** is to be gloomy. Rancor is bitter anger. Cheerful is also incorrect.

25. To **confound** is to baffle or stupefy. To find is a distracter based on the appearance of "found" in **confound**. To soothe means to mollify.

26. To **bemuse** is to confuse, stupefy, or confound. It is neither to amuse, nor to regret.

27. If something is **appalling** it is awful or frightful. The other two answers, legion (a great number) and vex (to irritate), are wrong.

28. **Opprobrious** means shameful and definitely not joyful or full.

29. To feel **doleful** is to feel sad. Glad is an antonym and lampoon (satire) is also the wrong choice.

30. To feel **choleric** is to feel irritable and short-tempered. It is not to be irreverent (disrespectful), nor cantankerous (crabby).

Sizing It Up

Bigger, smaller, shorter, taller, it's all here

BUILDING BLOCK QUIZ

This "building block" quiz tests the information you will learn in this chapter, plus two words from the previous chapter. By answering the 12 questions below, you will get a sense of how closely you'll have to study this chapter in order to master the vocabulary used to describe differences in size. Should you happen to choose incorrect answers for the final two questions, you'll want to go back to chapter 12 for some review.

DIRECTIONS: Fill in the blanks, using the most appropriate of the four multiple-choice answers. The correct answer will always fit into the sentence grammatically.

1. Whenever Jan's weight began to _____, she quickly switched from cookies to fruit after lunch and dinner.

   (A) wane   (B) abate

   (C) wax   (D) allay

2. Mrs. Grady reminded the class that _____ words in a research paper can often lower its grade.

   (A) finite   (B) infusion

   (C) superstar   (D) superfluous

3. Vince liked to _____ his fruit with his Swiss Army knife.

   (A) pare (B) eradicate

   (C) proliferate (D) inundate

4. Mick _____ the empty potato chip bag as he'd told his little brother that he didn't have any food left.

   (A) mitigated (B) jettisoned

   (C) razed (D) chided

5. Ken knew that unlike his mother, his father had _____ patience, so he stopped arguing.

   (A) finite (B) capacious

   (C) behemoth (D) superfluous

6. The crowd began to _____ after the security guards dragged the two girls away.

   (A) collage (B) surfeit

   (C) remnant (D) dissipate

7. As there was a(n) _____ of talent at the talent show, most people went home early.

   (A) abundance (B) legion

   (C) dearth (D) inflation

8. Lila could see Ursula _____ at the offer of dessert and knew that she would want to leave the dinner party soon.

   (A) burgeon (B) balk

   (C) augment (D) allay

9. Kara gave her little sister a Band-Aid to
   _____ the paper cut.
   (A) assuage (B) debase
   (C) wax (D) augment

10. In order to _____ the class's anxiety
    before the SAT, Miss Harmon turned her
    review classes into a mini-Olympics.
    (A) faux pas (B) crescendo
    (C) vex (D) allay

11. Mr. Jackson hoped to _____ the disgrun-
    tled employees by offering behavior incentives.
    (A) rankle (B) mollify
    (C) degrade (D) jettison

12. Jean's _____ to school lunches was
    almost comical, except to her mother who had
    to pack a lunch every day.
    (A) voracious (B) zenith
    (C) aversion (D) partiality

Answers and Explanations

1. C. Jan would have fruit for dessert when her weight started to **wax**, or increase gradually. The opposite is to decrease, or lessen, which is the definition for wane, abate, and allay.

2. D. **Superfluous** means extra, or more than necessary, and is the best choice. Finite (limited) doesn't make quite as much sense in context: a paper can't have an infinite number of words. An infusion is a mix or combination and makes as little sense here as superstar.

3. A. To **pare** is to trim, as in the skin of fruit, which is how Vince used his knife. To eradicate (eliminate) is incorrect as is proliferate (multiply or grow) and inundate (overwhelm).

4. B. Jettisoned means discarded. Mitigated (lessened), razed (destroyed), and chided (scolded) are all inappropriate choices.

5. A. Ken's father's patience was limited, or **finite**. It was neither capacious nor behemoth, both of which mean large. Superfluous, which means more than necessary, also fails to fit the sentence's intended meaning.

6. D. The crowd began to **dissipate**, or vanish. The other three answers don't fit grammatically or in context, as surfeit means an excessive amount, remnant means left over, and collage means assemblage.

7. C. There was a **dearth**, or lack, of talent, so people were not motivated to stay. There certainly wasn't an abundance, a legion (crowd), or an inflation (increase).

8. B. Ursula **balked** at the offer of dessert, meaning she refused it. Burgeon means multiply, augment means supplement, and allay means dispel, none of which makes sense here.

9. A. Kara wanted to ease, or **assuage**, her sister's pain. She did not want to debase (demean) it, augment (increase) it, or cause it to wax (gradually increase).

10. D. Only **allay** (to lessen or ease) makes sense. A faux pas is a social error, to crescendo is to increase, and to vex is to annoy.

11. B. He hoped to **mollify**, or soothe in temper and disposition, his employees with the rewards. He certainly didn't want to rankle (irritate) or degrade (humiliate) them, nor did he want to jettison (get rid of) them. If you answered this question incorrectly, you might want to go back to chapter 12 for some review.

12. C. Jean had an **aversion** to, or intense dislike of, school lunches. Voracious is an adjective meaning huge or insatiable, while the sentence calls for a noun. Zenith means peak, but you can't have a "zenith to" something. Partiality means bias towards, and it conveys the opposite of the sentence's intended meaning. If you answered this question incorrectly, you might want to go back to chapter 12 for some review.

PART ONE

abate v. (uh BAYT)—to decrease, to reduce
Gwen's hunger *abated* when she saw the chef's filthy hands.

accretion n. (uh KREE shuhn)—a growth in size, an increase in amount
The *accretion* of the college's endowment meant more scholarships could be offered.

allay v. (uh LAY)—to lessen, ease, reduce in intensity
Nurse Fanny sat with Sally all night, trying to *allay* Sally's fears.

amenity n. (uh MEN it tee)—pleasantness; something increasing comfort
After his third massage of the week, Joel really began to appreciate the resort's *amenities*.

amortize v. (uh MORE tiyze)—to diminish by installment payments
Jess would *amortize* her debt with automatic deductions from each paycheck.

assuage v. (uh SWAGE)—to make less severe, to ease, to relieve
After a bad day at work, Phil liked to go to the movies to *assuage* his stress.

attenuate v. (uh TEN oo ate)—to soothe; to lessen; to make thin or slender; to weaken
To make sure that states ratified the Constitution, the framers *attenuated* the power of the federal government.

augment v. (awg MENT)—to expand, extend
Ben looked to *augment* his salary by applying for overtime hours.

balk v. (BAWK)—to refuse, shirk; prevent
The horse *balked* at jumping over the high fence, going so far as to throw his rider off.

behemoth n. (buh HEE muhth)—something of monstrous size or power; huge creature
The Ford LTD was a *behemoth* and took up half the driveway.

bereft adj. (bee REHFT)—deprived or lacking of something
The reality show was *bereft* of anything resembling dignity or intelligence.

blight v. (BLIYT)—to afflict, destroy
The locusts *blighted* the crop in a matter of hours.

burgeon v. (BER gehn)—to sprout or flourish
The size of suburban schools *burgeoned* as more and more people moved out of the city.

capacious adj. (kah PAY shus)—large, roomy; extensive
Capacious houses quickly constructed in the suburbs are often called "McMansions."

colossal n. (kuh LAH suhl)—immense, enormous
Joseph made a *colossal* error by skipping school; he failed the final exam and was forced to retake the course.

Practice 1

DIRECTIONS: In completing the sentences, use 12 of the 15 words below. Use each of the words just once.

blight	attenuate	allay	amortize	assuage
behemoth	abate	bereft	burgeoned	capacious
accretion	colossal	amenity	augment	balk

1. The teacher tried to _____ the class's fear of exams by reviewing with a game of Hangman.

2. Participation in the Spanish Club _____ after the piñata party.

3. Mrs. Loller tried to _____ the theater group's budget with a candy sale.

4. The new cafeteria was _____ and well lit, and Mr. Drake knew the students were going to love it.

5. Only the presence of police officers could _____ the gang violence in the inner-city neighborhood.

6. Carol felt _____ of an advisor and friend when Miss Fenwick retired.

7. The judge held Louis responsible for $1,000 worth of damage to the church and said he could _____ his debt by paying $50 a month.

8. To _____ the sadness in the house after Grandma's funeral, Grandpa asked everyone to remember and share happy stories about her.

9. For the class, the poster project was a _____ of an assignment that would be impossible to complete over the weekend.

10. Due to the _____ in class size, the district planned on building a new elementary school.

11. Although there was no rule against pets, many of the residents feared that the woman's ten cats and seven dogs would _____ the apartment building.

12. The nurse urged everyone to get flu shots so as to _____ the chances of a flu epidemic during the winter.

Your Words, Your World

Don't have time to sit around repeating these words to yourself, over and over again, in order to remember them? Well, you don't have to! The following exercise tests your knowledge of the material . . . without requiring that you take a test! So your job now is to really *think* about what you read, and to really cement an image in your mind. You never know when you'll need that image to pop up again.

Amenity—Recall the *nicest* hotel you ever stayed in and try to remember the **amenities**. These might include a swimming pool, a gym, a *comfortable* bed, or the *pleasant* staff. Think of that hotel and you will remember that an **amenity** is anything to *improve your experience*.

Balk—In baseball, the term **balk** refers to a pitcher *stopping* in the middle of his motion. This is a useful image, as balk means to *refuse, shy away from, shirk,* or *prevent*. When the pitcher shies away from delivering the pitch, that's called a **balk**.

Colossal—Picture an *immense* blimp floating through the sky. Or a *huge* cruise ship, **colossal** compared to all the other boats around it. There is also the idea of a *tremendous* mistake as **colossal** doesn't just describe things in the physical world.

PART TWO

crescendo n. (kruh SHEN doh)—gradual increase in volume, force, or intensity
Due to the way the song *crescendoed*, the audience was left emotionally exhausted.

cumulative adj. (KYOOM yuh lah tiv)—resulting from gradual increase
The *cumulative* study included statistics not just from one year, but from the past ten years.

dearth n. (DUHRTH)—a lack, scarcity, insufficiency
The *dearth* of teachers made it difficult for principals to staff their classrooms.

debase v. (dee BAYS)—to degrade or lower in quality or stature
President Clinton's perjury *debased* the stature of his office.

debilitating adj. (dee BIL uh tay ting)—impairing the strength or energy
The 25 percent cut in staff proved *debilitating* to IntelliCo, and within a month profits had suffered.

degradation n. (deh gruh DAY shun)—reduction in worth or dignity
When Sarah broke up with Charlie at the dance, he had never felt such *degradation*.

MEMORY TIP

The **de-** in the preceding four words indicates a *lessening* or a *decrease*.

---

dissipate v. (DIHS uh payt)—to vanish; to waste
The fog gradually *dissipated*, revealing all of the ships docked in the harbor.

disseminate v. (dih SEM uh nayt)—to spread far and wide
The Associated Press quickly *disseminated* the story of Princess Di's tragic accident.

distract v. (dihs TRAKT)—to cause to lose focus, to divert attention
Music didn't *distract* Jeremy from his studies; it actually helped him to stay focused.

eradicate v. (ee RAHD ih kayt)—to erase or wipe out
Evan's economics thesis involved *eradicating* poverty in a Costa Rican village.

finite adj. (FIY niyt)—having bounds, limited
Professor Helms reminded the class that there were a *finite* number of jobs available and that they would all be competing against one another.

hindrance n. (HIN drehns)—impediment, clog; stumbling block
Not wishing to be a *hindrance*, Gary played outside while his father cleaned up for the party.

inflation n. (in FLAY shun)—undue amplification, often economic
Mr. Ogelvie's example of *inflation* was the increase in the cost of a cheeseburger over five years.

infusion n. (in FYOO zhun)—the introduction of, the addition of
The United States has benefited from the *infusion* of many different cultures.

inundate v. (IN uhn dayt)—to cover with a flood; to overwhelm as if with a flood
These days, college students are *inundated* with credit card offers.

MEMORY TIP

The **in-** in the previous three words indicates an *increase* or *growth*.

Practice 2

DIRECTIONS: After reading the three choices, circle the one that you think is the *antonym*.

13. **finite:**	unlimited	fine	limited
14. **dearth:**	scarcity	insufficiency	adequacy
15. **hindrance:**	assistance	impediment	clog
16. **debilitating:**	impairing	helping	debating
17. **crescendo:**	augment	increase	decrease
18. **dissipate:**	appear	vanish	anticipate
19. **infusion:**	dispersal	increase	absolute
20. **disseminate:**	spread	conceal	distribute
21. **debase:**	glorify	demean	degrade
22. **eradicate:**	dictate	construct	eliminate

Your Words, Your World

Don't have time to sit around repeating these words to yourself, over and over again, in order to remember them? Well, you don't have to! The following exercise tests your knowledge of the material . . . without requiring that you take a test! So your job now is to really *think* about the following words and the role they play in your day-to-day life.

Inflation—Think of a fully **inflated** balloon to remind yourself that **inflation** means *increase, rise,* or, at its worst, *unnecessary amplification.* As an adult, you know that **inflation** means an increase in prices such that one dollar buys less than it did before.

Cumulative—**Cumulative** means resulting from a *gradual increase.* A **cumulative** grade point average represents a student's grades in all of his or her classes. The hope is that grades will always get *bigger* and *better!* Similarly, as an adult, one's salary should reflect a **cumulative** *growth* as *raises* and *promotions* come your way.

Degradation—This word can be used to describe one's self-image (a *reduction in dignity*) or, even worse, one's actual lifestyle (a *reduction in worth*). If someone, for example, is living in **degradation**, he or she is living in poverty. Have you ever felt your life *slipping* into a pattern of **degradation**? Maybe your financial situation *declined* and *got worse*. One hopes this didn't last for long!

Distract—A concert or movie may *sidetrack* you from your work or studies. A friend may look to *divert*, or entertain, you when you're feeling down, and there's nothing wrong with that. Just be sure to avoid getting too **distracted** from this book!

Inundate—Although the image of a *flood* is the best way to remember that **inundate** means *overwhelmed*, you might prefer a *sea* of pens and pencils, calculators, a laptop, computer printouts, and all other material required for your job or schoolwork.

PART THREE

jettison v. (JEHT ih zuhn) (JEHT ih suhn)—to discard, to get rid of as unnecessary or encumbering
The sinking ship *jettisoned* its cargo in a desperate attempt to reduce weight.

legion n. (LEE jun)—a great number, a multitude
As soon as Lester got his first big role, he had *legions* of fans.

Lilliputian adj. (lih ee PYOO shun)—very small
Amy looked *Lilliputian* next to her roommate, a former basketball star.

mitigate v. (MIHT ih gayt)—to make less severe, make milder
Judge Leland decided to *mitigate* the first-timer's sentence.

modicum n. (MAHD ih kuhm)—a small portion, limited quantity
Bebe asked for even a *modicum* of a raise and her boss agreed to give her $2 more per hour.

palatial adj. (puh LAY shuhl)—relating to a palace; magnificent
After the cramped studio apartment, the one-bedroom apartment seemed *palatial*.

pallid adj. (PAHL id)—lacking color or liveliness
Tyler often exaggerated his illnesses, but his *pallid* skin color was a sure sign that he was sick.

paltry adj. (PAWL tree)—pitifully small or worthless
Bernardo paid a boy the *paltry* sum of 25 cents to sweep the restaurant every day.

pare v. (PAYR)—to trim off excess, reduce
Mrs. Rodgers could *pare* down the essays in the writing contest by eliminating the ones with spelling and punctuation mistakes.

proliferate v. (proh LIH fuhr ayt)—to grow by rapid production of new parts; increase in number
The cancer cells *proliferated* so quickly that even the doctor was surprised.

raze v. (RAYS)—to tear down, demolish
When Ricky returned, the house had been *razed* and there was nothing left on the lot.

remnant n. (REHM nent)—something left over, surviving trace
Mike was late to the dinner, but he still managed to grab the *remnants* of the appetizer platter.

repress v. (ree PRESS)—to restrain or hold in
Sheila *repressed* the urge to tell Glen to shut up, as he was one of her best customers.

superfluous adj. (soo PUHR floo UHS)—extra, more than necessary
The job counselor told Georgio that the extra reference letters were *superfluous* and he should pick just three.

surfeit n. (SUR fiht)—excessive amount
Because of the *surfeit* of pigs, pork prices fell to record lows.

voluminous adj. (vah LOO mehn us)—large, having great volume
The bachelor's *voluminous* mug was filled with root beer as he no longer drank alcohol.

voracious adj. (vor AY shus)—having a great appetite
The *voracious* boys ate three pizzas all by themselves.

wax v. (WAAKS)—to increase gradually; to begin to be
The moon was in its *wax* phase, after waning.

zenith n. (ZEE nihth)—the point of culmination; peak
The singer considered her appearance at the Metropolitan Opera
House to be the *zenith* of her career.

Practice 3

DIRECTIONS: Consider the two word choices in the parentheses and
circle the one that best fits in the context of the sentence.

23. Izzy thought that the standing ovation was
    (voracious OR superfluous), but thanked
    the crowd, nonetheless.

24. Bus duty was always a battle as the teachers
    tried to (repress OR impress) the exercise-
    starved kids.

25. Dr. Harvey hoped to (proliferate OR mitigate)
    the effects of the teacher strike by using assis-
    tant teachers and substitutes.

26. The (zenith OR modicum) of Verna's high
    school soccer career came with the win at the
    state championship.

27. Chris's house seemed (palatial OR paltry)
    compared to Eddie's apartment.

28. There was a (surfeit OR dearth) of pizza
    after the dance and the class president decided
    to donate it to the homeless.

29. The superintendent decided to (augment OR
    pare) the budget by cutting all freshman
    sports programs.

30. Whenever the pile of papers began to (wax
    OR abate) on her desk, Mrs. Borne would
    take an hour and file them.

31. The exterminator warned that the vermin would (dissipate OR proliferate) quickly, so Gail decided to hire him immediately.

32. A (zenith OR legion) of fans waited for the volleyball team to return from the sectional championship.

33. The new swimming pool was (voluminous OR paltry) in that it was, indeed, Olympic-sized.

34. The school paper was actually the first to reveal the town's plans to (raze OR repress) the old soccer stadium.

35. The (inflations OR remnants) of the new city hall construction project were enough to build a small community center.

36. Usually (pallid OR Lilliputian), Tina was darkly tan after her Caribbean vacation.

37. In his campaign for student council president, Paul promised to get the cafeteria to provide more than a (blight OR modicum) of dessert with lunch.

Your Words, Your World

Don't have time to sit around repeating these words to yourself, over and over again, in order to remember them? Well, you don't have to! The following exercise tests your knowledge of the material . . . without requiring that you take a test! So your job now is to really *think* about what you read, and to really think about the questions that follow.

Lilliputian—Is there a *miniaturized* version of something in your house? Maybe you have a *tiny* replica of an antique car, or a *very small* portrait of an ancestor in a locket? Anything *super small* is considered **Lilliputian**.

Jettison—The next time you clean out your room, what will be the first thing to get *thrown out*? Will you get *rid* of old clothing or books? Will you have a hard time **jettisoning** anything?

Paltry—Over the past year, have you been paid a **paltry** sum for a job well done? Did somebody give you a check that was *pitifully small*? Did they make you feel *worthless* by paying you *less* than you're *worth*? Maybe you can use this unfortunate experience to remember the meaning of **paltry**.

Voracious—Who is the most **voracious** person you know? Who in your circle of friends has the *greatest appetite*? Whoever it is, if you think of that person's face when faced with the word **voracious**, you'll know exactly what it means.

PRACTICE ANSWERS AND EXPLANATIONS

Practice 1

1. To **assuage** is to ease or make less severe and the teacher was hoping to calm the class with some Hangman. (NOTE: allay, abate, and attenuate are all acceptable answers, as well.)

2. Participation in the Spanish Club **burgeoned**, or flourished.

3. With the candy sale, Mrs. Loller hoped to **augment** (expand) the budget.

4. The new cafeteria was **capacious**, which means large and roomy.

5. Everyone hopes the police will be able to **abate** (decrease or reduce) gang violence. (NOTE: assuage, allay, and attenuate are all acceptable answers, as well.)

6. Carol felt **bereft**, which means deprived.

7. Louis would **amortize**, or diminish, his debt with monthly payments.

8. To **allay** is to lessen or ease and Grandpa was hoping to ease everyone's mourning. (NOTE: assuage, abate, and attenuate are all acceptable answers, as well.)

9. The assignment was a **behemoth** in that it seemed monstrous—too large to complete in a weekend.

10. An **accretion** is a growth in size, thus necessitating school construction.

11. To **blight** is to impair or destroy. The neighbors feared the animals would be a nuisance and possibly damage the building.

12. She wanted to **attenuate**, or lessen, the chances of everyone getting the flu. (NOTE: assuage, abate, and allay are all acceptable answers, as well.)

Practice 2

13. The antonym of **finite** is unlimited. Limited is a synonym while fine is irrelevant.

14. Adequacy is the antonym of **dearth**. The synonyms are scarcity and insufficiency, so neither of those answers is correct.

15. The antonym of **hindrance** is assistance, while impediment and clog are synonyms.

16. The antonym of **debilitating** is helping. One synonym is impairing. Debating is irrelevant.

17. The antonym of **crescendo** is decrease. Augment and increase are synonyms.

18. Appear is the antonym of **dissipate**. Vanish is a synonym, while anticipate is unrelated.

19. The antonym of **infusion** is dispersal. The synonym is increase (as a noun). Absolute has no relation to **infusion**.

20. The opposite of **disseminate** is conceal. The synonyms are spread and distribute.

21. Glorify is the antonym of **debase** as to debase means to demean and degrade.

22. The antonym of **eradicate** is construct. Eliminate is a synonym while dictate is a sound-alike distracter.

Practice 3

23. Izzy was being humble in that he thought the standing ovation was **superfluous**, or more than necessary. Voracious means insatiable, which doesn't make as much sense as **superfluous**.

24. The teachers were trying to **repress**, or restrain, the kids. At bus duty, they were done trying to impress them!

25. Dr. Harvey hoped to **mitigate**, or lessen the severity of, the teacher strike. He did not want to proliferate (reproduce, increase, or spread) it.

26. The **zenith** is the peak, or culmination, and the state championship was the high point of Verna's high school soccer career. A modicum is a small amount, so that's incorrect.

27. Chris's house looked **palatial** (relating to a palace; magnificent) in comparison to Eddie's apartment, which must have looked paltry (worthless and measly) compared to Chris's house.

28. A **surfeit** (excessive amount) of pizza means there was a lot left over for the homeless. A dearth, or shortage, would mean no pizza.

29. In cutting the budget, the superintendent decided to **pare** or reduce freshman sports. To augment is to supplement.

30. The pile of papers would have to **wax** (increase gradually) before Mrs. Borne would file them. Abate is an antonym meaning decrease.

31. Hearing that the vermin would **proliferate**, or spread rapidly, was enough to convince Gail that the exterminator was needed. If the vermin were going to dissipate or disperse, the meaning would be the opposite.

32. A **legion** of fans is a great number; a multitude. A zenith is a peak or summit and does not apply to quantity.

33. The Olympic-sized pool was **voluminous**, meaning large and having great volume. The pool was not paltry (worthless and small).

34. To **raze** is to tear down and that was what the town planned for the soccer stadium. Repress means suppress.

35. Remnants are leftovers; in this case, building materials. Inflations is not a word, but inflation means increase.

36. Before her vacation, Tina was **pallid** (lacking color or liveliness), but not afterward. She may have been small, but it is doubtful she was Lilliputian.

37. A **modicum** is a small portion. To blight is to destroy.

CHAPTER 13 TEST

Okay, it's time to put your memory to the test! Take your time not only with the questions but in reading the answer explanations that follow. Set a goal for yourself—80% (24 correct answers) is recommended—and if you don't reach that goal, go back and read through the chapter again. Good luck!

DIRECTIONS: For questions 1–15, circle T for True or F for False. For questions 16–30, circle the synonym.

1. T   F   **behemoth**—something tiny
2. T   F   **debase**—to raise in quality or stature
3. T   F   **zenith**—point of culmination
4. T   F   **cumulative**—resulting from gradual increase
5. T   F   **proliferate**—to shrink due to decreased production
6. T   F   **voracious**—having a great appetite
7. T   F   **palatial**—magnificent
8. T   F   **finite**—unlimited
9. T   F   **crescendo**—a gradual increase
10. T   F   **infusion**—the addition of
11. T   F   **allay**—to increase in intensity
12. T   F   **capacious**—large
13. T   F   **debilitating**—impairing the strength
14. T   F   **disseminate**—to spread
15. T   F   **abate**—to increase

16. **wax:**	decrease	increase	wane
17. **augment:**	to reduce	to withdraw	to expand
18. **blight:**	to destroy	to improve	to augment
19. **repress:**	to restrain	to release	to burgeon
20. **eradicate:**	to construct	to mitigate	to wipe out
21. **legion:**	a multitude	a miniature	a few
22. **attenuate:**	to increase	to soothe	to wax

23. **mitigate:**	less severe	more severe	to crescendo
24. **pallid:**	effervescent	colorful	lacking color
25. **assuage:**	to ease	to burden	to increase
26. **raze:**	to burgeon	to demolish	to assemble
27. **hindrance:**	an assist	an impediment	an aid
28. **distract:**	to divert	to focus	to debase
29. **bereft:**	prosperous	affluent	deprived of
30. **accretion:**	growth	depreciation	dearth

Answers and Explanations

1. False. A **behemoth** is something monstrously huge, like an elephant, and not something tiny.

2. False. To **debase** is to belittle or humiliate (demean is a synonym). It is not to raise in quality or stature.

3. True. The **zenith** is the point of culmination. Think of the **zenith** of the sun in the sky at noon.

4. True. The adjective **cumulative** means resulting from gradual increase.

5. False. To **proliferate** is to grow due to increased production, the opposite of the given answer (to shrink due to decreased production).

6. True. To be **voracious** is to have a great appetite. Some people, for example, are voracious eaters.

7. True. **Palatial** means magnificent.

8. False. If something is **finite** it is limited.

9. True. A **crescendo** is a gradual increase.

10. True. An **infusion** is the addition of something, but the word isn't used in mathematical contexts. It refers to things like color, light, taste, scent, or fun.

11. False. To **allay** is to decrease or to calm. It is not to increase and certainly not to increase in intensity.

12. True. To be **capacious** is to be large, as in the size of a room.

13. True. When something is **debilitating** it is impairing the strength of something else.

14. True. To **disseminate** is to spread.

15. False. To **abate** is to decrease and not to increase.

16. To **wax** is to increase. It is not to decrease, which means the same as wane.

17. To **augment** is to expand. It is not to reduce or to withdraw.

18. To **blight** is to destroy. In this case, it is a verb, but the word may also be used as a noun. To blight is not to improve or to augment (supplement).

19. To **repress** is to restrain and not to release or to burgeon (proliferate or flourish).

20. To **eradicate** is to wipe out, which is the opposite of to construct and nearly the opposite of to mitigate (to ease or lessen).

21. A **legion** is a multitude, which is the opposite of a few. A miniature is close to being synonymous with a few and to being an antonym of **legion**.

22. To **attenuate** is to soothe or lessen. It is not to increase, which is synonymous with to wax.

23. To **mitigate** is to make less severe. More severe and to crescendo (increase) are both incorrect.

24. If something is **pallid** it is lacking in color. Effervescent (shiny and bubbly) and colorful are antonyms of **pallid**.

25. To **assuage** is to ease. It is not to burden or to increase. **Assuage** is most often used regarding people's emotions, like **assuaging** someone's fears.

26. To **raze** is to demolish. To burgeon means to flourish and to assemble is to construct, the opposite of **raze**.

27. A **hindrance** is an impediment. An assist and an aid are both antonyms of **hindrance**.

28. To **distract** is to divert, especially attention. To focus is the opposite. To debase is to humiliate.

29. To be **bereft** is to be deprived of something. Prosperous and affluent both mean wealthy.

30. An **accretion** is an accumulation or growth. Depreciation (reduction) and dearth (lack or shortage) have the opposite meaning.

CHAPTER 14

Foreign Words

Vocabulary from the melting pot

BUILDING BLOCK QUIZ

This "building block" quiz tests the information you will learn in this chapter, plus two words from the previous chapter. By answering the 12 questions below, you will get a sense of how closely you'll have to study this chapter in order to master the vocabulary you'll need to navigate the global village. If you choose incorrect answers for the final two questions, you'll want to go back to chapter 13 for some review.

DIRECTIONS: Fill in the blanks, using the most appropriate of the four multiple-choice answers. The correct answer will always fit into the sentence grammatically.

1. Eduardo had a _____ for General Tsao's Chicken.
   (A) bing (B) bang
   (C) yen (D) yang

2. Mr. Pauling asked the superintendent for a _____ regarding the funding for field trips.
   (A) tea-to-tea (B) tête-à-tête
   (C) two-à-two (D) tête

3. The judge informed the two debate clubs that loyalty and the Marine Corps code of _____ was the day's topic.

   (A) temper fatalis (B) siempre fidalis

   (C) simper infidelis (D) semper fidelis

4. In finalizing their plans to elope, Helen and Gabe made the lake their _____.

   (A) rendezvous (B) voulez vous

   (C) voilà (D) vestibule

5. Part of the comedian's appeal was the way he interrupted himself with silly _____ throughout the routine.

   (A) nonsensicals (B) non-refundables

   (C) non sequiturs (D) nonplusseds

6. The principal was not pleased when Zabrina promised that the administrators would have to be more _____ if she were student body president.

   (A) lazy-fair (B) laissez-faire

   (C) savoire-faire (D) lackadaisical

7. Jan tried to convince her father to buy the prom dress by saying it was _____ to spend no less than $500.

   (A) du jour (B) de rigeur

   (C) de rigorous (D) du ponte

8. The class quickly tired of Mr. Winterbottom's
   old _____.
   (A) passés (B) clicky
   (C) cliques (D) clichés

9. All of the teachers noticed the amazing sense of
   _____ shared by the senior class.
   (A) concoctory (B) camaraderie
   (C) camouflagery (D) imparity

10. When Freddy was suspended, even his friends
    had to admit that the punishment was

    _____.

    (A) à propose (B) à pro bono
    (C) à professionale (D) à propos

11. The math teachers all admitted to the students
    that the additional statewide test was more of a
    _____ than a help.
    (A) hindrance (B) hind leg
    (C) reference (D) hypocritical

12. The elementary school was _____ of
    musical instruments until the anonymous
    donation of $3,000.
    (A) cleft (B) deft
    (C) bereft (D) bedraggled

Answers and Explanations

1. C. A **yen** is a strong desire or craving, and Eduardo had one for General Tsao's Chicken. Bing, bang, and yang are all silly answers. In this Building Block Quiz, most of the incorrect answers are nonsensical!

2. B. A **tête-à-tête** is a situation in which two people talk in private. In this case, the two people were Mr. Pauling and the superintendent. Tea-to-tea, two-à-two, and tête are all incorrect.

3. D. Semper fidelis is a Latin phrase—and the motto of the United States Marine Corps—that means to always be loyal. Siempre fidalis, simper infidelis, and temper fatalis are made-up answers.

4. A. A **rendezvous** is a place where a meeting has been arranged. Voulez vous (would you like?), voilà (ta da!), and vestibule (entrance hall) are all incorrect in this situation.

5. C. Non sequiturs are statements that do not logically follow what was said before. In this case, a comedian was using them to be funny. He was not using non-refundables. Nonsensicals and nonplusseds are not real words, although nonsensical (meaningless) and nonplussed (puzzled) are adjectives.

6. B. Zabrina was saying she would make the administrators be more **laissez-faire** (a governmental position of non-interference), which means they wouldn't make as many rules for the students. What a politician! It goes without saying that lazy-fair and lackadaisical (also meaning lazy) are way off. Savoire-faire means ability gained from having experienced something.

7. B. De rigeur means required by tradition or fashion. Do you think Jan's father fell for it? Du jour means of the day, and de rigorous and du ponte are made-up answers.

8. D. Mr. Winterbottom's **clichés** (overused expressions) might have been passé, but passés isn't a word, nor is clicky. Cliques are groups of friends, but that doesn't make sense in this context.

9. B. Camaraderie is a sense of comfort and trust shared between people. Imparity means inequality. Concoctory and camouflagery are concocted (made-up, artificial) words.

10. D. To say that something is **à propos** is to say that it is appropriate. The other three choices—à propose, à pro bono, à professionale—don't mean anything in French or English!

11. A. The math teachers thought the testing was more **hindrance** (impediment; trouble) than help. Hind leg, reference, and hypocritical (deceitful) are all incorrect. If you answered this question incorrectly, you might want to go back to chapter 13 for some review.

12. C. Bereft means deprived of or lacking. Cleft (partially split or divided), deft (dexterous), and bedraggled (disheveled) are all irrelevant. If you answered this question incorrectly, you might want to go back to chapter 13 for some review.

PART ONE

à propos adj. (ah pruh POH)—pertinent; appropriate. French for "to the purpose."
The punishment of washing cars was *à propos* as Heidi had spray-painted several cars.

ad hoc adj. (ad HAHK)—for a certain purpose. Latin for "for this."
An *ad hoc* committee formed with the goal of raising money for a new playground.

aficionado n. (uh fish ee yuh NAH doh)—a fan, usually of sports. Spanish for "affectionate one."
Catherine considered herself a baseball *aficionado* and had the statistical knowledge to prove it.

al fresco adj. (al FRES koh)—out in the fresh air. Italian for "in the fresh."
Tim preferred to dine *al fresco* and asked for a table on the patio.

au courant adj. (oh koo RAWN)—to be informed; knowledgeable of current events. French for "in the current."
Mitch read the paper every day and was considered *au courant* by all his friends.

avant-garde adj. (AH vant GARD)—a radically new or original movement, especially in the arts. French for "advance guard."
Maya Deren's *avant-garde* films broke the rules of classical cinema.

bourgeois adj. (boor ZHWAH)—middle-class. French for "of the town."
The *bourgeois* family was horrified when the lower-class family moved in next door.

camaraderie n. (kahm RAH da ree)—trust, sociability among friends. French for "comrade."
The photo clearly shows the *camaraderie* as the team sits smiling at the airport.

carte blanche n. (kahrt BLANCH)—full authority and freedom to do whatever one wants. French for "blank card."
When Mr. Thomas returned from Florida, he told his class that Disney World was *carte blanche* for kids.

cliché n. (klee SHAY)—overused expression or idea
The movie wasn't very original, as the characters continually uttered *clichés*.

collage n. (ko LAZH)—assemblage of diverse elements. French for "pasting."
Dean Wintner used a *collage* of newspaper clippings to decorate the wall of her office.

déjà vu n. (DAY zhah vu)—the illusory feeling of having been in a situation before. French for "already seen."
Standing on the deck of the cruise ship, Renee had an overwhelming sense of *déjà vu*.

de rigeur adj. (duh ri GUHR)—required by tradition or fashion. French for "indispensable."
The limousine and corsage had become *de rigeur* for the prom.

fait accompli n. (fet uhkohm PLEE)—something that cannot be undone. French for "accomplished fact."
Given Tony's work ethic and his close relationship with the manager, by the time of his annual review his promotion was a *fait accompli*.

Practice 1

DIRECTIONS: Match the foreign word (left column) with its translation or English meaning (right column).

1.	**au courant**	accomplished fact
2.	**cliché**	pasting
3.	**de rigeur**	familiar with current events
4.	**collage**	indispensable
5.	**ad hoc**	in the fresh air
6.	**bourgeois**	fellowship, trust
7.	**fait accompli**	middle-class
8.	**à propos**	overused expression
9.	**camaraderie**	for a certain purpose
10.	**al fresco**	appropriate

Your Words, Your World

Don't have time to sit around repeating these words to yourself, over and over again, in order to remember them? Well, you don't have to! The following exercise tests your knowledge of the material . . . without requiring that you take a test! So your job now is to really *think* about what you read, and to really cement an image in your mind. You never know when you'll need that image to pop up again.

Déjà vu—Déjà vu is not just a feeling of having been somewhere or having done something before, it is the feeling of having *already seen* what you are now seeing. So, more than a feeling, **déjà vu** is like a *vision*, come around for *another view*. Can you think of a time you have experienced **déjà vu**?

Carte blanche—Picture a *blank card*. Can you see it? A business card without any print? Well, if you can see it, you can remember it. **Carte blanche** is a *blank card*. More specifically, it is like "having" a *blank check*, meaning if you have it, you can help yourself to whatever you would like. Picture not just the *blank card* (or *blank check*), but the fun you would have using it.

Avant-garde—Put more emphasis on the *advance* than the *guard*. When something is **avant-garde**, it is a *glimpse of the future*. It is an indicator of something *up and coming*, usually in the art world. Think of *advance* and you'll remember this definition.

Aficionado—Remember these words: *"official fan."* **Aficionado** almost sounds like *"official fan,"* doesn't it? Can you see this person, wearing the team's full uniform, with his or her face painted in the team's colors, carrying a sign in each hand? **Aficionado** is Spanish for *"affectionate one"* and is most often applied to a *die-hard fan* of a certain team (though the meaning isn't limited to sports). Are you an **aficionado**?

PART TWO

faux pas n. (foh PAH)—an embarrassing mistake in a social setting. French for "false step."
When Missy dropped the baked beans all over her skirt at the cocktail party, it was the worst *faux pas* of her life.

joie de vivre n. (zhwah duh VEE vruh)—the enjoyment of life, usually shared with others. French for "joy of living."
Dr. Bingham always reminded her students that family, not work, was the way to achieve *joie de vivre*.

laissez-faire n. (lay zay FAIR)—a governmental position of non-interference, most often in terms of business. French for "let do."
The president's *laissez-faire* policies temporarily aided the economy.

MEMORY TIP

The laissez of **laissez-faire** is pronounced "lazy." Let this remind you that, in a way, *a position of non-interference* is . . . lazy.

---

non sequitur n. (nahn SEK wi tur)—a statement that does not logically follow what was said before. Latin for "it does not follow."
Mr. Edham's *non sequiturs* made his math lessons hard to follow.

outré adj. (oo TRAY)—bizarre. French for "carried to excess."
Liza's *outré* outfits were ridiculous and her friends told her so.

panache n. (puh nahsh)—flamboyance or dash in style and action. French for "plume."
Leah's *panache* made her very well known within her department.

raison d'être n. (ray zohn DET ruh)—the reason for living or existing. French for "reason to be."
As soon as his daughter was born, Calvin knew his *raison d'être*.

rendezvous n. (RAHN day voo)—a place where a meeting has been arranged; a meeting at such a place. French for "present yourself."
The lake was a popular summer *rendezvous*.

savoire-faire n. (sav wahr FEHR)—the ability gained from having experienced something. French for "to know how to do."
Everybody said Kirk came back from his term abroad with a surprising maturity and *savoire-faire*.

semper fidelis n. (sem puhr fi DEHL is)—undying loyalty. Latin for "always loyal."
Part of the team's success was its feeling of *semper fidelis*.

tête-à-tête n. (TET ah TET)—two people talking in private. French for "head-to-head."
Neil wouldn't tell anybody what was said in his *tête-à-tête* with Principal Lowell.

vis-à-vis prep. (VEE zah VEE)—as compared with or in relation to. French for "face-to-face."
Bernie was slow in finding his first job, *vis-à-vis* his go-getter of a brother.

yen n. (yehn)—a strong desire, craving. Cantonese for "smoke."
Pregnant women commonly have a *yen* for pickles.

zeitgeist n. (ZIYT giyst)—in the spirit of the times. German for "time spirit."
At the 1950s theme dance, the girls wore poodle skirts for fun and in accordance with the *zeitgeist*.

Practice 2

DIRECTIONS: In completing the sentences, use 10 of the 12 words below. Use each of the words just once.

vis-à-vis	semper fidelis	tête-à-tête	zeitgeist
faux pas	yen	outré	rendezvous
laissez-faire	raison d'être	non sequiturs	joie de vivre

11. Rapping was part of the _____, so Miss McGill agreed to do it for the talent show.

12. Mr. Robertson had a _____ for M&Ms, so students who wanted to get in his good graces would give him some.

13. Derek's classroom was across the hall _____ Lilly's classroom.

14. Whenever her father said he wanted a _____, Jacqueline knew that she was in trouble.

15. The gang's spirit of _____ fell apart as soon as the first member was arrested and turned the others in.

16. Miss Masters told anyone who asked that the works of Jane Austen were her _____.

17. Lenny's scheme was completely _____, but he believed in it so wholeheartedly that others were willing to help out.

18. Mr. Pasquali advised Ben to avoid _____ when speaking publicly.

19. Sasha believed that the government's _____ approach would be good for business.

20. Mrs. Joyce asked each student to write a definition of _____ and include personal examples of happiness.

Your Words, Your World

Don't have time to sit around repeating these words to yourself, over and over again, in order to remember them? Well, you don't have to! The following exercise tests your knowledge of the material . . . without requiring that you take a test! You will find that each of these foreign words has a place in your day-to-day life.

Faux pas—If you have never, ever made a **faux pas**, congratulations. Chances are, though, there is at least one *social blunder* on your mind right now. At some point, you did something *foolish* in front of other people. Put that *embarrassing* memory to use now and, in a way, your **faux pas** will have been worth it.

Panache—If you know someone who has **panache**—*style, grace*, a socially acceptable *flamboyance*—let that person be your guiding light when confronted with this word. Think of how you look up to this person, whether you'd like to admit it or not. This could be due to his or her *sense of fashion*, ability to *hold the attention* of a group of people, or *confidence*. . . . Oh, to have **panache**!

Savoire-faire—In a way, **savoire-faire** is similar to *panache*, except that it is knowledge that comes from *experience*. If the person you associate with *panache* has lived abroad, spends lots of time in the city, or has had a particular job for a long time, perhaps he or she has more than *panache*: he or she has **savoire-faire**. In simplest terms, think of the most *mature, experienced* person you know: a peer who *knows more* than the rest of your peers.

PRACTICE ANSWERS AND EXPLANATIONS

Practice 1

1. **Au courant** means familiar with current events (literally "in the current").

2. A **cliché** is an overused expression.

3. **De rigeur** means indispensable.

4. A **collage** is an assemblage of diverse elements (literally "pasting").

5. **Ad hoc** means for a certain purpose.

6. Something **bourgeois** is related to the middle class (literally "of the town").

7. A **fait accompli** is an accomplished fact.

8. If something is **à propos** it is appropriate (literally "to the purpose").

9. **Camaraderie** is fellowship and trust (literally "comrade").

10. **Al fresco** means out in the fresh air (literally "in the fresh").

Practice 2

11. Rapping seemed to be part of the **zeitgeist**, or spirit of the times.

12. Mr. Robertson had a **yen**, or a liking, for M&Ms.

13. Derek's classroom was across the hall in relation to (**vis-à-vis**) Lilly's.

14. Whenever her father wanted a **tête-à-tête**, or private face-to-face conversation, Jacqueline had reason to worry.

15. The spirit of **semper fidelis** (loyalty) could not survive the arrest.

16. Jane Austen's books were her **raison d'être**, or reason for living.

17. Lenny's scheme was **outré**, which means bizarre or outrageous.

18. Ben needed to avoid all **non sequiturs**, or random digressions, when speaking publicly.

19. Sasha liked the government's policy of non-interference (**laissez-faire**) regarding business and industry.

20. Mrs. Joyce wanted to know about the students' **joie de vivre**, or how they would define the joy of living.

CHAPTER 14 TEST

Okay, it's time to put your memory to the test! Take your time not only with the questions but in reading the answer explanations that follow. Set a goal for yourself—80% (16 correct answers) is recommended— and if you don't reach that goal, go back and read through the chapter again. Good luck!

DIRECTIONS: For questions 1–10, circle T for True or F for False. For questions 11–20, circle the synonym.

1. T F **zeitgeist**—trust
2. T F **non sequitur**—an illogical statement
3. T F **fait accompli**—something that can be undone
4. T F **ad hoc**—Latin for "always loyal"
5. T F **collage**—an artistic assemblage
6. T F **déjà vu**—a nice view
7. T F **joie de vivre**—the enjoyment of life
8. T F **cliché**—an overused expression
9. T F **avant-garde**—unoriginal
10. T F **savoire-faire**—ability gained from experience

11. **yen:** desire zen yang
12. **tête-à-tête:** teatime fistfight private conversation
13. **faux pas:** past tense blunder false friend
14. **camaraderie:** trust mistrust defeat
15. **bourgeois:** upper-class middle-class lower-class
16. **au courant:** informed uninformed ocean current
17. **al fresco:** of tomatoes at its freshest in the fresh air
18. **à propos:** appropriate inappropriate a proposal
19. **rendezvous:** code name meeting place French fries
20. **panache:** a dessert humility flamboyance

Answers and Explanations

1. False. **Zeitgeist** is the spirit of the times and not trust.

2. True. A **non sequitur** is an illogical statement in that it does not fit with what was said before.

3. False. A **fait accompli** is something that cannot be undone.

4. False. **Ad hoc** means for a certain purpose. Semper fidelis is Latin for "always loyal."

5. True. A **collage** is an artistic assemblage.

6. False. **Déjà vu** is the illusory feeling of having been in a situation before. It is definitely not French for "a nice view."

7. True. **Joie de vivre** means the enjoyment of life.

8. True. A **cliché** is an overused expression or idea.

9. False. If something is **avant-garde** it is not unoriginal. Quite the opposite, it is radically original.

10. True. **Savoire-faire** is general ability gained from having experienced something.

11. Yen means a strong desire. Zen and yang are unrelated.

12. A **tête-à-tête** is a private, one-on-one conversation, not a fistfight. People may talk at teatime, but this answer is wrong as well.

13. A **faux pas** is a social blunder. It is neither a false friend nor the past tense.

14. Camaraderie is a sense of trust within a group of people. Mistrust is an antonym and defeat is unrelated.

15. Bourgeois is French for "related to the middle class." Upper-class and lower-class are both incorrect.

16. Au courant means to be informed or current. Uninformed is the opposite and ocean current uses a different meaning of the word current.

17. **Al fresco** is Italian for "in the fresh" (air). In English it means "outside." At its freshest is incorrect as is of tomatoes.

18. The translation of **à propos** is "appropriate." Inappropriate and a proposal are both wrong choices.

19. A **rendezvous** is a meeting place. It is not a code name, nor is it French fries.

20. **Panache** means flamboyance. It is not a dessert, and humility has a strongly opposed meaning.

CHAPTER 15

Most Frequently Tested SAT Words

The words you need to ace the SAT

BUILDING BLOCK QUIZ

This "building block" quiz tests the information you will learn in this chapter, plus two words from the previous chapter. By answering the 12 questions below, you will get a sense of how closely you'll have to study this chapter in order to master the vocabulary that commonly shows up on the SAT! Should you happen to choose incorrect answers for the final two questions, you'll want to go back to chapter 14 for some review.

DIRECTIONS: Fill in the blanks, using the most appropriate of the four multiple-choice answers. The correct answer will always fit into the sentence grammatically.

1. Jeff didn't realize how much his little brother
   _____ him until his mother pointed it
   out.
   (A) rescinded (B) supplanted
   (C) emulated (D) rejected

2. Lezlie was a(n) _____ expert on all
   things MTV and VH1.
   (A) veritable (B) bogus
   (C) excoriate (D) amalgamate

3. The _____ way the kitten hid behind the chair instantly won everyone's heart.

(A) abstruse (B) courageous

(C) tremulous (D) plucky

4. The photos really captured the baby's _____ face.

(A) devilish (B) seraphic

(C) unsightly (D) insular

5. Maureen was _____ with her teachers and not always in a good way.

(A) timid (B) timorous

(C) audible (D) audacious

6. Dean's _____ mind made him a good research scientist.

(A) credulous (B) incredulous

(C) naïve (D) incorrigible

7. Bert's _____ attitude earned him no friends, but plenty of enemies.

(A) haughty (B) emphatic

(C) incredulous (D) viscous

8. Michelle's singing style was _____ of Mariah Carey.

(A) unwarranted (B) unwitting

(C) derivative (D) prodigal

9. The boy's _____ ways made all the teachers wonder if he was a victim of abuse.

   (A) precocious (B) chary

   (C) loquacious (D) facile

10. Lenny enjoyed _____ the other players as it made him feel better about his skills.

   (A) compounding (B) adroiting

   (C) unavailing (D) abasing

11. The _____ had been established by the gang leader one hour before the meeting.

   (A) stalwart (B) rendezvous

   (C) feral (D) utilitarian

12. As assistant principal, Merle had _____ to reprimand students and teachers alike.

   (A) carte blanche (B) card blanque

   (C) acuity (D) allusion

Answers and Explanations

1. C. Jeff's little brother **emulated** (copied and imitated) him. He did not reject, supplant (displace), or rescind (cancel) him.

2. A. Lezlie was a **veritable** (without question) expert. She was not an amalgamate (combine), excoriate (criticize), or bogus (fake) expert.

3. C. Tremulous, or trembling, is appropriate for describing the scared kitten. Plucky is synonymous with courageous and both are inappropriate, as the kitten was hiding. Abstruse means obscure, so that doesn't fit either.

4. B. The baby's face was **seraphic** (angelic) and not insular (narrow-minded), unsightly, or devilish.

5. D. Maureen was **audacious**, or bold. Although she might have been audible, this is an incorrect choice, as are timorous and timid, both of which are antonyms to audacious. It's hard to see how any of the incorrect answers could apply "not in a good way."

6. B. As a researcher, Dean must have had an **incredulous** (skeptical) mind. It wouldn't have helped his research if his mind had been incorrigible (incapable of being corrected), naïve (overly trusting), or credulous (a synonym of naïve).

7. A. Bert was unpopular because he was **haughty**, or arrogant and condescending. This is a better choice than viscous (syrupy), incredulous (skeptical), or emphatic (forceful).

8. C. To be **derivative** is to have copied or adapted from someone else. It is to be unoriginal. Michelle was not prodigal (wasteful), unwitting (unsuspecting), or unwarranted (unnecessary).

9. B. The boy was **chary**, which means cautious and extremely shy. There is no evidence of his having been facile (superficial), loquacious (wordy), or precocious (intelligent).

10. D. Lenny enjoyed **abasing** (disgracing) the other players. Unavailing and compounding are irrelevant and adroiting isn't a word.

11. B. The meeting point is the **rendezvous**. Utilitarian (useful), stalwart (strong), and feral (animalistic) are all incorrect. If you answered this question incorrectly, you might want to go back to chapter 14 for some review.

12. A. Merle had **carte blanche**, which means full authority and freedom. She did not have allusion (hint), acuity (insight), or card blanque (a made-up phrase). If you answered this question incorrectly, you might want to go back to chapter 14 for some review.

PART ONE

abase v. (ah BEYS)—to demean; humble; disgrace
John's immature behavior *abased* him in my eyes.

aberration n. (ab er A shun)—something different from the usual
Due to the bizarre *aberrations* in the author's behavior, her publicist
decided that the less the public saw of her, the better.

acuity n. (uh KYOO ih tee)—sharp vision or perception
With unusual *acuity*, she was able to determine that the masterpiece
was a fake.

adroit adj. (uh DROYT)—skillful; accomplished; highly competent
The *adroit* athlete completed even the most difficult obstacle course
with ease.

allusion n. (uh LOO shun)—indirect reference
The player was sometimes referred to as The Slugger, an *allusion* to his
ability to hit the baseball very hard.

anachronistic adj. (uh NAK ru NISS tik)—outdated; occurring out of its
proper time
The hippie's clothes, with their beads and dangling tassels, were
anachronistic in style.

FLASHBACK

In chapter 1: Word Roots, you learned that **chron** means
time. Remembering this will help you to recall that
anachronistic means *out of time* or *outdated*.

---

audacious adj. (ah DAY shus)—bold, daring, fearless
The *audacious* freshman ignored the senior's request.

banal adj. (bah NALL)—trite, overly common
Corey often used *banal* phrases that made people think he was less
intelligent than he really was.

brazen adj. (BRAY zen)—bold, shameless, impudent; of or like brass
Slapping the teacher was just one of the *brazen* things Melody did
before being expelled.

bucolic adj. (byoo CAH lihk)—pastoral, rural
My aunt likes the hustle and bustle of the city, but my uncle prefers a more *bucolic* setting.

chary adj. (CHAHR ee)—watchful, cautious; extremely shy
Mindful of the fate of the Titanic, the captain was *chary* of navigating the iceberg-filled sea.

circuitous adj. (suhr KYOO ih tuhs)—indirect, roundabout
The venue was only a short walk from the train station, but due to a roadblock I had to take a *circuitous* route.

commodious adj. (kuh MODE ee us)—roomy, spacious
Raeqwan was able to stretch out fully in the *commodious* bathtub.

compound v. (kom POWND)—to combine, augment
After spitting out his food, Marv *compounded* the insult to the hostess by giving his plate to the dog to finish.

derivative adj. (di RIV uh tiv)—copied or adapted; not original
The TV show was so obviously *derivative* of "Seinfeld" that viewers were not interested in watching it.

Practice 1

DIRECTIONS: After reading the three choices, circle the *antonym*.

1. **abase:**	to shame	to humble	to praise
2. **aberration:**	different	ordinary	unusual
3. **acuity:**	naïve	insight	perception
4. **allusion:**	mention	reference	avoidance
5. **audacious:**	bold	fearful	daring
6. **banal:**	unique	trite	common
7. **bucolic:**	pastoral	urban	rural
8. **chary:**	cautious	shy	audacious
9. **circuitous:**	undeviating	indirect	roundabout
10. **compound:**	break down	combine	augment

Your Words, Your World

Don't have time to sit around repeating these words to yourself, over and over again, in order to remember them? Well, you don't have to! The following exercise tests your knowledge of the material . . . without requiring that you take a test! So your job now is to really *think* about what you read, and to really think about the questions that follow.

Adroit—Who is the most *skillful* person you know? And what is his or her *skill*? When a person is **adroit**, he or she is *accomplished* (*highly competent*) in a certain area. Who comes to mind when you think of this word?

Anachronistic—Is there somebody in your family whose clothing is *out of style* and **anachronistic**? Often, people will think of grandparents who haven't gone shopping in twenty years! Who will remind you that **anachronistic** means *outdated*?

Brazen—What is the *boldest*, most *shameless* thing you have ever seen another person do? Where did it happen? Did anyone get *hurt* or just (hopefully) *embarrassed*? Did this person get in trouble or was the **brazen** act more of a *laughable* matter? Whatever the case, use this memory to help yourself.

Commodious—Everybody has a favorite room: what's yours? Is it in your house or is it someplace else? Is it a tiny little space or is it *roomy*? A *spacious*, or **commodious**, room might be your favorite if you're a fan of *wide-open*, *ample* spaces. What room will you think of to remind yourself that **commodious** means *large*?

Derivative—Who is your favorite singer or band? Is that person or group completely original or **derivative** of another singer or band? Whose style was a major *influence*? Think of either the original artist or your favorite and you will remember that **derivative** means *copied* or *unoriginal*.

PART TWO

dilapidated adj. (dih LAAP ih day tihd)—in disrepair, run-down
The architect saw great potential in the *dilapidated* house.

emphatic adj. (em FAT ik)—forceful and definite
When asked if they wanted to come to school over the weekends, the students answered with an *emphatic* "NO!"

emulate v. (EM yoo layt)—to copy, imitate
Heather tried to *emulate* her mother in every way possible.

exacting adj. (eg ZAK ting)—requiring a lot of care or attention; demanding
Baking bread is an *exacting* task because too much or too little attention can kill the yeast.

feral adj. (FEHR ul)—suggestive of a wild beast, not domesticated
Though the animal-rights activists did not want to see the *feral* dogs harmed, they offered no solution.

facile adj. (FAS ul)—easy; simplistic
The test ended up being far more *facile* than Mrs. Grier intended.

implausible adj. (im PLAWS uh bul)—improbable, inconceivable
Max found his neighbor's claim that he'd seen a UFO highly *implausible*.

impudent adj. (ihm PYUH duhnt)—marked by cocky boldness or disregard for others
Considering the judge had been lenient in her sentence, it was *impudent* of the defendant to refer to her by her first name.

FLASHBACK

In chapter 1: Word Roots, you read about **im-** and how it means *not*. In **implausible**, the negative emphasis is on *not being conceivable or probable*. In **impudent** the negative emphasis is on *not regarding others* and *not being humble*.

---

haughty adj. (HAW tee)—arrogant and condescending
The teacher resented Sally's *haughty* attitude and gave her a D for the semester.

hubris n. (HYOO brihs)—excessive pride or self-confidence. Greek for "to rush into."
Nathan's *hubris* spurred him to say things that many considered insensitive.

incorrigible adj. (ihn KOHR ih juh buhl)—incapable of being corrected or amended; difficult to control or manage
Bobby's mother complained all the time about how *incorrigible* he was.

incredulous adj. (ihn KREH juh luhs)—unwilling to accept what is true, skeptical
The Lasky children were *incredulous* when their parents told them they were moving to Alaska.

indiscriminate adj. (in dis KRIM uh nit)—haphazard; random; chaotic
John didn't want to make an *indiscriminate* choice, so he visited ten different colleges before applying.

insular adj. (IHN suh luhr)—characteristic of an isolated people, especially having a narrow viewpoint
It was a shock for Kendra to go from her small high school, with her *insular* group of friends, to a huge college with students from all over the country.

insuperable adj. (ihn SUH puhr uh buhl)—incapable of being surmounted or overcome
Insuperable as Quinchon's problems seemed, he refused to be grumpy or pessimistic.

Practice 2

DIRECTIONS: Consider the definition and then circle T for True or F for False.

11. T   F   **emphatic**—vigorous
12. T   F   **emulate**—to imitate
13. T   F   **exacting**—easy
14. T   F   **facile**—simplistic
15. T   F   **implausible**—inconceivable
16. T   F   **impudent**—cocky, disregarding
17. T   F   **hubris**—a lack of confidence
18. T   F   **incorrigible**—capable of correction
19. T   F   **incredulous**—skeptical
20. T   F   **indiscriminate**—haphazard
21. T   F   **insuperable**—surmountable

Your Words, Your World

Don't have time to sit around repeating these words to yourself, over and over again, in order to remember them? Well, you don't have to! The following exercise tests your knowledge of the material . . . without requiring that you take a test! So your job now is to really *think* about what you read, and to really cement an image in your mind. You never know when you'll need that image to pop up again.

Insular—Insulation is pink and fluffy. And itchy! Picture insulation around a person, having surrounded that person for the past ten years. This *isolated* person would have *no idea* about politics, changes in technology, new music and fashions, or anything else current. This person would have a *narrow viewpoint* because he or she would *know nothing* about modern-day living. This is typical of **insular** people. NOTE: **Insular** is usually used in regards to a group of people; not to an individual.

Haughty—Although it will be mildly annoying, summon the image of the most *obnoxious, arrogant, condescending* person you know and implant it in your mind. This way, you will never, ever forget what **haughty** means.

Feral—Feral just sounds like a *wild* animal, doesn't it? If you love animals, picture a *wild* animal, but if you don't, simply think of the most *uncouth, untamed, uncultivated, undomesticated* person you know. He or she is **feral**.

Dilapidated—Every town has a haunted house, or, at least, a *decrepit* place where no one would ever think of living again. Imagine the place near where you live that is in the worst state of *disrepair* and let this serve as your reminder: **dilapidated** means *ramshackle* and *run-down*.

PART THREE

interminable adj. (in TER mi nu bul)—endless
By the time the seemingly *interminable* school play ended, half the audience was gone.

loquacious adj. (loh KWAY shuhs)—talkative
Patty was *loquacious*, which was always a problem as she worked in the library.

nebulous adj. (NEH byoo luhs)—vague, undefined
Jerry's *nebulous* promise to get fast food for school lunches made many voters skeptical.

precipitous adj. (PREE sih puh tuhs)—steeply; hastily
The night before finals, John *precipitously* began to study.

precocious adj. (pri KOH shiss)—unusually advanced or talented at an early age
The fact that Beatrice got married at eighteen shocked no one, as she'd always been a bit *precocious*.

prodigal adj. (PRAH dih guhl)—recklessly extravagant, wasteful
The *prodigal* spending of the class secretary earned her a suspension and removal from office.

seraphic adj. (seh RAH fihk)—angelic, sweet
Selena's *seraphic* appearance belied her bitter personality.

stalwart adj. (STAHL wuhrt)—marked by outstanding strength and vigor of body, mind, or spirit
Hank's 85-year old grandmother went to the market every day, impressing everyone with her *stalwart* routine.

timorous adj. (TIM uh rus)—timid, shy, full of apprehension
A *timorous* child, Lois too often relied on adults to help her out.

> **FLASHBACK**
>
> Often synonyms will have word roots in common. This is the case with **timorous**, which means *timid*. It is also true of the next word: **tremulous** means *trembling*.

tremulous adj. (TREM yoo luss)—trembling; quivering; fearful, timid
The *tremulous* boy was found in the staff bathroom, hiding from the bullies.

unavailing adj. (uhn ah VAYL ing)—hopeless, useless
Sally's efforts to drag her antique dresser out of the flooded house were *unavailing*.

unwarranted adj. (uhn WAAR ehn ted)—groundless, unjustified
The student art show received criticism that was *unwarranted* in its harshness.

unwitting adj. (uhn WIH ting)—unaware; unintentional
The *unwitting* students had no idea that Mr. Brady was planning a pop quiz.

utilitarian adj. (yoo TIL eh TAR ee uhn)—efficient, functional, useful
The school website became even more *utilitarian* when the students began to maintain it.

veritable adj. (VEHR ih tuh buhl)—absolute; being without question, often used figuratively
Chris's neighbor was a *veritable* gold mine of information for his term paper on the civil rights movement, as she had been a student organizer and protester.

viscous adj. (VIHS kus)—thick, syrupy, and sticky
The *viscous* sap trickled slowly down the trunk of the tree.

Practice 3

DIRECTIONS: Read the three possible synonyms, then circle the word you think best defines the word in bold.

22. **interminable:**	predetermined	finite	endless
23. **nebulous:**	vague	defined	distinct
24. **precipitous:**	leisurely	abrupt	mild
25. **prodigal:**	wasteful	vigilant	cautious
26. **seraphic:**	devilish	sweet	rapscallion
27. **timorous:**	timid	audacious	impudent
28. **tremulous:**	fearless	courageous	trembling
29. **unavailing:**	hopeless	hopeful	optimistic
30. **unwarranted:**	justified	necessary	unjustified
31. **unwitting:**	unsuspecting	wary	cautious
32. **veritable:**	phony	absolute	counterfeit

Your Words, Your World

Don't have time to sit around repeating these words to yourself, over and over again, in order to remember them? Well, you don't have to! The following exercise tests your knowledge of the material . . . without requiring that you take a test! So your job now is to really *think* about the following words and how they apply to your everyday life.

Loquacious—If someone were to describe you as **loquacious**, you might take offense. That's because you are being accused of being *long-winded*. The other person might mean to say that you are a good *communicator*, but **loquacious** does have a negative connotation. It means *overly talkative*.

Stalwart—Now, if someone were to call you **stalwart**, you might also take offense, but you'd be misunderstanding the compliment. If you are stalwart, you possess a *strength of body, mind, and spirit*; this word is also used to describe someone who is *rugged* and *athletic*. So if somebody notices your **stalwart** nature, be happy!

Utilitarian—Don't be upset if someone calls you **utilitarian** either. It simply means that you are *highly efficient*. Usually, this word is used to describe organizations, groups, or systems that are *functional* and *useful*.

Precocious—When you were young, people may have called you **precocious**. And for some reason, this is often thought of as a criticism. But in reality, to be called **precocious** is to be called *mature*. It is to be thought of as *unusually advanced at an early age*. It is to be *bright*, *gifted*, and *talented*. So hopefully, if someone called you a **precocious** child, your mother was proud and not angry.

Viscous—You may have heard the word **viscous** and thought it sounded gross. But if you drive, then you need to change your mindset. Picture the oil that helps your car run smoothly. **Viscous** describes that oil. It describes things that are *thick*, *syrupy*, and *sticky*.

PRACTICE ANSWERS AND EXPLANATIONS

Practice 1

1. To **abase** is to humble or shame, so the answer is to praise.

2. An **aberration** is something different or unusual. So ordinary is correct.

3. **Acuity** is a noun that means insight and perception and not naïve.

4. An **allusion** is when someone mentions something or makes an indirect reference. So the word with an opposite charge is avoidance.

5. To be **audacious** is to be bold, daring, and fearless, not fearful.

6. If something is **banal**, it is trite and common. Unique is the antonym.

7. **Bucolic** is used to describe a place that is pastoral and rural, so urban (relating to the city) is the opposite.

8. To be **chary** is to be cautious and shy, but certainly not audacious (daring).

9. To go somewhere, or do something, in a **circuitous** manner is to be indirect about it. Roundabout is a synonym while undeviating is an antonym.

10. To **compound** is to combine or augment and not to break down.

Practice 2

11. **True.** To be **emphatic** is to be forceful and vigorous.

12. **True.** To **emulate** is to imitate.

13. **False.** When a task is **exacting**, it requires great care. It is anything but easy.

14. **True.** **Facile** means simplistic.

15. **True.** If something is **implausible** it is improbable and inconceivable.

16. True. If someone is **impudent**, she or he is bold and cocky, with little regard for others.

17. False. **Hubris** is excessive pride and confidence.

18. False. To be **incorrigible** is to be incapable of correction.

19. True. To be **incredulous** is to be skeptical.

20. True. If something is **indiscriminate** it is random or haphazard.

21. False. If a task is **insuperable**, it isn't easy or surmountable. The task is insurmountable or impossible.

Practice 3

22. Interminable is synonymous with endless, so predetermined and finite are antonyms.

23. Nebulous is synonymous with vague, while defined and distinct are antonyms.

24. Precipitous is synonymous with abrupt. Leisurely is the opposite and mild, in one of its meanings, evokes a far different feeling and idea.

25. Prodigal is synonymous with wasteful and reckless. Vigilant and cautious are near-antonyms.

26. Seraphic is synonymous with sweet or angelic. Devilish and rapscallion are antonyms of **seraphic**.

27. Timorous means timid. An audacious and impudent person is not timid!

28. Tremulous is synonymous with trembling. Fearless and courageous are both antonyms.

29. Unavailing is synonymous with hopeless, so hopeful and optimistic are more like opposites, even though you wouldn't call a situation hopeful or optimistic.

30. Unwarranted is synonymous with unjustified, thus making justified an antonym. Necessary is another antonym of **unwarranted**.

31. Unwitting is synonymous with unsuspecting; wary and cautious are its antonyms.

32. Veritable is synonymous with absolute. Phony and counterfeit are its antonyms.

CHAPTER 15 TEST

Okay, it's time to put your memory to the test! Take your time not only with the questions but in reading the answer explanations that follow. Set a goal for yourself—80% (24 correct answers) is recommended—and if you don't reach that goal, go back and read through the chapter again. Good luck!

DIRECTIONS: For questions 1–15, circle T for True or F for False. For questions 16–30, circle the synonym.

1. T F **prodigal**—recklessly extravagant
2. T F **aberration**—unusual
3. T F **derivative**—original
4. T F **feral**—sterile
5. T F **impudent**—humble
6. T F **incorrigible**—uncorrectable
7. T F **indiscriminate**—random
8. T F **precocious**—immature
9. T F **stalwart**—strong and brave
10. T F **unwarranted**—justified
11. T F **insuperable**—insurmountable
12. T F **dilapidated**—renovated
13. T F **bucolic**—pastoral
14. T F **brazen**—shameless
15. T F **implausible**—conceivable

16. **veritable:**	questionable	absolute	unverifiable
17. **unwitting:**	unintentional	conscious	intentional
18. **nebulous:**	vague	defined	concrete
19. **interminable:**	restricted	endless	predetermined
20. **incredulous:**	unsuspecting	innocent	skeptical
21. **emphatic:**	vigorous	timid	quiet

22. **compound:**	to separate	to pound	to combine
23. **circuitous:**	indirect	electrical	direct
24. **anachronistic:**			
	avant-garde	outdated	couture
25. **banal:**	trite	uncommon	original
26. **adroit:**	novice	skillful	incompetent
27. **abase:**	to compliment	to revere	to demean
28. **haughty:**	arrogant	humble	modest
29. **tremulous:**	fearless	assertive	trembling
30. **unavailing:**	useful	ineffective	effective

Answers and Explanations

1. **True.** **Prodigal** describes someone or something that is recklessly extravagant.

2. **True.** An **aberration** is unusual.

3. **False.** To be **derivative** is to imitate and copy; it is to be unoriginal.

4. **False.** When something is **feral** it is characteristic of a wild animal.

5. **False.** **Impudent** means marked by disregard for others. It is not synonymous with humble.

6. **True.** To be **incorrigible** is to be uncorrectable.

7. **True.** If someone is **indiscriminate**, he or she does things haphazardly and randomly.

8. **False.** To be **precocious** is not to be immature. It is to be unusually advanced at an early age.

9. **True.** If someone is **stalwart**, he or she is strong and brave.

10. **False.** When something is **unwarranted** it is not justified. It is groundless and unjustified.

11. **True.** To be **insuperable** is to be insurmountable.

12. **False.** When a building is **dilapidated** it is anything but renovated. It is run-down and in a state of disrepair.

13. **True.** A **bucolic** scene is pastoral and rural (related to the countryside).

14. **True.** To be **brazen** is to be shameless and bold.

15. **False.** To be **implausible** is not to be conceivable. It is to be improbable and inconceivable.

16. **Veritable** means absolute, not questionable or unverifiable (impossible to prove).

17. **Unwitting** is unintentional. Conscious and intentional are its antonyms.

18. To be **nebulous** is to be vague and not defined or concrete.

19. Interminable means endless, which is contrary to restricted and predetermined.

20. To be **incredulous** is to be skeptical. Unsuspecting and innocent are its antonyms.

21. When someone is **emphatic**, he or she is vigorous and not timid or quiet.

22. Compound means to combine. To separate is the opposite and to pound is irrelevant.

23. When something is done in a **circuitous** way, it is done in an indirect manner, making direct an incorrect choice. Electrical is a distracter based on the confusion of circuit (electrical) and circuitous.

24. The adjective **anachronistic** means outdated. Avant-garde and couture are two French words associated with up-to-the-minute art and fashion, respectively.

25. To be **banal** is to be common or trite, so uncommon and original are both wrong.

26. When someone is **adroit**, that person is neither a novice, nor incompetent. Quite the opposite, when someone is adroit, he or she is skillful.

27. To **abase** someone is to demean him or her. It is far from complimenting or revering (admiring) that person.

28. To be **haughty** is to be arrogant. Humble and modest are both antonyms.

29. If someone is **tremulous**, that person is trembling and neither fearless nor assertive.

30. If someone's efforts can be described as **unavailing**, they are ineffective. Useful and effective are antonyms of **unavailing**.

CHAPTER 16

Most Frequently Tested GRE Words

The words you need to ace the GRE

BUILDING BLOCK QUIZ

This "building block" quiz samples the information that you will learn in this chapter, plus two words from the previous chapter. By answering the 12 questions below, you will get a sense of how closely you should study this chapter in order to master the vocabulary you'll need for the GRE! Keep in mind, should you happen to choose incorrect answers for the final two questions, you'll want to go back to chapter 15 for some review.

DIRECTIONS: Fill in the blanks, using the most appropriate of the four multiple-choice answers. The correct answer will always fit into the sentence grammatically.

1. The speech Dean Finch gave after the tragic events of September 11, 2001 was _____ and provided everyone a bit of relief.

    (A) disparate (B) felicitous
    (C) didactic (D) chimerical

2. When the football team won the first game, it was a(n) _____ after four losing seasons.

    (A) normality (B) anonymity
    (C) juxtaposition (D) anomaly

3. Gina finally ended her _____ relationship with Rich after he punched her car and dented it.
   (A) prodigy (B) tempestuous
   (C) vernal (D) cathartic

4. Lynn's one fault was that she lived life in a _____ way and was always surprised by changes.
   (A) myopic (B) assiduous
   (C) fallacious (D) abstruse

5. Even though Francine and Shaniqua came from _____ backgrounds, they were the best of friends.
   (A) didactic (B) ambidextrous
   (C) ephemeral (D) disparate

6. What Dave lacked in _____, he had in street smarts, so he rarely got into trouble.
   (A) continence (B) continents
   (C) malapropisms (D) circumlocution

7. Mrs. Reagan _____ her daughter to get married, which only made dating more difficult.
   (A) scolded (B) aplombed
   (C) beseeched (D) amalgamated

8. After graduating from business school, Jeffrey
   _____ his academic success to his grandfather.
   (A) blamed (B) disparated
   (C) excoriated (D) imputed

9. For her twenty-first birthday, Meg's parents
   sent her on a _____ to Europe.
   (A) confluence (B) continence
   (C) sojourn (D) celerity

10. At the _____ of the school year, the
    highways near the university became filled with
    packed cars covered in college stickers.
    (A) cessation (B) acumen
    (C) celerity (D) presage

11. Alberto's little brother was _____, so
    they were able to do a lot of things together.
    (A) obdurate (B) precocious
    (C) salacious (D) propagate

12. When Nick's father called his A+ a(n)
    _____, it almost made him cry.
    (A) volition (B) pundit
    (C) aberration (D) platitude

Answers and Explanations

1. B. The speech Dean Finch gave after the September 11, 2001 attacks was **felicitous**, meaning suitable and appropriate (with a secondary meaning of "pleasurable"). Disparate means dissimilar, didactic means instructive, and chimerical means fanciful, none of which is appropriate.

2. D. The victory was an **anomaly**, or irregularity. Normality (ordinariness), anonymity (the state of being unknown or unnamed), and juxtaposition (combination) are all incorrect.

3. B. The relationship was **tempestuous**, meaning stormy and turbulent. Prodigy (genius), vernal (springtime), and cathartic (therapeutic) are all poor choices in context.

4. A. Lynn lived life in a **myopic** way, meaning she lacked foresight and so was surprised by change. Assiduous (persevering), fallacious (misleading), and abstruse (obscure) are all incorrect.

5. D. The girls came from **disparate** (dissimilar) backgrounds. None of the other answers—didactic (instructive), ambidextrous (able to use either the left or right hand), and ephemeral (short-lived)—makes sense.

6. A. Dave lacked **continence**, which means self-control. Continents makes no sense in this context. Malapropisms (mistaking one word for another in a comic way) and circumlocution (the act of doing something in a roundabout way) are both incorrect.

7. C. Mrs. Reagan **beseeched** (begged and pleaded) her daughter, which probably sounded a lot like scolding, but that answer is incorrect. Aplombed is not a real word and amalgamated (compounded) doesn't fit.

8. D. Jeffrey **imputed** (credited) his success to his grandfather. He didn't blame his grandfather, nor did he criticize (excoriate) him. Disparate mean dissimilar, but disparated isn't a word.

9. C. Meg went on a **sojourn**, which is a temporary stay or visit. Confluence (coming together), continence (self-control), and celerity (rapidity) are all incorrect.

10. A. Those packed cars marked the **cessation**, or end, of the school year. Acumen (insight), celerity (speed), and presage (to foretell) don't work in the context of the sentence.

11. B. Alberto's little brother was **precocious**, which means he was unusually advanced for his age. He was neither obdurate (stubborn) nor salacious (scandalous in a sexual way), and propagate (reproduce and spread) does not fit grammatically. If you answered this question incorrectly, you might want to go back to chapter 15 for some review.

12. C. An **aberration** is something different from the norm, and it hurt Nick's feelings when his father said that about his good grade. Volition is a wish, a pundit is an expert, and a platitude is a cliché. If you answered this question incorrectly, you might want to go back to chapter 15 for some review.

PART ONE

abstruse adj. (ahb STROOS)—difficult to comprehend; obscure
Stan's presentation was so good that he turned an *abstruse* subject into one the rest of the class could understand.

acumen adj. (AH kew men)—sharpness of insight
Charlie's literary *acumen* helped him to do very well on the Advanced Placement exam, so he got to skip Freshman English.

amalgamate v. (ah mal gah MATE)—to mix, combine
Giant Industries *amalgamated* with Mega Products to form Giant-Mega Products Incorporated.

ambidextrous adj. (am bih DEX truss)—able to use both hands equally well
The *ambidextrous* chef was able to chop vegetables with both hands, simultaneously.

anomaly n. (ah NOHM ah lee)—irregularity or deviation from the norm
The single albino deer in the herd was an *anomaly*.

anonymity adj. (ah noh NIHM eh tee)—condition of having no name or an unknown name
The actor said he wanted to return to the *anonymity* of his school days.

aplomb n. (uh PLAHM), (uh PLUHM)—self-confidence, assurance
For such a young dancer, Daria had great *aplomb*, making her perfect to play the young princess.

arduous adj. (AR joo uhs)—extremely difficult, laborious
Amy thought she would pass out after completing the *arduous* hike.

assiduous adj. (uh SIH joo ihss)—diligent, persistent, hardworking
The chauffeur scrubbed the limousine *assiduously* on the morning of the wedding.

beseech v. (bah SEECH)—to beg, plead, implore
Taylor *beseeched* Mr. Jones to give her a second chance at the music store, but he refused.

catharsis n. (KAH thar sis)—purification, cleansing
Plays can be more satisfying if they end in some sort of emotional *catharsis* for the characters involved.

celerity n. (seh LEH rih tee)—speed, haste
The track team practiced with great *celerity*.

cessation n. (se SAY shun)—termination; halt; end
The *cessation* of the attacks meant that people could start using the park again at night.

chimerical adj. (kie mehr ih kuhl), (kie meer ih kuhl)—fanciful; imaginary, impossible
The inventor's plans seemed *chimerical* to the conservative venture capitalist.

circumlocution n. (SIR kuhm low KYOO shin)—roundabout, lengthy way of saying something
Ogden used endless *circumlocutions* to avoid discussing emotional issues.

FLASHBACK

Circum means *around*, so remember this word root when asked about **circumlocution**. It's a lengthy word that refers to a *lengthy way of saying something*, usually to *talk around* an issue.

Practice 1

DIRECTIONS: Consider the two word choices in the parentheses and circle the one that best fits in the context of the sentence.

1. Mary wrote a series of (chimerical OR assiduous) poems on the theme of lost love.

2. Because only his rap name was famous, G Boy enjoyed (ambidextrous OR anonymity) when making dinner and hotel reservations under his given name.

3. With amazing (circumlocution OR celerity), Kristina told everyone in school about the early dismissal.

4. Kenny was able to (amalgamate OR beseech) his English paper with his geography project, thus fulfilling both requirements at once.

5. Writing his graduate school application essay was a(n) (arduous OR timorous) task for Andy.

6. It was a sure sign that Paulette was nervous whenever she fell into a pattern of (rhetoric OR circumlocution).

7. Jacques wasn't the smartest boy in his class, but he was so (assiduous OR precious) that his grades were usually good.

8. Theo promised his supervisor that the recent tardiness was an (aplomb OR anomaly) and that it would never happen again.

9. The memorial service provided (catharsis OR anonymity) for everyone involved.

10. The (aplomb OR cessation) of the soccer season meant Yol had more time for her non-athletic friends.

11. Gary's political (acumen OR abstruse) always impressed his teachers.

Your Words, Your World

Don't have time to sit around repeating these words to yourself, over and over again, in order to remember them? Well, you don't have to! The following exercise tests your knowledge of the material . . . without requiring that you take a test! So your job now is to really *think* about what you read, and to really think about the questions that follow.

Abstruse—What is the most *confusing* class you have ever taken? What subject matter was the most *difficult for you to comprehend*? Well, if you think of that nightmarish year—all of that *perplexing*, *puzzling*, *obscure* information—you will remember what **abstruse** means.

Ambidextrous—Do you know anyone who is **ambidextrous**? Or is it you, yourself, who can do things with *both hands*? If you have this *ability*, what is it that you like to do with your *left and right hands*?

Aplomb—Do you know someone who does everything with **aplomb**? Does someone come to mind when you think of *self-confidence*, *assurance*, and *poise*? Hopefully, the answer is yes. Because if that person can help you to remember what **aplomb** means, all of his or her *style* and *composure* will have helped you as well.

Beseech—When was the last time you had to *beg* for something? And what was it you *pleaded* for or *implored* another person to do for you? To *grovel* like that is to **beseech** and it never feels very good, so if you can remember that feeling at least you'll also remember the meaning of **beseech**.

PART TWO

confluence n. (KAHN floo uhns)—the act of two things flowing together; the junction or meeting place of two things
At the Young Democrats meeting, the head of the Young Independents signed an agreement, leading to a *confluence* of ideas between the two organizations.

continence n. (KAHN tih nihns)—self-control, self-restraint
Lucy exhibited impressive *continence* in steering clear of fast food, and she quickly lost ten pounds.

didactic adj. (di DAK tik)—excessively instructive
Helen's father was overly *didactic*, turning every family activity into a lesson.

MEMORY TIP

Didactic rhymes with tactic and to be *excessively instructive* is a tactic some people take. Somewhat boring in the classroom, it is especially lethal in a book or movie. Remember, it is a mistake to take a tactic that's **didactic**.

---

disparate adj. (DIS par it)—dissimilar, different in kind
Although the two sisters looked like identical twins, their personalities were quite *disparate*.

ephemeral adj. (eh FEM ehr ihl)—momentary, transient, fleeting
The lives of mayflies seem *ephemeral* to us, since the flies' average lifespan is a matter of hours.

excoriate v. (ehk SKOHR ee ayt)—to censure scathingly; to express strong disapproval
The three-page letter to the editor *excoriated* the magazine for printing the rumor without verifying it.

extrapolation n. (ihk STRAP uh lay shuhn)—the use of known data and information to determine what will happen in the future, prediction
Through the process of *extrapolation*, the study group was able to develop a theory.

fallacious adj. (fuh LAY shuhs)—tending to deceive or mislead; based on incorrect logic (a fallacy)
The *fallacious* statement "the earth is flat" was the subject of Matthew's essay.

felicitous adj. (feh LIH sih tus)—suitable, appropriate; well-spoken
The father of the bride made a *felicitous* speech at the wedding, contributing to the overwhelming success of the evening.

imperturbable adj. (IHM puhr TUHR buh buhl)—unshakably calm and steady
No matter how disruptive the children became, the babysitter remained *imperturbable*.

impute v. (im PYOOT)—to attribute, to credit
When Greg found the puddle, he quickly *imputed* it to his puppy.

juxtaposition n. (juks ta po ZISH un)—side-by-side placement for comparison
Marty's presentation included the *juxtaposition* of an acorn and a walnut.

laudable adj. (LAW du buhl)—deserving of praise
Kristin's dedication was *laudable*, but she just didn't have the skills to be a professional soccer player.

malapropism n. (MAAL uh prahp ihz uhm)—the accidental, often comical, use of a word that resembles the one intended but has a different, often contradictory, meaning
Everybody laughed at the *malapropism* when the announcer said "public boredcasting" instead of "public broadcasting."

myopic adj. (mie AHP ihk), (mie OH pihk)—lacking foresight, having a narrow view or lack of long-range perspective
The *myopic* business owner didn't want to spend money on advertising, and as a result his store went out of business.

Practice 2

DIRECTIONS: Match the word (left column) with its definition (right column).

12. **laudable**	to attribute
13. **felicitous**	momentary
14. **excoriate**	self-control
15. **continence**	comical use of the wrong word
16. **fallacious**	appropriate
17. **ephemeral**	excessively instructive
18. **impute**	determining what will happen
19. **malapropism**	deserving of praise
20. **didactic**	to censure harshly
21. **extrapolation**	misleading

Your Words, Your World

Don't have time to sit around repeating these words to yourself, over and over again, in order to remember them? Well, you don't have to! The following exercise tests your knowledge of the material . . . without requiring that you take a test! So your job now is to really *think* about what you read, and to really cement an image in your mind. You never know when you'll need that image to pop up again.

Confluence—Although **confluence** usually refers to people or ideas, it also can be used to describe something in nature. The image of two streams *joining* to form a river will probably serve you best. By picturing the two bodies of water *flowing as one*, you will remember that **confluence** means *two things coming together*.

Disparate—When two people are *different*, they are **disparate**. Think of twins who don't look alike (fraternal). They are probably *dissimilar* in a number of ways. Even identical twins have *contrasting* traits.

Juxtaposition—A **juxtaposition** is a *side-by-side comparison* of two things. Imagine two different iPods held up for *evaluation* and *judgment*. Imagine looking at a magazine article *comparing* them as you try to decide which you want to buy. The image in that magazine, one iPod next to the other, should symbolize the word **juxtaposition** for you. (Also realize that the word **juxtaposition** contains "position.")

Myopic—Think of the most *judgmental* person you know. Now, picture his or her *tiny* little brain. **Myopic** means *small-minded*, but not in a physical sense. In a more intellectual way, **myopic** is used to describe someone who *lacks vision and foresight*. But the image of a *little brain* should do the trick!

Imperturbable—Picture a small, rocky island rising out of the ocean. No matter how much it is buffeted by the wind and waves, it remains firmly rooted and unmoved. This image should help you remember that to be **imperturbable** is to be *calm* and *steady*. It is to be *unflappable* and *in control*. It is to be a *pillar of strength*.

PART THREE

obdurate adj. (AHB door it)—stubborn, hardhearted; inflexible
Professor Raimes was *obdurate* on the issue and no amount of
persuasion could change his mind.

perfunctory adj. (pir FUNK tu ree)—done in a routine manner;
indifferent; automatic
The secretary listened to the boy's story, gave a *perfunctory* smile, and
told him to sit and wait.

platitude n. (PLAA tuh tood)—overused and trite remark
Instead of voicing the usual *platitudes* in his commencement remarks,
the comedian gave a memorable and inspiring speech to the
graduating class.

presage n., v. (PREH sihj)—something that foreshadows, a feeling of
what will happen in the future; to predict or foretell
The Persian Gulf War was a *presage* to the fall of Saddam Hussein.

prodigy n. (PRAHD ih jee)—person with exceptional talents
Her parents noticed very early in her childhood that Lezlie was a math
prodigy, capable of doing the most complex computations in her head.

propagate v. (PROP uh gayt)—to spread out; to have offspring
While Gary only told one person about his new girlfriend, news of the
relationship *propagated* around the school within an hour.

pundit n. (PUHN diht)—one who gives opinions in an authoritative
manner
Victor wanted to be a *pundit* of the arts when he grew up, and he
practiced by writing reviews in the campus paper.

revile v. (rih VEYE uhl)—to criticize with harsh language, verbally abuse
The new plant manager had several plans in the works, all of which
were *reviled* by the workers' union.

salacious adj. (suh LAY shuhs)—appealing to sexual desire
The audience was shocked by the comedian's *salacious* routine.

sojourn n. (SOH jurn)—a temporary stay, visit
After graduating from college, Iliani embarked on a *sojourn* to China.

stasis n. (STAY sihs)—a state of static balance or equilibrium, stagnation
The rusty World War II tank in the town park had obviously been in *stasis* for years.

> ## MEMORY TIP
> The first syllable of **stasis** is pronounced "stay" and this might help you to remember that **stasis** means to "stay" *in balance* or to be in a *sta(y)te of equilibrium.*

supersede v. (soo puhr SEED)—to cause to be set aside; to force out of use as inferior, replace
Ellen's computer was still running version 2.0 of the software, which had long since been *superseded* by three more versions.

supplant v. (suh PLAANT)—to replace (another) by force, to take the place of
After the military officers overthrew the government, a dictator *supplanted* the democratically elected president.

tempestuous adj. (tehm PEHS choo uhs)—stormy, turbulent
The camping trip was cut short when the drizzle turned into a *tempestuous* downpour.

transitory adj. (TRAAN sih tohr ee)—short-lived, existing only briefly
The football team's championship victory was *transitory* because it was disqualified when officials discovered that players had used steroids.

vernal adj. (VUHR nuhl)—related to spring; fresh
Bea basked in the balmy *vernal* breezes, happy that winter was coming to an end.

volition n. (vole ISH un)—free choice, free will; act of choosing
Of his own *volition*, Darius admitted to cheating on the test.

zephyr n. (ZEH furh)—a gentle breeze; something airy or insubstantial
The *zephyr* from the ocean made the intense heat on the beach bearable.

Practice 3

DIRECTIONS: In completing the sentences, use 14 of the 15 words below. Use each of the words just once.

pundit	salacious	volition	perfunctory	supplanting
platitude	prodigy	obdurate	propagate	reviled
transitory	sojourn	stasis	presage	superseded

22. Nelson's parents told everyone he was a _____ on the piano, but most people secretly disagreed.

23. On Jill's _____ to Africa, she came to see the world in a different light.

24. For Jamal, studying for the science exam _____ studying for the math quiz.

25. Mr. Meyers told his sons that they could sleep away the sunny day according to their own _____.

26. Professor Lieberson's _____ had little effect on her students as they had heard her give others the exact same compliment.

27. After _____ the dean, the associate dean moved into the bigger office and began to run the college as he saw fit.

28. To _____ word of the school orchestra's appearance at the mall, the group posted flyers around the campus.

29. By October things had calmed down and the professors felt the university had reached a point of acceptable _____.

30. Marv was the college's unofficial political
_____ and even had a weekly column
in the school newspaper.

31. The fans _____ the visiting team so
much that Coach George issued an apology on
behalf of the home team.

32. By the second week, Nancy was able to deliver
the daily announcements in a _____,
highly professional manner.

33. Luke was so _____ that even his ailing
grandfather couldn't get through to him.

34. The cast was disappointed when Dean Gardner
decided that their play was too _____ for
the college, but many of them understood.

35. Frieda's six months at Morgan Middle School
seemed _____ at the time, but she would
always remember them fondly.

Your Words, Your World

Don't have time to sit around repeating these words to yourself, over
and over again, in order to remember them? Well, you don't have to!
The following exercise tests your knowledge of the material . . . without
requiring that you take a test! So your job now is to really *think* about
the following words and how they apply to your everyday life.

Vernal—Just saying the word **vernal** should trigger a memory of how
the *first warm breeze* of the year feels. And if you need more than a
physical reminder, just think of the *vernal equinox* (usually March 20th
or 21st), when the hours of daylight and darkness are of equal length.
Vernus is Latin for "*belonging to spring*" and **vernal** always *relates to
spring*.

Zephyr—The first *vernal* breeze might be a **zephyr**. The root of the
word **zephyr** can be found in the Greek *Zephyrus*, a god personified by
the western *wind*. Most of the time, **zephyr** is used in reference to a
gentle breeze, but it can also mean something *light* and *insubstantial*.

Tempestuous—This adjective can be used to describe a raging *storm* or figuratively to represent things like relationships and situations (*stormy, turbulent*). To trigger your memory, just think of one of those *thunderstorms* that comes in the summer. If you need further help in remembering what **tempestuous** means, think of Mother Nature as having a *"temper"* during these *powerful storms*.

Presage—**Presage** means *to foreshadow* or to give *a feeling of what will happen in the future*. There is always a day or two in the winter when the sun comes out, a warm wind blows (perhaps a vernal zephyr), and the birds begin to sing. And this **presages**, or *signifies*, the coming spring

PRACTICE ANSWERS AND EXPLANATIONS

Practice 1

1. Mary wrote **chimerical**, or fanciful, poems. While she may have worked hard to write them, the poems themselves can't be assiduous (hardworking).

2. G Boy appreciated his **anonymity**, or ability to go unrecognized, under his given name. Ambidextrous means being able to use both hands equally well, so it is irrelevant in this context.

3. Kristina spread the word with **celerity** (speed). If she'd done it with circumlocution, it would have been in a long, roundabout way, and it's unlikely the news would have reached everyone in school.

4. To **amalgamate** is to combine, which is exactly what Kenny did with his assignments. To beseech is to beg and plead and has nothing to do with Kenny's work.

5. An **arduous** task is an extremely difficult task, and it was very tough for Andy to write the essay. Timorous means timid and makes no sense—Andy may have been timid in writing his essay, but the task itself can't be afraid.

6. **Circumlocution** (roundabout) is nearly the opposite of rhetoric (oratory skills); whenever Paulette took a long time getting to her point, it was because she was nervous.

7. Jacques was **assiduous**, which means he was persistent and a hard worker. Precious (valuable and dear) is a distracter as it sounds like precocious, which means mature.

8. Theo called his late arrival an **anomaly**, which means an irregularity. Aplomb is self-confident assurance, so it makes no sense in context.

9. The memorial service provided **catharsis**—a cleansing release of emotions—for the mourners. The other choice, anonymity, would mean that the mourners were unrecognized, which doesn't make sense.

10. **Cessation** means termination or end, while aplomb means self-assurance and doesn't work in the sentence. Yol had more time because her soccer season ended, so **cessation** is the answer.

11. Gary's political **acumen** (insight) earned him the respect of his teachers. Abstruse means difficult to comprehend or obscure, and is incorrect.

Practice 2

12. To be **laudable** is to be deserving of praise.

13. When something is **felicitous**, it is appropriate and fortunate.

14. To **excoriate** is to censure harshly.

15. **Continence** means self-control.

16. Someone or something **fallacious** is misleading and tending to deceive.

17. **Ephemeral** means momentary, fleeting, or brief.

18. To **impute** is to attribute or credit.

19. A **malapropism** is a comical misuse of a word or phrase. Yogi Berra is famous for his malapropisms.

20. Someone or something **didactic** is excessively instructive.

21. An **extrapolation** is a way of determining what will happen.

Practice 3

22. Nelson might not have been a **prodigy** (person with exceptional talents) on the piano, but his parents certainly were proud!

23. Jill's trip to Africa was merely a **sojourn**, or temporary stay, but it had a big impact on her.

24. Preparing for the exam **superseded** (took the place of or overruled) reviewing for the quiz.

25. **Volition** is free will and Mr. Meyers was giving his sons a choice.

26. A **platitude** is an overused remark and Professor Lieberson seems to have been using her compliments a bit too much. "Tired" is a current phrase that refers to something overused, such as a **platitude**.

27. **Supplanting** means replacing (usually by force), and this is what the associate dean did to the dean (probably not by force!).

28. To **propagate** is to spread and in this case, the orchestra was spreading word of its gig.

29. **Stasis** is a state of balance or equilibrium and when the university calmed down, it had reached this state.

30. To be a political **pundit** is to give opinions in an authoritative voice, which is exactly what Marv did.

31. The fans **reviled** the other team, which means they criticized the players with harsh language.

32. Nancy delivered the announcements in a **perfunctory** (routine and automatic) manner.

33. To be **obdurate** is to be stubborn.

34. The **salacious** (appealing to sexual desire) play was called off and rightly so, according to some of the cast members.

35. Frieda's memories of the school were good, even though her time there was **transitory**, or short-lived.

CHAPTER 16 TEST

Okay, it's time to put your memory to the test! Take your time not only with the questions but in reading the answer explanations that follow. Set a goal for yourself—80% (24 correct answers) is recommended—and if you don't reach that goal, go back and read through the chapter again. Good luck!

DIRECTIONS: For questions 1–15, circle T for True or F for False. For questions 16–30, circle the synonym.

1. T F	**myopic**—lacking foresight
2. T F	**prodigy**—an untalented person
3. T F	**sojourn**—a long vacation
4. T F	**pundit**—an opinionated authority
5. T F	**fallacious**—tending to mislead
6. T F	**continence**—self-control
7. T F	**acumen**—lacking insight
8. T F	**excoriate**—to censure
9. T F	**platitude**—original remark
10. T F	**presage**—to foreshadow
11. T F	**revile**—to criticize
12. T F	**volition**—free will
13. T F	**didactic**—lacking instruction
14. T F	**zephyr**—a storm
15. T F	**juxtaposition**—an upside-down position

16. **anomaly:**	regularity	irregularity	contact
17. **supersede:**	to take over	to cede	to be great
18. **celerity:**	celebrity	slothfulness	speed
19. **transitory:**	short-lived	severe	permanent
20. **impute:**	to discredit	to attribute	to relieve
21. **chimerical:**	fanciful	realistic	possible
22. **beseech:**	to search	to beg	to demand

23. **cessation:**	termination	commencement	initiation
24. **ephemeral:**	eternal	momentary	skin
25. **laudable:**	appalling	unworthy	deserving praise
26. **arduous:**	affluent	uncomplicated	extremely difficult
27. **obdurate:**	stubborn	flexible	compliant
28. **supplant:**	to support	to replace	to concede
29. **imperturbable:**			
	calm	impulsive	high-strung
30. **aplomb:**	aghast	insecurity	self-confidence

Answers and Explanations

1. True. To be **myopic** is to be lacking foresight. Associate "opic" with optical to help recall the sight part of this definition.

2. False. A **prodigy** is a person, usually a young person, with exceptional talent. Young or old, this person definitely is not untalented.

3. False. A **sojourn** is actually a short stay or visit, so a long vacation is wrong.

4. True. A **pundit** is, indeed, an opinionated authority. The authority of **pundits** derives from their informed and insightful opinions.

5. True. To be **fallacious** is to tend to deceive or mislead. A con man is **fallacious**.

6. True. **Continence** is synonymous with self-control.

7. False. **Acumen** refers to a sharpness of insight and not a lack of insight. John Madden has athletic acumen and thus is one of the most popular football analysts ever.

8. True. To **excoriate** is to censure scathingly.

9. False. A **platitude** is not original. It is an overused remark. Cliché is a synonym.

10. True. To **presage** is to foreshadow.

11. True. To **revile** is to criticize with harsh language.

12. True. If one does something by one's own **volition**, it is an act of free will.

13. False. To be **didactic** is not to be lacking instruction, but to be excessively instructive. A novel might be criticized as being overly didactic.

14. False. A **zephyr** is a gentle breeze and not a storm.

15. False. A **juxtaposition** is a side-by-side placement for comparison and has nothing to do with an upside-down position.

16. An **anomaly** is an irregularity. Regularity is an antonym while contact is irrelevant.

17. To **supersede** is to take the place of something or to take over, and not to cede (yield) or to be great.

18. **Celerity** is speed, so slothfulness is an antonym. Celebrity is a look-alike distracter.

19. To be **transitory** is to be short-lived. Severe (extreme; harsh) is incorrect while permanent is an antonym of **transitory**.

20. To **impute** is to attribute or credit, so to discredit and to relieve are incorrect.

21. **Chimerical** means fanciful, therefore realistic and possible are its antonyms.

22. To **beseech** is to beg. To demand is an antonym and to search is unrelated.

23. A **cessation** is a termination, so commencement and initiation are antonyms.

24. To be **ephemeral** is to be momentary or transitory. Eternal is the opposite while skin is irrelevant.

25. **Laudable** means deserving praise; appalling and unworthy have the opposite meaning.

26. If a task is **arduous** it is extremely difficult and therefore anything but uncomplicated. Affluent means wealthy, so that is also incorrect.

27. To be **obdurate** is to be stubborn, so flexible and compliant are its antonyms.

28. To **supplant** is to replace. To support and to concede are incorrect because they are near-antonyms of **supplant**.

29. **Imperturbable** means calm, definitely not impulsive or high-strung!

30. **Aplomb** is self-confidence and poise. Insecurity suggests the opposite, while aghast means horrified.

CHAPTER 17

Most Commonly Misused Words

You'll never mix up "affect" and "effect" again

BUILDING BLOCK QUIZ

This "building block" quiz samples the information that you will learn in this chapter, plus two words from the previous chapter. By answering the 12 questions below, you will get a sense of how closely you should study this chapter in order to master the vocabulary words that people commonly mispronounce, misspell, and confuse with other words. Keep in mind, should you happen to choose incorrect answers for the final two questions, you'll want to go back to chapter 16 for some review.

DIRECTIONS: Fill in the blanks, using the most appropriate of the four multiple-choice answers. The correct answer will always fit into the sentence grammatically.

1. When the bully tried to _____ Jimmy's lunch money, Jimmy wisely told the teacher.

   (A) abject (B) expropriate

   (C) equivocate (D) expatriate

2. Laura looked really _____ after Gabe broke up with her.

   (A) object (B) fulsome

   (C) abject (D) incipient

3. Hillary was a bright girl, but for some reason she told the most _____ lies.

(A) patent (B) obscure

(C) temporal (D) titular

4. *Schindler's List* _____ the class in ways Mr. Verrone hadn't predicted.

(A) disassembled (B) dissembled

(C) effected (D) affected

5. Xavier's constant _____ was a source of anger and upset for his parents.

(A) duplication (B) Spartan

(C) propensity (D) duplicity

6. When Heather and Jack stopped arguing in public, it was a(n) _____ sign that their marriage counseling was working.

(A) ostensible (B) discomfit

(C) apathetic (D) osteoporosis

7. The newspaper's refusal to publish the environmentalist's editorial about global warming _____ him.

(A) exacerbated (B) excoriated

(C) exasperated (D) unadulterated

8. Mrs. Klein had to admit that her class was indeed _____ when only three of its members showed up for the car wash fundraiser.

(A) pathetic (B) empathetic

(C) salient (D) apathetic

9. At the wedding, Nina's parents were impressed
   with how _____ all her friends were.
   (A) urbane (B) urban
   (C) querulous (D) abject

10. Dr. Jennings quickly tired of Sandra's
    _____ ways and canceled all future
    appointments with her, citing the importance
    of honest communication in therapy.
    (A) frank (B) inveterate
    (C) surreptitious (D) intemperate

11. Mr. Goings often _____ his students and
    no one was saddened by the announcement of
    his retirement.
    (A) replete (B) reviled
    (C) enjoined (D) apprised

12. Umberto's efforts on behalf of homeless chil-
    dren were _____ and at the end of the
    year, he won the Community Service Award.
    (A) unequivocal (B) tractable
    (C) laughable (D) laudable

Answers and Explanations

1. B. To **expropriate** is to forcibly take property (just what you'd expect from a bully). Equivocate (be evasive), expatriate (live abroad), and abject (hopeless) are all incorrect.

2. C. If someone is **abject**, like Laura, then she is miserable and not incipient (just beginning), fulsome (flattering), or an object.

3. A. A **patent** lie is an obvious lie. An obscure lie would be vague and although that's close, patent is better. Temporal means sequential and titular means supposed, neither of which works.

4. D. Not to be confused with an effect (a consequence), **affect** means to produce an emotional response, as *Schindler's List* did. Effect can be used as a verb meaning to bring about, but it has nothing to do with emotions. Dissembled (pretended) and disassembled (taken apart) are both incorrect.

5. D. Xavier's deception, or **duplicity**, upset his parents. Duplication (repetition), Spartan (simple, sparse), and propensity (tendency) make no sense in context, even if Xavier had a propensity to lie.

6. A. Heather and Jack had reached an **ostensible** (apparent, but possibly hiding a deeper meaning) resolution of their differences: they no longer argued, at least not in public. Discomfit (to embarrass) and apathetic (uninterested) are both incorrect while osteoporosis (a health condition in which the bones become brittle) is just a distracter.

7. C. The environmentalist was **exasperated**, or frustrated, because the newspaper would not publish his opinion. The newspaper's decision did not exacerbate him (make him worse), excoriate him (harshly criticize him), or unadulterate him (an adjective meaning absolutely pure, not a verb).

8. D. Mrs. Klein had to admit that her students were **apathetic**, meaning they had little care, or feeling, for others. Although their turnout was pathetic (pitiful), they were not personally pathetic. Neither were they salient (outstanding) nor empathetic (understanding the feelings of others).

CHAPTER 17: MOST COMMONLY MISUSED WORDS 369

9. A. Nina's parents thought her friends were **urbane**, which means courteous and refined and not urban (related to a city), querulous (argumentative), or abject (hopeless).

10. C. Sandra's **surreptitious** (sneaky) ways ruined Dr. Jennings's trust in her. To be intemperate is to be extreme, to be frank is to be honest (thus an antonym), and to be inveterate is to be confirmed.

11. B. To **revile** is to criticize with harsh language, which nobody likes to hear. Enjoined (commanded), apprised (informed), and replete (stuffed) are all incorrect. If you answered this question incorrectly, you might want to go back to chapter 16 for some review.

12. D. **Laudable** means deserving of praise and definitely applies to Umberto. Unequivocal (plain and clear), tractable (good), and laughable are not good choices. If you answered this question incorrectly, you might want to go back to chapter 16 for some review.

PART ONE

abject adj. (AAB jekt)—miserable, pitiful
After finding the *abject* bird on the ground, we took it inside and called the Audubon Society.

apprise v. (uh PRIYZ)—to inform. French for "to teach" or "to inform."
Emanuel had to *apprise* his boss when a package arrived.

enjoin v. (ehn JOYN)—to direct or impose with urgent appeal, to order with emphasis; to forbid
Patel explained that he is *enjoined* by his culture from eating the flesh of a cow, which is sacred in India.

enmity n. (EN mih tee)—hostility, antagonism, ill will
After the car accident, there was so much *enmity* between the two families that the Bells decided to move away.

equivocate v. (ih KWIHV uh kayt)—to avoid committing oneself in what one says, to be deliberately unclear
Officer Cardea had no patience for suspects who wasted his time *equivocating*.

expropriate v. (eks PRO pree ayt)—forcibly take one's property; to seize
Missy explained she'd missed the past two weeks of school because her family's apartment and car had been *expropriated* by the government for taxes owed.

fulsome adj. (FOOL suhm)—abundant, flattering in an insincere way
Right before grades were given, many *fulsome* students stopped by Mrs. Leibowitz's office.

MEMORY TIP

Sometimes compliments come with strings attached. Chock-full of strings! So let the "ful" in **fulsome** remind you that this word describes someone who gives compliments, but in an insincere way (because he or she wants something).

---

incipient adj. (ihn SIHP ee uhnt)—beginning to exist or appear; in an initial stage
The *incipient* idea seemed brilliant, but the Spanish Club officers knew it needed much more development.

intemperate adj. (in TEM per ut)—not moderate
The *intemperate* climate in the desert meant boiling hot days and bitter cold nights.

inveterate adj. (ihn VEHT uhr iht)—firmly established, especially with respect to a habit or attitude; unchangeable
An *inveterate* risk-taker, Lori tried her luck at bungee-jumping.

malingerer n. (muh LIN gehr ehr)—one who evades responsibility by pretending to be ill
Andrew had the reputation of being a *malingerer* just because his older brother was one.

patent adj. (PAA tehnt)—obvious, evident
Moe could no longer stand Frank's *patent* fawning over Heather and told him so.

portentous adj. (pohr TEHN tuhs)—self-important; arrogant
The minister always spoke in a *portentous* way, which irritated many congregants.

propensity n. (proh PEHN suh tee)—a natural inclination or preference
Natalie had a *propensity* for lashing out at others when stressed, so her family and friends stayed away at exam time.

Practice 1

DIRECTIONS: After reading the three choices, circle the one that you think is the *antonym*.

1. **abject:**	joyous	unhappy	miserable
2. **apprise:**	to inform	to conceal	to tell
3. **enjoin:**	to order	to command	to beg
4. **expropriate:**	to confiscate	to purchase	to seize
5. **fulsome:**	critical	overgenerous	flattering
6. **incipient:**	developing	established	initial
7. **intemperate:**	rational	immoderate	extreme
8. **inveterate:**	adaptable	established	unchangeable
9. **patent:**	obvious	apparent	unclear
10. **portentous:**	pompous	humble	pretentious

Your Words, Your World

Don't have time to sit around repeating these words to yourself, over and over again, in order to remember them? Well, you don't have to! The following exercise tests your knowledge of the material . . . without requiring that you take a test! So instead of memorizing, your job now is to really *think* about what you read, and to really think about the questions that follow.

Enmity—When was the last time a story in the news made you angry? When did something upset you to the point of *hostility*? Is this a regular occurrence? Do you often find yourself in a state of **enmity** as you fling the remote control in disgust? Hopefully not! **Enmity** equates a state of *antagonism*. If the news makes you feel this way, if it's so bad that you feel *irritated* after watching, maybe you should turn off the TV and spend some more time with this book!

Equivocate—What chore, errand, or job do you **equivocate** about more than any other? What is it that you hate so much, you *beat around the bush, make excuses,* and *avoid doing it at all costs*? What, more than anything else in the world, makes you want to *avoid committing yourself*? To be *deliberately unclear* when giving your answer? Perhaps it's baby-sitting, having lunch with a certain friend or relative, or walking the dog.

Malingerer—Do you go so far as to be a **malingerer** to get out of doing the above task? Whether it's going to school or mowing the lawn, do you *willingly deceive* so that you don't have to do it? Do you *evade responsibility by pretending to be ill*?

Propensity—If given the *choice*, what is your *preference*? What do you *like* to do when you have free time? What is your *natural inclination*? Do you have a **propensity**, or *preference*, when it comes to activities? Perhaps your **propensity** is for listening to music, talking to friends on the phone, using IM, visiting chat rooms, or watching TV. What are you *predisposed* to do with your free time?

PART TWO

querulous adj. (KWER uh lus)—complaining, grumbling
Nick's boss was tired of his *querulous* attitude and threatened to dock an hour's pay if he complained again.

replete adj. (rih PLEET)—abundantly supplied, complete
Even though Tim's music collection was *replete* with over a thousand CDs, he decided to purchase an iPod.

salient adj. (SAY lee uhnt)—prominent, of notable significance
Joan finally told Hank that his most *salient* characteristic was his tendency to dominate every conversation.

Spartan adj. (SPAHR tihn)—highly self-disciplined; careful, strict; marked by simplicity
While training, Cheech preferred to live in a *Spartan* room so he could shut out all distractions.

specious adj. (SPEE shuhs)—having the ring of truth but actually being untrue; deceptively attractive
The students were disappointed to learn that the band's mention of a show in the auditorium was just a *specious* promise.

surreptitious adj. (sir up TISH iss)—secret, stealthy
George had to be *surreptitious* when he slipped the birthday card in Janet's handbag.

tangential adj. (tan JEN shul)—digressing, diverting
Dave's arguments were always *tangential* to the conversation, and people began to ignore him after a while.

temporal adj. (TEHMP ore uhl)—having to do with time
The history test would include a *temporal* fill-in-the-blank section, so Margaret studied a time line she'd created herself.

titular adj. (TIHCH yoo luhr)—existing in title only; having a title without the functions or responsibilities
Carla was thrilled to be voted Homecoming Queen until somebody explained that the *titular* honor didn't mean she could boss anybody around.

tractable adj. (TRAK te bul)—easily managed or controlled
During the second quarter, Francine's classes were *tractable* and so she decided to get a part-time job.

> **MEMORY TIP**
>
> Ask a farmer if he'd prefer to go back to the days of having his plow pulled by oxen or horses and he'll tell you . . . tractors make things much more **tractable**!

umbrage n. (UHM brij)—offense, resentment
Becky took *umbrage* with the principal's accusation that she'd been smoking in the bathroom.

unadulterated adj. (uhn ah DUL ter ay ted)—absolutely pure
Jenny liked to tell people she only drank bottled water because it was *unadulterated*.

unequivocal adj. (uhn eh KWEV ih kul)—absolute, certain
The jury's verdict was *unequivocal*: the sadistic murderer would be locked up for life.

urbane adj. (erh BANE)—courteous, refined, suave
Although Tom thought of himself as an *urbane* college student, everybody at home just thought he was full of himself.

veracious adj. (ver AH shus)—truthful, accurate
Suspecting her son's excuse for coming home late wasn't *veracious*, Sue decided to check his story.

Practice 2

DIRECTIONS: Consider the definition and then circle T for True or F for False.

11. T F   **replete**—complete
12. T F   **salient**—insignificant
13. T F   **specious**—deceptively false
14. T F   **surreptitious**—truthful
15. T F   **tangential**—digressing
16. T F   **titular**—exciting
17. T F   **tractable**—easily managed
18. T F   **umbrage**—inoffensive
19. T F   **unequivocal**—absolute
20. T F   **veracious**—inaccurate
21. T F   **unadulterated**—unchanged

Your Words, Your World

Don't have time to sit around repeating these words to yourself, over and over again, in order to remember them? Well, you don't have to! The following exercise tests your knowledge of the material . . . without requiring that you take a test! So your job now is to really *think* about what you read, and to really cement an image of each of these confusing words in your mind. You never know when you'll need that image to pop up again.

Spartan—The **Spartans** were a warlike people, highly *self-disciplined* and *austere* (stern) in their ways. Sparta was a powerful city-state in ancient Greece and if you can recall its *prudent* people, you'll have no problem answering any questions about **Spartan**.

Temporal—If you are musical, you can keep *tempo*. Picture a metronome on top of a piano or even the snapping of fingers to keep *time*. This will help you to recall that **temporal** means *having to do with time*. **Temporal** refers more often to *chronological order* than to rhythm, but if music is your thing, use the association with *tempo* to help yourself out.

Urbane—Imagine the most *polite* city in the world. There is no crime and no one is rude. The streets are *clean* and the people are *courteous* and *kind*. In addition, they are all *highly educated*, *suave*, and *refined*. The inhabitants of this city, if it ever could exist, would be considered **urbane**. So to remember **urbane**, just think of this urban setting and its *cultured*, *sophisticated*, and *stylish* inhabitants.

Querulous—In your life, there is, more likely than not, a King of Complaining. This is someone who is always grumbling about something. This king's soul mate is the Queen of **Querulous**, who is always *argumentative* and *irritable*. Who would want to hang out with that kind of king and queen?

PART THREE

NOTE: The following list pairs words commonly confused for one another.

access n. (AK ses)—ability to obtain or make use of
The student council president fought, unsuccessfully, to get Internet *access* in the cafeteria.

excess n. (ek SES)—overload, overindulgence; extra
Jill partied to *excess* and had to miss the family reunion the next day.

affect v. (ah FEKT)—to produce an emotional response; to influence
Manny was really *affected* by the play and couldn't stop thinking about it all week.

effect v. (eh FEKT)— to cause; to produce
Although many worried that the World Trade Center tragedy would drive people out of New York City, the terrorist attack did not *effect* this migration.

apathetic adj. (ahp ah THET ik)—having little feeling, emotion, or interest
Yulitza's joke made her mother fear that Yulitza was truly *apathetic* about poverty and hunger.

empathetic adj. (ehm pah THEH tihk)—sympathetic; compassionate; understanding the feelings of others
Kenny showed just how *empathetic* he was when he donated all of his graduation money to AIDS relief.

censor v. (SEN sir)—to examine in order to suppress or delete anything considered objectionable
It was clear the declassified government documents had been *censored*, as several paragraphs had been crossed out.

censure v. (SEN shur)—to find fault; to criticize; to find blameworthy
While Congress decided whether or not to *censure* the president, the reporters waited eagerly outside.

disassemble v. (dis ah SEM buhl)—to take apart
From a young age, Carmen liked to *disassemble* her toys and then put them back together.

dissemble v. (dih SEM bul)—to pretend, disguise one's motives
With his parents and the principal staring at him, Billy could only *dissemble* for so long.

discomfit v. (dis KUM fit)—to put into a state of embarrassment and humiliation
Darren liked to *discomfit* everyone with his dirty jokes, but one day a teacher overheard and sent him to detention.

discomfort v. (dihs KUM fort)—to make uneasy; embarrass
Sometimes the best books *discomfort* the reader, showing that person something about the world that he or she had never considered before.

MEMORY TIP

Discomfit and **discomfort** are sometimes confused with one another and this isn't just because they sound the same. Their definitions are actually quite similar. Just think of people being embarrassed and uncomfortable when you're asked about **discomfit** and **discomfort** and chances are you'll get the question right.

---

duplicity n. (doo PLISS ih tee)—deception, dishonesty
The two girls claimed to be best friends, but their relationship was always being tested by *duplicity*.

duplication n. (dup li KAY shun)—the act of making an exact copy of something
Henry used his artistic talents for *duplication*, and everyone was always impressed with his reproductions of famous paintings.

exacerbate v. (ig ZAS ur bayt)—to aggravate, intensify the bad qualities of
Often times, when people try to self-medicate with illegal drugs, it only *exacerbates* the problem.

exasperate v. (ex AHS per ate)—to cause irritation or annoyance to
By December, the students had *exasperated* Mr. Meyers to the point that he was ready to quit.

ostensible adj. (ah STEN sihbel)— apparent, perceived; for display
Endorsed by the school paper, Tammy was the *ostensible* front-runner in the race for student council president; however, Ryan actually had more student support.

ostentatious adj. (ahs sten TAY shus)—flamboyant and arrogant; eye-catching; pretentious
The number of BMWs in the parking lot was an *ostentatious* display of the students' wealth.

Practice 3

DIRECTIONS: Read the three possible synonyms, then circle the word you think best defines the word in bold.

22. **excess:**	entrance	necessary	indulgence
23. **effect:**	to cause	to incite	to sadden
24. **empathetic:**	pathetic	sympathetic	unfeeling
25. **censure:**	to send	to blame	to suppress
26. **dissemble:**	to pretend	to take apart	to follow through
27. **discomfort:**	to make uneasy	to make happy	to comfort
28. **duplicity:**	imitation	truth	dishonesty
29. **exacerbate:**	to aggravate	to improve	to enhance
30. **ostentatious:**	modest	pretentious	obvious

Your Words, Your World

Don't have time to sit around repeating these words to yourself, over and over again, in order to remember them? Well, you don't have to! The following exercise tests your knowledge of the material . . . without requiring that you take a test! So your job now is to really *think* about the following words and how they apply to your everyday life. NOTE: You will notice that these are the words that are often confused with the ones in the previous synonym activity. After looking at them separately in two different activities, you should have an easier time telling them apart in the future.

Access—Internet **access**, **access** to that concert you're dying to see, **access** to the phone number of the pizza place, **access** to the information you need to finish your research paper: these days, it's not just about *being able to obtain* what you want or need, it's about being able to do it quickly and easily.

Affect—Think about what **affects** you most, about what *produces an emotional response*. Recall what **affects** you in a good way, what *makes you* sad, what *makes you* angry, and even what *makes you* hungry! These are all things that *influence how you feel*: things that **affect** you.

Apathetic—Pathetic is not a synonym of **apathetic** (but in the opinion of many, to be **apathetic** is to be pathetic). Try and remember the last time a story in the news made you mad because a person or group of people showed *little feeling, emotion, or interest in another person or group of people*. Whether it was a war or a case of domestic violence, you probably became angry because somebody involved had *total disregard* for another human being. This *lack of caring* is **apathy**.

Censor—Another thing that might affect you in a negative way is to be **censored**. Have you ever written anything for school or your job, and had it **censored** by your teacher or manager? Have you ever believed in something and been unable to describe and discuss it because somebody *suppressed* you? Think of **censorship** as the opposite of freedom of expression. Sometimes, there are legitimate reasons to *gag* somebody (as when a judge issues a gag order, or when the army protects sensitive information during wartime), but most of the time **censorship** is just an attempt to *stifle* an individual.

Disassemble—Simply put, to **disassemble** is to *take apart*. Imagine the pieces of a toy, spread out across the floor. The hard part is assembling it again, right? Often a paper for school or a report for work has to be *pulled apart* and put back together again during the editing process. If this has happened to you you'll surely remember what **disassemble** means.

Discomfit—One common phrase these days is "diss" as in "disrespect." If you have ever been *dissed* by somebody, you have been **discomfited**. You have been *embarrassed* in front of other people. You have been *humiliated* by another person. It's happened to everybody: just remember that to be *dissed* is to be **discomfited**.

Duplication—If you've ever had to make photocopies, then you know what **duplication** is. Burning a CD is an act of **duplication** that leaves you with the original CD and an *identical* **duplicate**. To print two *copies* of a photo also is *to make two things that are exactly alike*.

Exasperate—Often the worst days are those days when you come home feeling *annoyed* and *upset*. These are the days when something happened at school, at work, or out with family or friends, to **exasperate** you. Just remember, without those *frustrating* times, the good days wouldn't seem so good.

Ostensible—At its best, **ostensible** means *apparent*, but at its worst something that is **ostensible** is *disappointing* in that it leads you to believe something that turns out not to be true on closer examination. The actual thing is not what you originally *perceived*, thus the *disappointment*. When a friend promises to do something but then bails out on you at the last minute, claiming to be sick, you might consider this excuse to be **ostensible**, to say the least.

PRACTICE ANSWERS AND EXPLANATIONS

Practice 1

1. The antonym of **abject** is joyous. Miserable and unhappy are synonymous with **abject**.

2. Inform and tell are synonymous with **apprise**, while conceal is the antonym. No one ever says "Keep me **apprised** of the situation" because he or she wants the truth of the matter to be concealed.

3. The antonym of **enjoin** is to beg, while to order and to command are its synonyms.

4. To **expropriate** is to seize and to confiscate, so to purchase is an antonym.

5. The antonym of **fulsome** is critical, while overgenerous and flattering are its synonyms.

6. The antonym of **incipient** is established. Developing and initial both refer to origins and are synonyms of **incipient**.

7. The antonym of **intemperate** is rational. Immoderate and extreme are definitely not rational; they are **intemperate**.

8. The antonym of **inveterate** is adaptable. Established and unchangeable are synonyms of **inveterate**.

9. The antonym of **patent** is unclear, since obvious and apparent are its synonyms.

10. The antonym of **portentous** is humble. Pompous and pretentious are its synonyms.

Practice 2

11. **True.** **Replete** means complete. Let the rhyme remind you.

12. **False.** **Salient** is defined as significant and is definitely not insignificant.

13. **True.** **Specious** means deceptively false.

14. **False.** **Surreptitious** means secret and stealthy, not truthful.

15. True. **Tangential** is synonymous with digressing and diverting.

16. False. **Titular** means existing in title only, so exciting is not the definition.

17. True. **Tractable** means easily managed or easy to do. Put the emphasis on the "able" in trac*able*.

18. False. To take **umbrage** is to take offense. Inoffensive is incorrect.

19. True. Absolutely, positively . . . **unequivocal** means absolute.

20. False. If something is **veracious**, it is accurate, so inaccurate is incorrect.

21. True. **Unadulterated** means pure, untainted, and unchanged.

Practice 3

22. Excess is synonymous with indulgence, so necessary is an antonym. Entrance should be associated with access and not **excess**.

23. To **effect** is to cause. Although to incite and to sadden have similar meanings, they relate to emotions and therefore are more properly associated with affect, not **effect**.

24. To be **empathetic** is to be sympathetic and not pathetic (pitiful, sad) or unfeeling.

25. To **censure** is synonymous with to blame. To suppress is synonymous with censor, and to send is irrelevant.

26. To **dissemble** is to pretend and not to follow through. To take apart is to disassemble and should not be confused with **dissemble**.

27. To **discomfort** is to make uneasy, so to make happy and to comfort are antonyms.

28. Duplicity is synonymous with dishonesty and the opposite of truth. Imitation should be associated with duplicate and not **duplicity**.

29. To **exacerbate** is to aggravate and not to improve or to enhance.

30. If someone, or something, is **ostentatious** it is pretentious. Modest is an antonym and obvious has more to do with ostensible than **ostentatious**.

CHAPTER 17 TEST

Okay, it's time to put your memory to the test! Take your time not only with the questions but in reading the answer explanations that follow. Set a goal for yourself—80% (24 correct answers) is recommended—and if you don't reach that goal, go back and read through the chapter again. Good luck!

DIRECTIONS: For questions 1–15, circle T for True or F for False. For questions 16–30, circle the synonym.

1.	T	F	**propensity**—a natural tendency
2.	T	F	**tangential**—quite important
3.	T	F	**enjoin**—to order emphatically
4.	T	F	**inveterate**—new
5.	T	F	**exasperate**—to annoy
6.	T	F	**discomfit**—to praise
7.	T	F	**dissemble**—to pretend
8.	T	F	**surreptitious**—sincere
9.	T	F	**tractable**—easily managed
10.	T	F	**access**—ability to obtain
11.	T	F	**expropriate**—to undo
12.	T	F	**fulsome**—excessive
13.	T	F	**Spartan**—undisciplined
14.	T	F	**salient**—prominent
15.	T	F	**apprise**—to inform

16. **enmity:**	enemy	hostility	cooperation
17. **intemperate:**	immoderate	sensible	moderate
18. **patent:**	unclear	obscure	obvious
19. **querulous:**	complaining	tractable	amiable
20. **urbane:**	unrefined	courteous	uncouth
21. **veracious:**	hungry	truthful	inaccurate
22. **effect:**	to cause	to consume	to make emotional

23. **empathetic:**	unsympathetic	ambivalent	compassionate
24. **censor:**	to suppress	to sponsor	to promote
25. **duplicity:**	honesty	deception	to copy
26. **ostensible:**	perceived	authentic	imperceptible
27. **unequivocal:**	ambivalent	ambiguous	absolute
28. **abject:**	miserable	optimistic	to protest
29. **umbrage:**	admiration	resentment	acclaim
30. **portentous:**	unassuming	insignificant	ominous

Answers and Explanations

1. True. A **propensity** is a natural inclination or preference. Every person has a **propensity** for something.

2. False. If something is **tangential** it is a digression from the main topic and not quite important.

3. True. To **enjoin** is to order, or command, emphatically.

4. False. If something is **inveterate** it is not new, but firmly established and set in its ways.

5. True. To **exasperate** is to annoy.

6. False. To **discomfit** is to perplex and embarrass, not to praise.

7. True. To **dissemble** is to deceive by pretending. Don't confuse this word with disassemble, to take apart.

8. False. If something is done in a **surreptitious** manner, it is done in a secret, stealthy way. Sincere means honest and is obviously incorrect.

9. True. If a thing is **tractable** it is easily managed or controlled.

10. True. To have **access** is to have the ability to obtain or make use of something. It's nice to have **access** . . . in excess!

11. False. To **expropriate** is to forcibly take property. It is not to undo.

12. True. The adjective **fulsome** means abundant or excessive, especially in terms of flattery.

13. False. When a person is described as **Spartan**, he or she is self-disciplined and austere, so undisciplined is the opposite of **Spartan**.

14. True. To be **salient** is to be prominent and of notable significance.

15. True. To **apprise** is to inform.

16. Enmity means hostility. Cooperation is a near-antonym and enemy is a closely related word: an enemy is one who bears **enmity**.

17. To be **intemperate** is to be immoderate (over the top, excessive). Moderate and sensible mean the opposite.

18. If something is **patent** it is blatant or obvious. It is definitely not unclear or obscure (vague).

19. A **querulous** person is always complaining, and not amiable (friendly) or tractable (easily managed).

20. To be **urbane** is to be courteous and sophisticated. Unrefined and uncouth are antonyms of **urbane**.

21. Veracious means truthful. Voracious describes a strong appetite, so hungry is a distracter. Inaccurate is an antonym.

22. To **effect** is to cause. To make emotional is to affect, so that is wrong. To consume is irrelevant.

23. If someone is **empathetic**, he or she is compassionate. Unsympathetic and ambivalent are antonyms of **empathetic**.

24. To **censor** is to suppress. It is the opposite of to sponsor and to promote.

25. Duplicity means deception. Honesty is the opposite and to copy is the definition of duplicate.

26. Ostensible means perceived, but it often refers to an inauthentic or misleading perception. So both authentic and imperceptible are incorrect.

27. Unequivocal means absolute. Ambiguous and ambivalent are defined as unclear and unsure, respectively.

28. Abject means miserable. Optimistic has an opposed meaning and to protest is the definition of object.

29. To take **umbrage** is to be in a state of resentment. Admiration and acclaim refer to positive feelings for something, and are near-antonyms of **umbrage**.

30. Portentous means ominous and significant, so unassuming and insignificant are both incorrect.

CHAPTER 18

Fifty-cent Words You Can Actually Use

For the show-off in all of us

BUILDING BLOCK QUIZ

This "building block" quiz samples the information that you will learn in this chapter, plus two words from the previous chapter. By answering the 12 questions below, you will get a sense of how closely you should study this chapter in order to master the vocabulary that will help you even after you graduate from the school that accepted you upon learning that you aced the SAT or GRE! Keep in mind, should you happen to choose incorrect answers for the final two questions, you'll want to go back to chapter 17 for some review.

DIRECTIONS: Fill in the blanks, using the most appropriate of the four multiple-choice answers. The correct answer will always fit into the sentence grammatically.

1. The Health Department would only reveal that there was a fear of _____ chemicals in the area, and that was why the nature preserve was being inspected.

   (A) pathetic (B) pathogenic

   (C) anodyne (D) altruism

2. Professor Wheatley tried to teach _____
   and selflessness in addition to math.

   (A) altruism (B) selfishness

   (C) alto (D) compunction

3. Willy had always wanted a _____, but
   "Stinky" wasn't quite what he'd had in mind.

   (A) euphemism (B) milieu

   (C) exhortation (D) sobriquet

4. When Duane realized that his new doctor was
   completely _____ he asked his friends to
   recommend another physician.

   (A) inefficacious (B) efficacious

   (C) competent (D) effective

5. Larry joked about breaking into the credit card
   company's computer system to _____
   all of his debt.

   (A) convalesce (B) plunge

   (C) expunge (D) adumbrate

6. It was Anne's _____ that led her to
   admit to taking the money from the fundraiser.

   (A) conjunction (B) amalgamation

   (C) compunction (D) corruptibility

7. From a young age, Glenn had been a master of
   _____ so no one was surprised when he
   became a magician.

   (A) prestidigitation (B) consanguineous

   (C) neonate (D) inchoate

8. Mrs. Traylor told Gwen's parents that Gwen was one of the most _____ students she'd ever had the pleasure of teaching.
   (A) inefficient (B) ineffective
   (C) inefficacious (D) efficacious

9. Even though Miss Unger was in her first year of teaching, her _____ ways made her seem more mature, and more in control, than most rookies.
   (A) abstemious (B) absent
   (C) alimentary (D) anthropomorphic

10. Once Victoria decided that the school nurse was a(n) _____, she stopped going to her for bandages, advice, or anything else.
    (A) interlocutor (B) vicissitude
    (C) palimpsest (D) charlatan

11. The professor advised all the prospective teachers to never _____ a student in front of his or her peers.
    (A) grandiloquence (B) discomfit
    (C) expunge (D) amalgamate

12. All of the parents warned their children of the _____ offers on the Internet.
    (A) variegated (B) abstemious
    (C) specious (D) punctilious

Answers and Explanations

1. B. There was a fear of **pathogenic** (disease-causing) chemicals, not pathetic (pitiful), anodyne (bland), or altruism (unselfishness) chemicals.

2. A. Professor Wheatley was concerned with **altruism**, or the unselfish concern for the welfare of others. An alto is a female singer with a low range. Selfishness is an antonym of selflessness, but the sentence calls for a synonym instead. Compunction means regret and is also incorrect.

3. D. Willy had always wanted a nickname (**sobriquet**). Euphemism is close in that it is a word substituted for another word, but it's not close enough. A milieu is a setting and an exhortation is a strong written or verbal appeal.

4. A. This doctor was **inefficacious**, which means ineffective and incompetent. Efficacious, competent, and effective are all antonyms of **inefficacious**, thus incorrect.

5. C. Larry wanted to **expunge** (erase completely) his debt from the system. Convalesce (recover from illness), adumbrate (give a hint), and plunge don't work in the context of the sentence.

6. C. It was Anne's **compunction**, or feelings of regret, that led her to admit her guilt. Conjunction and amalgamation both mean merger or combination, so they're not right. Corruptibility fits the theme but refers to someone who can be convinced to commit a crime. It's unlikely that such a person would feel any **compunction**.

7. A. Glenn had been a master of **prestidigitation**, which is a cleverly executed trick or deception. Inchoate means unclear, consanguineous means of similar lineage, and neonate means a newborn, so all three are incorrect.

8. D. Gwen was **efficacious**, which means effective and efficient. Inefficient, ineffective, and inefficacious are all antonyms of the correct answer. They're also not the kind of thing that would make a student a "pleasure" to teach.

9. A. Miss Unger was **abstemious** (moderate and in control). If she had been absent, she wouldn't have been a very good teacher. Alimentary (pertaining to food) and anthropomorphic (assigning human characteristics to animals and inanimate things) are also incorrect.

10. D. Victoria thought that the school nurse was a **charlatan**, which means a quack or a fake. An interlocutor is a partner in conversation, so that's wrong. A vicissitude is a change and a palimpsest is an object that has been written on, erased, and written on again, so both of those answers are incorrect as well.

11. B. Teachers should never **discomfit**, or humiliate, their students. Expunge means obliterate and amalgamate means join together, neither of which makes sense here. Grandiloquence (a noun meaning pompous talk) does not fit the sentence, which requires a verb. If you answered this question incorrectly, you might want to go back to chapter 17 for some review.

12. C. All of the parents warned their kids of the **specious** (deceptively attractive) offers on the Internet. Variegated means multicolored, abstemious means self-disciplined, and punctilious means meticulous, so all three are wrong. If you answered this question incorrectly, you might want to go back to chapter 17 for some review.

PART ONE

abstemious adj. (aab STEE mee uhs)—done sparingly; consuming in moderation
Roger advised his children to be *abstemious* spenders, rather than blowing their allowances on candy and comic books.

adumbrate v. (AAD uhm brayt) (uh DUHM brayt)—to give a hint or indication of something to come
Whenever Miss Frey *adumbrated* about a test with an after-school review session, all of her students attended.

alimentary adj. (AAL uh mehn tuh ree) (AAL uh mehn tree)—pertaining to food, nutrition, or digestion
Frederique decided she wanted to work in an *alimentary* field, possibly as a nutritionist.

altruism n. (AL troo ihzm)—unselfish concern for others' welfare
Mitchell decided to become an Eagle Scout because of the group's focus on *altruism*.

amalgamation n. (ah MAL ga MAY shun)—consolidation of smaller parts
The concert was an *amalgamation* of songs from different pop artists.

anodyne n. (AAN uh diyn)—a source of comfort; a medicine that relieves pain
After a long day at the office, classical music was just the *anodyne* Regina needed.

anthropomorphic adj. (AAN thruh poh MOHR fihk)—suggesting human characteristics for animals and inanimate things
Many children's stories feature *anthropomorphic* animals such as talking pigs and wolves.

MEMORY TIP

To **morph** is a commonly used expression meaning to change and **anthro** means man, as in human. So it only makes sense that **anthropomorphic** refers to the *practice of assigning human characteristics* to animals and other nonhuman things.

charlatan n. (SHAR lah tan)—quack, fake
The *charlatan* of a doctor prescribed the wrong medication for hundreds of patients and found himself the subject of a class action suit.

compunction n. (kum PUHNK shun)—feeling of uneasiness caused by guilt or regret
When the principal didn't see any *compunction* in Daniel, she called the police to report that Daniel had slashed the tires of three teachers' cars.

consanguineous n. (kahn saang GWIHN ee uhs)—having the same lineage or ancestry; related by blood
Often, best friends will act as if they are *consanguineous*.

conundrum n. (ka NUHN druhm)—riddle, puzzle or problem with no solution
To Adam, algebra was a *conundrum*, and he believed he had no hope of ever passing the class.

convalesce v. (kahn vuhl EHS)—to recover gradually from an illness
After her bout with malaria, Tatiana needed to *convalesce* for a whole month.

convergence n. (kuhn VEHR juhns)—the state of separate elements joining or coming together
Mrs. Friedmann taught that a *convergence* of factors led to the start of World War I.

efficacious adj. (ef ih KAY shus)—effective, efficient
Nurse Gina was quite *efficacious*, and by the third day of school all of the student health files were in order.

emollient adj. (ee MOHL yent)—having soothing qualities, especially for skin
After using the *emollient* lotion on her sunburn, Dominique felt much more comfortable.

Practice 1

DIRECTIONS: Consider the two word choices in the parentheses and circle the one that best fits in the context of the sentence.

1. Kevin saved a lot of money because he was so (alimentary OR abstemious) in his spending.

2. Al's mother asked him to please just tell her what he wanted for lunch rather than (adumbrate OR convalesce).

3. Mr. Nednick used Peg's (anodyne OR altruism) as an example for all the other students.

4. The new band was an (amalgamation OR anthropomorphic) of two other bands that had just broken up.

5. Mike was revealed as a(n) (efficacious OR charlatan) when none of the people who had bought tickets from him could get into the show.

6. Rakeem's strong feelings of (compunction OR adumbrate) kept him from ever doing drugs again.

7. When Marty and Evan figured out that they were (abstemious OR consanguineous), they began to call one another "cousin."

8. Mr. Hall always told his students that there were no (alimentary OR conundrums) in math.

9. The Board of Education meeting turned out to be the site of a(n) (convergence OR anodyne) of several religious groups, all concerned with the new curriculum.

10. Principal Yee's new discipline system was (efficacious OR emollient) and the teachers and parents were thrilled.

Your Words, Your World

Don't have time to sit around repeating these words to yourself, over and over again, in order to remember them? Well, you don't have to! The following exercise tests your knowledge of the material . . . without requiring that you take a test! So your job now is to really *think* about what you've read, and to really think about the questions that follow.

Convalesce—When was the last time you had to *recover from an illness*? Or, better yet, what was the worst sickness you ever had and how long did it take you to **convalesce**? To **convalesce** is to *gradually get over being sick*. Think of the *lengthiest recovery* you ever had, and you'll be sure to remember this word.

Emollient—When you think of something *soothing*, especially something *soothing on your skin*, do you think of a blanket or do you think of *moisturizer*? Do you have a favorite blanket, perhaps from your childhood? If so, think of it whenever faced with the word **emollient** and you'll be able to recall the definition. If not, just think of *lotion* or *moisturizer*, particularly if you use either on a daily basis.

Anodyne—Is your favorite shirt an **anodyne**, a *source of comfort*? A more literal definition of **anodyne** is *a medicine that relieves pain*. However, the word is commonly used in a figurative sense to mean *something comforting*. So a certain kind of music or even a particular food might qualify as your **anodyne**. After you've had a bad day, what *makes you feel better*?

Anthropomorphic—Can you remember being a child and reading books with *talking animals*? You also probably had a favorite movie that included this element. Whenever an *animal can talk*, that indicates an **anthropomorphic** trait. Whenever *something nonhuman has human characteristics*, it is **anthropomorphic**.

Alimentary—Do you love *food*, or just one particular type of *food*? If so, let that pizza, cheeseburger, chili, or chocolate-chip cookie serve as your reminder: all things **alimentary** *pertain to food and nutrition.* (Of course, the list above probably isn't the most *nutritious* group of foods ever assembled.)

PART TWO

euphemism n. (YOO fuh mihz uhm)—an inoffensive and agreeable expression that is substituted for one that is considered offensive
Mr. Herbert was a good health teacher because he used *euphemisms* to help the students feel more comfortable with the subject matter.

expunge v. (ihks PUHNJ)—to erase, eliminate completely
The parents' association *expunged* the questionable texts from the children's reading list.

exhortation n. (eg zor TAY shun)—speech that advises or pleads
The minister's *exhortation* convinced the mayor to show mercy toward the juvenile delinquents.

grandiloquence n. (graan DIHL uh kwuhns)—pompous talk; fancy but meaningless language
The headmistress was notorious for her *grandiloquence* at graduation, and everybody feared having to sit through her speech.

MEMORY TIP

Grandiloquence even sounds high and mighty! The word is defined as *pompous, fancy talk*, and the trick is to put together **grand** (magnificent and sometimes self-important) and **–loquence** (the last part of eloquence, which means expressiveness): **grandiloquence**.

---

immutable adj. (im MYOOT uh bul)—unchangeable, invariable
Poverty seemed an *immutable* fact of life for the Wood family, but fortunately Beverly earned an academic scholarship to college.

implacable adj. (ihm PLAY kuh buhl) (ihm PLAA kuh buhl)—inflexible; not capable of being changed or pacified
Despite complaints from students and parents, Mr. Jacobsen was *implacable* about having the test the day before vacation.

inchoate adj. (ihn KOH iht)—being only partly in existence; unformed
Jessie had an *inchoate* first draft of her novel, with a couple of characters and scenes roughly sketched.

inefficacious adj. (in ef ih KAY shus)—ineffective, incompetent
Miss Collins' attempts to quiet the class were *inefficacious* as they ignored her and continued to yell.

invariable adj. (in VAR ee uh bul)—constant, unchanging
The university switched to the quarter system, despite the fact that trimesters had been an *invariable* aspect of the school for years.

interlocutor n. (in ter LAHK yu tur)—someone taking part in a dialogue
Everybody knew that Stew was a willing *interlocutor* with a real gift of gab.

FLASHBACK

Inter means *between*—given the fact that a conversation happens between two people, this word root should remind you of the meaning of **interlocutor**.

---

macabre adj. (muh KAA bruh) (muh KAA buhr)—having death as a subject; dwelling on the gruesome
Martin enjoyed *macabre* tales about werewolves and vampires.

malleable adj. (MAAL ee uh buhl)—easily influenced or shaped, capable of being altered by outside forces
Mr. Foster felt that all young minds were *malleable*, so he never, ever gave up on a student.

milieu n. (mihl YOO)—the physical or social setting in which something occurs or develops, environment
Quinchon was uncomfortable with the *milieu* at the club, so he left.

mutability n. (myoo tuh BIHL uh tee)—the quality of being capable of change, in form or character; susceptibility to change
The actress lacked the *mutability* needed to perform in the improvisational play.

Practice 2

DIRECTIONS: Match the word (left column) with its definition (right column).

11. **euphemism**	to eliminate
12. **exhortation**	environment
13. **expunge**	constant
14. **grandiloquence**	a speech offering advice
15. **implacable**	inflexible
16. **inchoate**	pompous talk
17. **inefficacious**	easily influenced
18. **invariable**	unformed
19. **malleable**	ineffective
20. **milieu**	an agreeable expression

Your Words, Your World

Don't have time to sit around repeating these words to yourself, over and over again, in order to remember them? Well, you don't have to! The following exercise tests your knowledge of the material . . . without requiring that you take a test! So your job now is to really *think* about what you read, and to really cement an image in your mind. You never know when you'll need that image to pop up again.

Interlocutor—Think of the person in the world you most enjoy talking to. Whether it's a best friend, a teacher, or one of your parents, picturing this certain somebody will help to remind you that an **interlocutor** is *someone taking part in a dialogue*. Just think, you may be somebody's favorite *conversationalist*!

Macabre—Stephen King is an author of **macabre** books. Clive Barker is a film producer who always makes *horror* movies that use *death* as a subject. Even if you don't enjoy such *gruesome* stories, keeping them in mind can help you remember this word.

Mutability—When you think of **mutability**, think of someone who is *flexible*. Think of someone who can *change* at the drop of a hat. Think of the friend who most embodies the quality of *being capable of change*. These are usually fun people to have around. (**Mutability** has nothing to do with mute, which means being unable to talk.)

Expunge—To **expunge** is to *eliminate completely*. If you've ever had a manager or teacher who, at a crucial moment, decided to cut you a break and *erase* an assignment, picture him or her now. Or maybe one of your parents *relieved* you of some sort of responsibility at home so that you could go have fun. Perhaps you had a ticket **expunged** from your driving record. Although **expunge** can be used to describe a *very harsh wiping out*, or *obliteration*, it's better to focus on the positive when you try to remember the definition.

PART THREE

neonate n. (NEE uh nayt)—a newborn child
With all the talk of *neonates* in science class, Jerry began to imagine life as a father.

obstreperous adj. (ahb STREP uh res)—troublesome, boisterous, unruly
The *obstreperous* boys lost their bathroom privileges and had to be escorted by an adult.

palimpsest n. (PAHL ihmp sehst)—an object or place having diverse layers or aspects beneath the surface.
When paper was expensive, people would just write over existing writing, creating a *palimpsest*.

pathogenic adj. (paa thoh JEHN ihk)—causing disease
Bina hoped her research of *pathogenic* microorganisms would help stop the spread of disease in developing nations.

perspicacious adj. (pur spi KAY shuss)—shrewd, astute, keen-witted
In Arthur Conan Doyle's stories, Sherlock Holmes uses his
perspicacious mind to solve mysteries.

phlegmatic adj. (flehg MAA tihk)—having a sluggish, unemotional
temperament
Waylon's writing was energetic but his *phlegmatic* personality wasn't
suited for television, so he turned down the interview.

prestidigitation n. (PREHS tih dih jih TAY shuhn)—a cleverly executed
trick or deception; sleight of hand
Denise's father was known for his practical jokes and *prestidigitation*,
but she was a very serious young lady.

MEMORY TIP

At six syllables, **prestidigitation** is one of longest words in this
book, and certainly the most difficult to pronounce. So
remember, if you can pronounce **prestidigitation**, that's a
cleverly executed trick.

---

punctilious adj. (puhngk TIHL ee uhs)—concerned with precise details
of codes or conventions
Being a *punctilious* student, Sarah never made any spelling mistakes
on her essays.

seminal adj. (SEH muhn uhl)—influential in an original way, providing
a basis for further development; creative
Randall's graduate work was considered *seminal* in the area of
quantum physics, inspiring many other scientists.

sobriquet n. (SOH brih KAY) (SOH brih KEHT)—a nickname
Before becoming president, Ronald Reagan was an actor. One of his
roles earned him the *sobriquet* "The Gipper."

tautological adj. (tawt uh LAH jih kuhl)—having to do with needless repetition, redundancy
Teoni tried to clarify things, but her *tautological* statements just further confused everyone.

unconscionable adj. (uhn KAHN shuhn uh buhl)—unscrupulous; shockingly unfair or unjust
Although Evan had stolen the purse, he made the *unconscionable* decision to blame it on his sister.

variegated adj. (VAAR ee uh GAYT ehd)—varied; marked with different colors
Mrs. Quinlon showed the class that the *variegated* foliage of the rain forest allows it to support thousands of animal species.

verisimilitude n. (VEHR ah sih MIHL ih tood)—quality of appearing true or real
Because they achieved a level of *verisimilitude*, reality TV shows saw their ratings soar.

vicissitude n. (vih SIHS ih tood)—change or variation; ups and downs
In his economics class, Allen learned that the key to stable investing is waiting out the *vicissitudes* of the stock market.

Practice 3

DIRECTIONS: In completing the sentences, use 10 of the 12 words below. Use each of the words just once.

tautological	verisimilitude	obstreperous
perspicacious	phlegmatic	vicissitudes
neonate	punctilious	variegated
pathogenic	palimpsest	sobriquet

21. Maleeka's _____ study habits were one reason for her good grades.

22. Dean always flattered his teachers, but he had such skills of _____ that his teachers never realized it.

23. Mr. Thomas brought the _____ to the front office as proof that Janice had erased her paper and added the correct answers after the test was done.

24. Tim tired of the _____ of the stock market and decided to keep all of his money in his mattress instead.

25. The parents were worried that the kids had eaten something _____ in the cafeteria because so many were now ill.

26. The new superintendent was _____ and soon the teacher's union, the Board of Education, and even the parents' group were all on board with her agenda.

27. The sophomores had the reputation of being _____, but their behavior was surprisingly good all year.

28. The diagram in the science book showed the _____ soil sample from ground level to twenty feet beneath the surface.

29. Maureen was anything but _____,
bringing excitement into every room she
entered.

30. Always repeating the same facts about lacrosse,
Kelvin made _____ statements that
annoyed his friends and family.

Your Words, Your World

Don't have time to sit around repeating these words to yourself, over
and over again, in order to remember them? Well, you don't have to!
The following exercise tests your knowledge of the material . . . without
requiring that you take a test! So your job now is to really *think* about
the following words and how they apply to your everyday life.

Sobriquet—In your group of friends, there are probably a few *nicknames*,
right? Well, simply think of your favorite *nickname*—maybe even your
own, if you have one—and use it as a reminder: a **sobriquet** is a
nickname.

Prestidigitation—**Prestidigitation** is a noun and means *a deception* or
well-executed trick. What's the best *trick* you ever heard of? Did one of
your friends *play a joke* on another friend? In many families or groups
of friends, there is at least one person who likes to play *pranks* on
others. Keeping this person in mind may be the trick you need to help
you remember this word.

Neonate—Embed in your mind the image of the last *child* to enter
your family. Think of the *baby* of the family and you will surely recall
that a **neonate** is a *newborn child*. Also, remembering that **neo** means
new should help.

Seminal—Has there been a **seminal** book, movie, song, or band in
your life that has *influenced* you? Has it *shaped your future*? When
something is *influential in an original way*, it is **seminal**. The world is
full of people who chose a career because of a **seminal** movie; people
who moved to a certain place because of a **seminal** book; and artists
and writers who were *influenced* by a **seminal** work.

Unconscionable—Every person carries a *horrible* memory of the first time he or she witnessed or was hurt by an **unconscionable** act. Something *shocking* happened to make you see the world in a slightly different way. This may have been something *unscrupulous* that a teacher did or maybe even a supposed friend. When an act is **unconscionable**, it is *shockingly unfair*, and unfortunately these acts are a fact of life.

PRACTICE ANSWERS AND EXPLANATIONS

Practice 1

1. Kevin was **abstemious**, which means he did things sparingly. Alimentary refers to food and is incorrect.

2. Rather than give hints (**adumbrate**), Al should just have told his mother what he wanted. To convalesce is to recover from illness, so that is an irrelevant answer.

3. Peg's **altruism** (unselfish concern for others) was held up as an example to all. An anodyne is a medicine that relieves pain, so that answer is incorrect.

4. An **amalgamation** is a consolidation or joining together, which is what the bands did. Anthropomorphic describes the assignment of human characteristics to nonhuman things.

5. Mike was not only a scalper but also a **charlatan**, or fake. Efficacious is an adjective meaning effective, but the sentence calls for a noun.

6. Rakeem's **compunction**, or feeling of guilt or regret, helped to keep him off drugs. To adumbrate means to hint and makes no sense in context.

7. **Consanguineous** means having the same ancestry, like Marty and Evan. Abstemious refers to doing something in moderation.

8. A **conundrum** is a problem with no solution, and Mr. Hall enjoyed telling his class that every math problem has a solution. Alimentary pertains to food and is both grammatically and contextually incorrect.

9. A **convergence** is a coming together, as the religious groups did at the meeting. An anodyne is something that provides relief, and the word doesn't fit the context.

10. The system was **efficacious**, which means effective, and not emollient, which means soothing to the skin.

Practice 2

11. A **euphemism** is an agreeable expression used to replace a distasteful expression.

12. An **exhortation** is an advisory speech arguing for a particular course of action.

13. To **expunge** means to eliminate.

14. **Grandiloquence** is pompous talk.

15. To be **implacable** is to be inflexible.

16. To be **inchoate** is to be unformed or just partially formed.

17. **Inefficacious** is synonymous with ineffective.

18. **Invariable** is the opposite of variable and means constant.

19. **Malleable** means easily shaped or influenced. It can be applied in a physical sense (to a substance like clay) or a mental sense (to an impressionable person).

20. **Milieu** means environment.

Practice 3

21. Maleeka was **punctilious**, which means concerned with details, especially rules, codes, and conventions.

22. Dean's **verisimilitude** (quality of appearing true) helped him to get away with flattering his teachers.

23. A **palimpsest** is an object that has layers, or a document that has been erased and written over. Through the layers, one can see what was originally written (in this case, Janice's original answers).

24. The **vicissitudes** (variation or ups and downs) of the stock market led Tim to give up on investing.

25. **Pathogenic** means causing disease, so it's easy to understand why the parents were concerned.

26. The superintendent was **perspicacious**, or shrewd and keen-witted.

27. **Obstreperous** is the answer as it means troublesome, boisterous, and unruly.

28. The diagram of the **variegated** (marked with different colors) soil layers helped to teach the science students to distinguish the different strata.

29. Maureen had an excitable personality, so she was not **phlegmatic** (having a sluggish, unemotional temperament).

30. Kelvin repeated the same information, which led his family and friends to be annoyed by his **tautological** (redundant) statements.

CHAPTER 18 TEST

Okay, it's time to put your memory to the test! Take your time not only with the questions but in reading the answer explanations that follow. Set a goal for yourself—80% (24 correct answers) is recommended— and if you don't reach that goal, go back and read through the chapter again. Good luck!

DIRECTIONS: For questions 1–15, circle T for True or F for False. For questions 16–30, circle the synonym.

1.	T	F	**verisimilitude**—appearing true
2.	T	F	**vicissitude**—variation
3.	T	F	**punctilious**—unconcerned with details
4.	T	F	**grandiloquence**—meaningful talk
5.	T	F	**abstemious**—done sparingly
6.	T	F	**anodyne**—a source of comfort
7.	T	F	**emollient**—not soothing
8.	T	F	**interlocutor**—a conversationalist
9.	T	F	**altruism**—selfish behavior
10.	T	F	**amalgamation**—consolidation of smaller parts
11.	T	F	**convergence**—a coming together
12.	T	F	**compunction**—guilt-free
13.	T	F	**unconscionable**—scrupulous behavior
14.	T	F	**conundrum**—a problem with no solution
15.	T	F	**inchoate**—undeveloped

16. **pathogenic:** trailblazing   healing   causing disease
17. **adumbrate:** to hint   to state   to berate
18. **charlatan:** a fake   a chieftain   a physician
19. **immutable:** variable   unchangeable   voiceless
20. **milieu:**   French food   environment   genre
21. **neonate:**   baby   senior citizen   octogenarian
22. **obstreperous:**
                    respectful   gracious   unruly

23. **sobriquet:**	a bouquet	a nickname	sobering
24. **expunge:**	to erase	to create	to plunge
25. **exhortation:**	press conference	advisory speech	conversation
26. **malleable:**	shapeless	resistant	easily influenced
27. **perspicacious:**	shrewd	naïve	obtuse
28. **invariable:**	inconsistent	erratic	unchanging
29. **inefficacious:**	unsuccessful	complete	efficient
30. **implacable:**	merciful	inflexible	makeshift

Answers and Explanations

1. **True. Verisimilitude** means appearing true.

2. **True. Vicissitude** is synonymous with change, variation, and ups and downs.

3. **False. Punctilious** actually describes someone who is concerned with details.

4. **False. Grandiloquence** is actually meaningless, pompous talk, not meaningful talk.

5. **True.** When something is done in an **abstemious** manner, it is done sparingly.

6. **True.** An **anodyne** is a source of comfort.

7. **False.** An **emollient** is also a source of comfort, most often in the form of a soothing lotion applied to the skin. Not soothing is therefore incorrect.

8. **True.** An **interlocutor** is a conversationalist, specifically someone taking part in a dialogue.

9. **False. Altruism** is unselfish concern for the welfare of others.

10. **True.** An **amalgamation** is the consolidation of smaller parts.

11. **True.** A **convergence** is a coming together of things.

12. **False.** A **compunction** is not guilt-free, but is distress caused by guilt or regret.

13. **False.** If an act is **unconscionable**, it is unscrupulous and shockingly unfair.

14. **True.** A **conundrum** is a problem with no solution.

15. **True. Inchoate** means unformed or only existing partially.

16. **Pathogenic** means causing disease, so healing is definitely out, as is trailblazing.

17. To **adumbrate** is to hint. It is not to state or to berate.

18. A **charlatan** is a fake and is often used in reference to a phony physician. Chieftain (leader) is also incorrect.

19. Immutable is synonymous with unchangeable. Voiceless is irrelevant and variable is an antonym of immutable.

20. A **milieu** is an environment. Like genre, the word is taken from the French, so genre (type or sort) and French food are both trick answers.

21. A **neonate** is a newborn baby, so senior citizen and octogenarian (someone in his or her eighties) are both incorrect.

22. Obstreperous means unruly, so respectful and gracious are its antonyms.

23. A **sobriquet** is a nickname. It is not a bouquet, nor is it sobering (a serious fact or incident that makes one thoughtful).

24. To **expunge** is to erase or delete. To create and to plunge (a sound-alike distracter) are both incorrect.

25. An **exhortation** is a catchphrase or an advisory speech. It is not a press conference; it isn't even a conversation, just a one-way speech.

26. To be **malleable** is to be easily influenced, so resistant is its antonym and shapeless is irrelevant.

27. Perspicacious means shrewd. Naïve and obtuse (overly trusting and stubborn, respectively) are its antonyms.

28. Invariable means unchanging, so inconsistent and erratic are both its antonyms.

29. To be **inefficacious** is to be unsuccessful. It is not to be complete and it definitely isn't to be efficient (a near-antonym of **inefficacious**).

30. Implacable means inflexible. Merciful is incorrect as to be merciful requires some flexibility and understanding. Makeshift, or crude and temporary, is also incorrect.

CHAPTER 19

Word Source Cumulative Test

Before moving on to bigger and better things, such as conquering an important exam or impressing family, friends, and potential employers with your new vocabulary, take the time to double-check your comprehension. Below, you will find a final Cumulative Test comprised of at least two words from each chapter of this book. From word roots all the way to "fifty-cent" words, you'll have the chance to flex your vocabulary muscle! Aim for 100% correct, and best of luck to you!

1.	T	F	**stoic**—indifferent
2.	T	F	**discretion**—disability
3.	T	F	**gregarious**—introverted
4.	T	F	**impugn**—to question
5.	T	F	**declaim**—to speak loudly
6.	T	F	**cataclysmic**—indestructible
7.	T	F	**evanescent**—momentary
8.	T	F	**assent**—to agree
9.	T	F	**amalgamation**—merger
10.	T	F	**requisition**—acquisition
11.	T	F	**actuate**—activate
12.	T	F	**dogmatic**—flexible
13.	T	F	**arbitrary**—consistent
14.	T	F	**condone**—to forgive
15.	T	F	**perfidious**—disloyal
16.	T	F	**avow**—to declare

17. T F **fait accompli**—to dine outside

18. T F **precocious**—precious

19. T F **ephemeral**—momentary

20. T F **apprise**—to misinform

21. **malleable:**
     maddening   easily influenced   difficult to convince

22. **dis**, as in dissemble:
     away from   close to   analyze

23. **mal**, as in malevolent:
     mediocre   superior   bad

24. **onus:**
     burden   solution   empowered

25. **vilify:**
     to promote   to contemplate   to slander

26. **cogent:**
     convincing   illogical   weak

27. **missive:**
     a problem   a letter   a mission

28. **vapid:**
     eye-catching   rapid   dull

29. **doleful:**
     sad   joyous   full

30. **opprobrious:**
     hopeless   shameful   optimistic

31. **augment:**
     to secure   to depend   to extend

32. **mitigate:**
     to ease   to sever   to relocate

33. **panache:**
     illogical statements   flamboyance   overused phrase

34. **beseech:**
     to implode   to beg   to acquiesce

35. **brazen:**
    shy   consistent   bold

36. **surreptitious:**
    stealthy   celebratory   repetitious

37. **affect:**
    to influence   to attend   to produce

38. **replete:**
    incomplete   complete   competent

39. **crescendo:**
    a gradual increase   a rapid ascent   a sparkle

40. **rankle:**
    to anger   to mediate   to meditate

Answers and Explanations

1. True. To be **stoic** is to be indifferent. A **stoic** person is rarely affected by emotions.

2. False. **Discretion** does not equate disability. When one uses **discretion** one demonstrates good judgment.

3. False. To be **gregarious** is not to be introverted. On the contrary, it is to be outgoing and sociable.

4. True. To **impugn** is to call into question.

5. True. To **declaim** is to speak loudly and vehemently, as in a dramatic recitation or a persuasive speech.

6. False. **Cataclysmic** does not mean indestructible. It describes an event that is severely destructive.

7. True. If something is **evanescent** it is momentary or short-lived.

8. True. To **assent** is to express agreement. Wouldn't you agree?

9. True. An **amalgamation** is a merger or a consolidation of smaller parts.

10. False. Acquisition is incorrect even though it rhymes with **requisition** and has a related meaning. **Requisition** describes a demand for something, while acquisition describes the act of actually obtaining it. The **requisition** is the request.

11. True. To **actuate** is to activate or to put into motion.

12. False. To be **dogmatic** is to be rigidly fixed in one's opinions. To be flexible is the opposite.

13. False. **Arbitrary** is an antonym of consistent. Its correct definition is inconsistent or random.

14. True. To **condone** is to forgive or overlook a fault.

15. True. If someone is **perfidious**, he or she is disloyal, faithless, and untrustworthy.

16. True. To **avow** is to state openly or declare.

17. False. Al fresco comes from Italian and means "in the fresh (air)" (outside). **Fait accompli** is French for "accomplished fact" and refers to something that cannot be undone.

18. False. A **precocious** child is unusually advanced for his or her age. He or she may be precious, but that is not the correct definition.

19. True. **Ephemeral** is synonymous with evanescent and means momentary, transient, or fleeting.

20. False. To **apprise** is to give notice or inform, while to misinform is the opposite.

21. When someone is **malleable**, he or she can be influenced easily. Material things such as clay or molten glass can also be malleable, or easily shaped. Difficult to convince is the opposite and maddening is unrelated.

22. The word root **dis** means away from. To **dissemble** is to disguise one's motives under a false appearance, as those who dissemble try to stay away from the truth. Close to means the opposite of **dis** and analyze is not correct.

23. Mal is a word root meaning bad as in **mal**evolent, which means spiteful and vicious. Both mediocre (of average or poor quality) and superior (better than or above) express different meanings.

24. Onus is synonymous with burden. Solution and empowered describe opposed concepts.

25. To **vilify** is to slander and defame. It is neither to promote nor to contemplate.

26. To be **cogent** is to be logically forceful and convincing. Neither illogical nor weak can be correct.

27. A **missive** is a written note or letter. It is not a problem. A mission is a sound-alike distracter.

28. If something is **vapid**, it is dull, tasteless, and unexciting. Eye-catching is the opposite and rapid is also wrong.

29. To be **doleful** is to be sad and mournful. It is not to be joyous or full.

30. To be **opprobrious** is to be disgraceful and shameful. Both hopeless and optimistic are irrelevant.

31. Augment means to expand or extend. Neither to secure nor to depend is correct.

32. Mitigate may sound harsh, but it actually means to ease. To sever (to cut off) and to relocate (to move) are both incorrect.

33. Panache is a French word that means flamboyance. The incorrect choices also come from the foreign words chapter. A non sequitur (Latin for "does not follow") is an illogical statement and a cliché (French) is an overused phrase.

34. To **beseech** is to beg and plead. It is not to implode (explode internally), nor is it to acquiesce (to agree).

35. To be **brazen** is to be bold! To be shy is the opposite, and **brazen** has nothing to do with being consistent.

36. Surreptitious means secret or stealthy. Celebratory describes a happy mood or setting, while repetitious refers to something that is repeating.

37. To **affect** is to influence. To produce is to effect and is incorrect. To attend is irrelevant.

38. To be **replete** is to be abundantly supplied or complete. Incomplete is an antonym of **replete**, and competent means adequate or qualified.

39. A **crescendo** is a gradual increase, as in the volume of music. It is not a rapid ascent (rise or climb), and it has nothing to do with a sparkle.

40. To **rankle** is to cause anger and irritate. To meditate means to contemplate and to mediate is to settle a dispute between two parties. Both wrong answers describe a cooling of anger and tension, the opposite of **rankle**.

SOURCE SERIES CONTEST RULES

NO PURCHASE NECESSARY.
Void in Quebec, in Puerto Rico, and wherever prohibited or restricted by law

Kaplan Publishing wants to know how Word Source made a difference in your life. What goal(s) did you accomplish with the help of Word Source?

1) ENTRY REQUIREMENTS:
Register to enter the contest by emailing your answer to sourcecontest@simonandschuster.com or mailing your response to Source Contest, Kaplan Publishing/Simon & Schuster, 1230 Avenue of the Americas, NY NY 10020. Enter by submitting your answer as specified below.

2) CONTEST ELIGIBILITY:
This contest is open to legal residents of the United States and Canada (excluding Quebec). Employees (or relatives of employees living in the same household) of Simon & Schuster, VIACOM, or any of their affiliates are not eligible. This contest is void in Quebec, Puerto Rico and wherever prohibited or restricted by law.

3) FORMAT:
Entries must not be more than 250 words long. The author's name, address, e-mail address, and phone number must appear on the first page of the entry. All entries must be original and the sole work of the Entrant and the sole property of the Entrant.

All submissions must be in English. Entries are void if they are in whole or in part illegal, incomplete, lost, late, illegible, technically corrupted, or damaged or if they do not conform to any of the requirements specified herein. Sponsor reserves the right, in its absolute and sole discretion, to reject any entries for any reason, including but not limited to based on sexual content, vulgarity and/or promotion of violence.

4) ADDRESS:
Entries must be submitted via email by 2/1/06 to: sourcecontest@simonandschuster.com or via mail to Source Contest, Kaplan Publishing/Simon & Schuster, 1230 Avenue of the Americas, NY NY 10020.

Each entry may be submitted only once. Please retain a copy of your submission.

5) PRIZES:
Five Grand Prize winners will receive:

Their choice of $100 worth of DVDs from Paramount Pictures. The sponsor will supply the DVD list for the winners to choose from. Total retail value of all prizes to be awarded: $500. All taxes on prizes will be the sole responsibility of the winners.

6) JUDGING:
Submissions will be judged on the originality of the story. Judging will take place on or about 3/1/06. The judges will include 5 employees of Sponsor, who are qualified to apply the aforementioned judging criterion. The decisions of the judges shall be final and binding. All prizes will be awarded provided a sufficient number of entries are received that meet the minimum criteria established by the judges.

7) NOTIFICATION:
The winners will be notified by email or phone on or about 3/15/06. All winners will be required to sign and return an Affidavit of Eligibility/Release within 30 days of notification, or prize will be forfeited. In the event any winner is considered a minor in his/her jurisdiction of residence, such winner's parent/legal guardian will be required to sign and return all required documents. In the event any prize notice is returned as undeliverable, such winner will forfeit the prize.

8) INTERNET:

If for any reason this Contest is not capable of running as planned due to an infection by a computer virus, bugs, tampering, unauthorized intervention, fraud, technical failures, or any other causes beyond the control of the Sponsor which corrupt or affect the administration, security, fairness, integrity, or proper conduct of this Contest, the Sponsor reserves the right in its sole discretion, to disqualify any individual who tampers with the entry process, and to cancel, terminate, modify or suspend the Contest. The Sponsor assumes no responsibility for any error, omission, interruption, deletion, defect, delay in operation or transmission, communications line failure, theft or destruction or unauthorized access to, or alteration of, entries. The Sponsor is not responsible for any problems or technical malfunctions of any telephone network or telephone lines, computer on-line systems, servers, or providers, computer equipment, software, failure of any e-mail or entry to be received by the Sponsor due to technical problems, human error or traffic congestion on the Internet or at any Web site, or any combination thereof, including any injury or damage to participant's or any other person's computer relating to or resulting from participating in this Contest or downloading any materials in this Contest. CAUTION: ANY ATTEMPT TO DELIBERATELY DAMAGE ANY WEB SITE OR UNDERMINE THE LEGITIMATE OPERATION OF THE CONTEST IS A VIOLATION OF CRIMINAL AND CIVIL LAWS AND SHOULD SUCH AN ATTEMPT BE MADE, THE SPONSORS RESERVE THE RIGHT TO SEEK DAMAGES OR OTHER REMEDIES FROM ANY SUCH PERSON(S) RESPONSIBLE FOR THE ATTEMPT TO THE FULLEST EXTENT PERMITTED BY LAW. In the event of a dispute as to the identity or eligibility of a winner based on an e-mail address, the winning entry will be declared made by the "Authorized Account Holder" of the e-mail address submitted at time of entry. "Authorized Account Holder" is defined as the natural person 18 years of age or older who is assigned to an e-mail address by an Internet access provider, on-line service provider, or other organization (e.g., business, education institution, etc.) that is responsible for assigning e-mail addresses for the domain associated with the submitted e-mail address. Use of automated devices are not valid for entry.

9) GENERAL INFORMATION:

All submissions, including answers, become sole property of Sponsor and will not be acknowledged or returned. By submitting an entry, all entrants grant Sponsor the absolute and unconditional right and authority to copy, edit, publish, promote, broadcast or otherwise use, in whole or in part, their entries, along with their names and addresses (city and state), in perpetuity, in any manner without further permission, notice or compensation. Entries that contain copyrighted material must include a release from the copyright holder. Prizes are non-transferable. No substitutions or cash redemptions, except by Sponsor in the event of prize unavailability.

In the event that there is an insufficient number of entries received that meet the minimum standards determined by the judges, all prizes will not be awarded. Void in Quebec, Puerto Rico and wherever prohibited or restricted by law. In the event any winner is considered a minor in his/her state of residence, such winner's parent/legal guardian will be required to sign and return all necessary paperwork.

By entering, entrants release the judges and Sponsor, and its parent company, subsidiaries, affiliates, divisions, advertising, production and promotion agencies from any and all liability for any loss, harm, damages, costs or expenses, including without limitation property damages, personal injury and/or death arising out of participation in this contest, the acceptance, possession, use or misuse of any prize, claims based on publicity rights, defamation or invasion of privacy, merchandise delivery or the violation of any intellectual property rights, including but not limited to copyright infringement and/or trademark infringement. Contest void in Quebec, Puerto Rico and where prohibited by law.

10) LIST OF WINNERS.

To obtain a list of winners, send a self-addressed, stamped envelope by 3/15/06 to: Helena Santini, Kaplan Publishing, 1230 Avenue of the Americas, NY NY 10020.

Sponsor: Kaplan Publishing, an imprint of Simon & Schuster, Inc.

1230 Avenue of the Americas, New York, NY 10020